THEN
NOW
and
IN THE
FUTURE

A Search for Honesty and Value-Based Living

JOE WOERNER

ISBN 978-1-68570-274-8 (paperback)
ISBN 978-1-68570-275-5 (digital)

Copyright © 2022 by Joe Woerner

All rights reserved. No part of this publication may be reproduced, distributed, or transmitted in any form or by any means, including photocopying, recording, or other electronic or mechanical methods without the prior written permission of the publisher. For permission requests, solicit the publisher via the address below.

Christian Faith Publishing
832 Park Avenue
Meadville, PA 16335
www.christianfaithpublishing.com

Printed in the United States of America

This book is dedicated to my grandchildren, the hope of the future who are already in the process of figuring things out and continue to teach, amaze, and inspire me.

- Michael (eight) would tell you to be friends with everybody.
- Sarah (seven) might tell you that even though you don't have to like everybody, trying is a good start.
- Virginia (five) would let you know to stand up for yourself.
- Faye (four) would explain that a person's true colors are shown when you love yourself and others and are kind to yourself and others.
- Audrey (three) would think it is important to be heard.
- Andrew (four months) is still working on life's lessons.

CONTENTS

Preface 13
Acknowledgments 19

Chapter 1: Getting It Right 21
    Metaphor: A Window to Truth 21
    The Boardwalk: A Metaphor for Life 23
    Atheism 25
    Anti-Semitism 28
    True Religion 31
    Thank God I Am Not Like the Rest of Men 33
    Religious Freedom and Love 37
    Fix the Children 40
    Sharing 44
    The Truth Will Set You Free 46
    War 49
    Nonnegotiable Beliefs 52
    The Morality of War 57
    Groundhog Day 59
    Black Lives Matter 62

Chapter 2: Christian Attitudes 65
- Service 65
- Image 67
- Worry and Christian Hope 69
- Patience 71
- Poor in Spirit 74
- Obedience 78
- Peacemaker 80
- Being Perfect 83
- Tez 85
- Giving Is Receiving 85
- Forgiveness 88
- Joy 91
- God's Mercy Is without End 92
- A God beyond Mercy and Forgiveness 94
- Diversity and Respect 98
- Enlightenment 103
- Jesus's Mission 107

Chapter 3: Christian Concepts 111
- Word of God, Bread of Life 111
- The Meaning of Creation 113
- Sacred Scripture 116
- Incarnation 119
- The Problem of Original Sin 122
- Image and Likeness of God 125

    Sacrament 128

    Christmastime 132

    Resurrection...135

    Communication Equals Transformation............139

Chapter 4: 9/11/2001 142

    September 11, 2001 142

    God in Our Lives...146

    Where Was God on 9/11? 150

    Reflections 154

    Opportunity 159

    Religious Fundamentalism 162

    Fundamentalism 166

    Creation: The Future 169

Chapter 5: Fragile and Sinful...................................173

    Hypocrisy 173

    Truth or Consequences 176

    Where Do We Go from Here? 180

    Final Thoughts..183

    The Eucharist and Abortion............................186

    Abortion 190

Chapter 6: Christian Attitudes Continued 195

    Lessons of Christmas.......................................195

    Relationship Equals Worship 198

    Does God Get Off the Hook Because of

    Free Will?..201

It's About Time	205
Desires of the Heart	207
Hope and Consolation	210
Happy, Healthy, and Holy	213
Interchangeability	216
What Do You Treasure?	220
Chapter 7: COVID-19	225
For Just Such a Time as This	225
Render to Caesar	229
An Opportunity Missed?	233
Common Sense: Not So Common	238
Herman Cain	242
Thanksgiving 2020 / John Fitzgerald	244
Chapter 8: Faith	248
Faith and Salvation	248
Thankful for Life	251
Give God Permission	255
Religion, Where Is Your Focus?	258
Faith: Not So Simple	261
God's Will	264
Faith and Good Works	267
Belief versus Unbelief	270
A Family of Faith	276
A Man of God	279
Possibilities	282

Chapter 9: A Little Different Look 285
    Jesus the Christian Prophet 285
    Relationship: War and Peace 288
    Suffering: A Partial Answer 294
    Love and Power 298
    Direction of Life 301
    Vulnerability 307
    Fear of the Lord 311
    Here I Go Again 313
    Hatred Is the Main Problem 316
    A Corrupt and Broken System 322
    The Devil and Evil 324
    The Front Four 326
    Religion and the Afterlife 330
    Defiance 333
    Compartmentalization 336
    Paradox 339

Chapter 10: Prayer 342
    Prayer on 9/11 342
    Glory and Praise to God 346
    Prayer: What Is It? 350
    Our Father: Matthew 6:5–15 355

Chapter 11: Racism 359
    Ahmaud Arbery 359
    You've Got to Be Carefully Taught 365

Angry and Selfish 369
SNAFU: Breonna Taylor 373
An Ugly Fact 375
Bloody Sunday: George Floyd 378
Peace on the Left, Justice on the Right 381
Rayshard Brooks: Why? 385
Stupid as in Angry and Selfish 389
Monuments 392
Jacob Blake 396
What Do You Have to Lose? 399
Shut Up and Dribble 403
Qualified Immunity 405
Walter Wallace Jr. 407
Anjanette Young 410

Chapter 12: Questions 414
Asking Questions 414
A Mystery 416
Religion: Not So Simple 419
Natural Law Theory and Religion 423
Natural Law and Related Topics 429
Why Did God Become Man? 434
Continuing Questions 442
Justice 444
Do We Really Want a Solution? 447
Paradox: What Is It? 454

    Free Will 457
    Would Religion Exist Even without God? 463
    Could God Have Done Better? 467
    COVID-19 versus Racism? 469
    What Does 70+ Million Mean? 471
    Conclusion: Where Am I Today? 474

Bibliography 481

PREFACE

The inspiration to write this book came as the result of the encouragement of close friends and family. It is an attempt to express and share the beliefs, thoughts, and experiences that have formed and shaped my life over the years. It reflects a natural movement of my life from "then" till "now." These essays are grouped by theme rather than chronology but are dated to help the reader achieve a sense of the movement from "then" till now. It has been an evolutionary process.

The question is, What am I trying to communicate to you, and how? The how is through these essays that represent a personal evolutionary process that began in earnest approximately twenty years ago. I would like to share that process or journey of moving from the status quo toward something beyond, moving to something more personal, toward a sensibility for the truth, and an openness to self-education and questioning.

As a Catholic and a priest, I held fast to much of what the church proclaimed and offered. In the chapters

"Christian Concepts," "Christian Attitudes," and "Faith" and "Prayer," I have dealt with themes that more or less reflect traditional Christian beliefs. These attitudes and concepts are included in this book to give the reader some perspective regarding where I was in the beginning—the "then." They also represent the foundation upon which the present rests—the "now." Some beliefs and concepts, I have rejected, and some I still see as fundamentally valid and valuable as a guide for my life.

At this point, I would like to make a distinction between attitudes and concepts because there is a significant difference between the two. Attitudes have more to do with values while concepts have more to do with belief and dogma. For me, attitudes, in this process, have become more important than concepts because attitudes affect behavior rather than theoretical belief; orthopraxy is more important than orthodoxy. The process or path of evolution requires a more critical and judgmental view of reality.

My best friend, Franklyn Casale—a priest, a classmate, and former president of St. Thomas University in Florida—has suggested that I pick and choose from religion and scripture what I judge works best for me, a smorgasbord Catholic as it were. I am guilty; he is absolutely right! However, it is now not a question of picking and choosing but rather a question of belief itself, a question more of "what do I believe personally, and how am I going to act upon my beliefs in the real world?" Who better to choose what is right for my life than me? Should some flawed institution or system be the sole interpreter of scripture for me? Should it determine how I relate to God, religion, truth, and life? Institutions and systems have their place but should not be used as infallible guides or absolute possessors and dispensers of truth. We should not accept hook, line and sinker what institutions offer and at times demand of us. We should not abdicate our obligations and responsibilities.

Ultimately, we are responsible for who we are and who we become, not the church, not a religion, not institutions and systems. We, as human beings, have been gifted with minds and hearts, reason and discernment, intellects, and wills that place upon us responsibility for what we believe and how we practice those beliefs.

If you can see the value of living life without pat answers to tough questions, perhaps these essays will help you along the way. In these pages, you will find reflections on theology, politics, faith, conscience, God, justice, prayer, race, war, spirituality, and many other topics.

I was ordained in 1967 for the Archdiocese of Newark, New Jersey; and transitioned to married life in 1974. As a member of St. Mark's Parish in Sea Girt, New Jersey, I moderated a Bible study group for approximately ten years, when Kathy Toohey, a member of the group, approached me about writing a book together. However, after several years, the project fell by the wayside, and Kathy and I stopped working on the book. Some years later, I began writing again and finally decided to go forward with this undertaking on my own.

Much of what I believed remained constant, and much has changed. It was during the Bible study group years that things started to evolve. I started to read and study authors (listed in the bibliography) who caused me to question the status quo and the idea of absolute truths held to be in the possession of certain institutions. Issues and events such as fundamentalism, religious orthodoxy, 9/11/2001, war, pedophilia, social justice, spirituality, racism, faith, prayer, hypocrisy, and truth became my pathway to a reality that made more sense than much of what I accepted for years.

The process requires awareness and effort, along with a strong desire to find that truth. I hope these essays help you find your own unique way along this path. Not all these essays will be helpful. You will have your own questions and find your particular path; these essays are possible windows to truth seeking and valued based living. Unflagging and unflinching questioning is the pathway to advancement in this process. We all have the wherewithal to take up the challenge of this evolutionary process.

The connecting thread throughout this book is a Christian scriptural viewpoint, rooted in openness and respect for all people. After September 11, 2001, themes were often dictated by world events rather than personal preferences. I realize a short essay can only scratch the surface of these complex issues. It is my hope that my journey will help you seek the truth, even when it is uncomfortable or unsettling. It is my desire to elicit value-based living, peace, and joy and encourage independence of spirit and obedience to conscience. It is actually a never-ending journey; it lasts into eternity.

Like Abraham who followed God's call, not knowing where it would lead him, we strike out in the same way in the hope that this journey might bring us closer to each other and to the transcendent. This is not a book of answers but rather a book to inspire questions. In the course of writing this book, I have grown in a sense of awe and mystery regarding the great gift of life. I hope that sharing this journey will shed some light on your own path toward peace, emotional growth, and intellectual and spiritual fulfillment.

ACKNOWLEDGMENTS

Without the support and aid of family and friends, I would have never completed this project. First and foremost are my wife Marilyn and our boys: Joey, Pat, and Jim. Whatever I asked of them, they did without complaint or hesitation.

My sister Rosemary helped enormously in the editing process along with her friend Judy Mahoney. Ellen Curran helped get the ball rolling and Bonnie Scolamiero helped put the finishing touches on the project.

My niece's husband, Greg Smith, supported me throughout the whole process, including reading and editing the manuscript.

Dan, my nephew, realized that my computer skills were pretty nonexistent and took control of much of that process.

Bob Andrew, a good friend, allowed me to bounce my feelings and ideas off him without complaint.

Last but not least is Bill Ward, a good friend who died this year. He supported and encouraged me not only regarding this book but in all aspects of my life.

Thanks to one and all.

CHAPTER 1

Getting It Right

Metaphor
A Window to Truth

Two great spiritual leaders, Buddha and Jesus, teach that unless we set aside ego and its wants, desires, and fears, spiritual freedom can't be achieved. Jesus, through selfless love, shows how to achieve life by dying. He demonstrates this by living and dying for others. For us to really understand the meaning of life, he allows his physical death, which leads to resurrection and life on a deeper level.

Buddha makes the same truth evident, using detachment from desires and fears to find freedom from the physical world and what it represents, liberating people to act in freedom rather than self-interest. Joseph Campbell, in his book *The Power of Myth*, speaks of Buddha and his teachings. He explains the freedom that is achieved when one releases himself or herself from the desire for the goods of this world and from the fear of their loss. He speaks of Nirvana being achieved when one frees oneself from irresistible desires, worries, and pressures of society: when one acts in freedom rather than from compulsion.

Jesus counsels in John 12:25, "*Those who love their life lose it, and those who hate their life in this world will keep it for eternal life.*" The teachings of both spiritual leaders connect with the transcendent and leave the self behind.

Sometimes God's promises are interpreted only in a literal sense, in a material or physical way rather than as signs and symbols of the spiritual. This inaccurate perception causes disappointment when what is asked for is not received. "*Whatever you ask for in prayer with faith, you will receive*" (Matt. 21:22).

The woman at the well and Nicodemus were perplexed by Jesus's use of water and rebirth in the metaphorical sense. They understood what Jesus said in a totally physical or materialistic sense. They were looking for water that would quench the physical thirst for all time and rebirth through reentering the physical womb. It is easy for us to make the same error because we are often so focused on the here and now and the physical world. If we are to understand Jesus, we must realize that he was never about this world only but about a reality over and above—a reality that vivifies and gives spirit to what we see and touch.

They look but do not see, and listen but do not hear or understand. (Matt. 13:13) (2015)

The Boardwalk: A Metaphor for Life

How happy we are at the beginning of this spring/summer season to have some of our boardwalks open and near completion after Superstorm Sandy. What does the boardwalk mean? Is it a sign of hope, a window to life, a place of relaxation and sharing, a place of wonder and awe? It is all of these things and more; it is in many ways a metaphor for life. Each of us has our unique experiences and memories of the boardwalk.

It is a place we go to see the sun rise. We see the beginning and end of each day, which raises our awareness of the beginning and end of life. No matter what our spiritual background may be, on the boardwalk we are exposed to the source of all life. There, we share in the awe of being in the presence of the sea, the origin of all life on this planet.

Children experience the anticipation of going to the beach, romping in the sand, exploring under the boards, and frolicking in the surf. For children to run along the boardwalk with the sun, sand, and sea in the background is not only a delight for the children but also for parents, grandparents, relatives, and friends; even perfect strangers enjoy watching the parade of life.

The boardwalk allows each and every one of us to go at our own pace. Young people and some older people jog along the boards to get in shape, to embrace life, and just for plain old exercise, all while enjoying nature. All manner of folks walk the boards for sheer pleasure. Early risers often ride their bikes in the breaking hours of the day. Young and older couples stroll the boards, sharing their love for each other. All these activities can be done at one's own pace—quickly or leisurely or at any speed in between.

In life, we get a few surprises along the way. So it is with the boardwalk. If we are lucky, we see a pod of porpoises making their way along the coast just offshore. During the winter, we might just happen upon seals sunning themselves on the rocks of a jetty, or perhaps we experience a rare whale sighting.

Many times, the boardwalk is a place we go to refresh and invigorate ourselves, a place to renew our spirits or to think through our problems and woes, a place of meditation and contemplation. Oftentimes, it takes a loss for us to really appreciate what we have.

All in all, life is a lot like a walk on the boards. It is someplace we love but at times take for granted, just as we do with life and those we love the most.

From childhood to old age, the boardwalk, like life, can be an experience that evokes gratitude and thanksgiving. (2012)

Atheism

Atheism—is it evil or just another belief system? It depends on how the term is defined, with or without connotation. *Webster* defines it as "a lack of belief or a strong disbelief in the existence of God or any Gods." There is, in this definition, no inference of right or wrong or good or evil. It is a straight forward statement of fact. No sense of morality is attached; there is no judgment whatsoever.

Just as with many other words we, in time, denote, connote, infer, and assign certain characteristics above and beyond the literal meaning of a word or concept. Atheism over time has come, in some sense, to be synonymous with evil and immorality, which is quite unfortunate and erroneous. For many people, atheists are the equivalent of bad people. They are ungodly and without a moral compass, people who would deny believers the right to worship God. This is not the case. The historical record of God and religion is spotty, to say the least. This is not to belittle the enormous good religion has done, but an honest look reveals enormous evil also. Ethical and moral behavior can be the domain of the atheist as much as the believer.

Just as Christianity or Islam is not monolithic, neither is atheism. There are good and moral people who believe in God, and there are good and moral people who do not believe in God. There are evil people who believe in God and belong to religious institutions and there are evil people who do not believe in God and religious institutions. We need to be careful not to paint with too broad a brush.

For two thousand years, throughout the world, doubters of religious dogma and the existence of God have been killed, persecuted, jailed, whipped, and ostracized. Atheism is a complex reality and should not be reduced to simplistic terms. For many, the term *atheism* encompasses more than just unbelievers. Some agnostics, deists, freethinkers, and disbelievers fall under the broad term of atheists and are suspected of nefarious beliefs and activities. All these groups of people have suffered, to a greater or lesser degree, under people of religion. This in no way minimizes the evil done by atheists. No group of people who persecute others is justified regardless of what they believe.

I have two very good priest friends who, I believe, have problems with atheism. They appreciate and value the right to practice, unencumbered, their faith and resent anyone who might try to limit that right. I firmly and fully agree with them regarding this right. On the other hand, I believe that the rights of atheists should be respected in the same way as the rights of believers.

The respect, which I see as owed to believers and disbelievers alike, has been violated by both parties. Much of the present-day reciprocal negative attitudes exist because believers have persecuted nonbelievers and vice versa. Atheistic regimes in Russia and China have persecuted believers while Christians have a long and ugly history of persecution against unbelievers and believers of a different persuasion than their own. For each side to indict the other is to miss the point.

In light of these atrocities, is it any wonder that there is great mistrust on both sides? Trust and respect become major issues. It seems that when both sides get together, they each try to convert the other to their way of thinking rather than just trying to understand and respect the other.

To encourage and allow believers and unbelievers to practice their beliefs in a peaceful and respectful manner is a legitimate approach to the issue. The Constitution of the USA endeavored to respect the rights of individuals to practice faith or nonfaith without interference by individuals, the state, or hostile groups as long as it did not impinge on the rights of others. These constitutional rights in many cases are aspirational.

It was and still is hard to be an atheist, especially in the USA. You are a person under suspicion, always a suspect, different, not to be trusted, one to be avoided, one to be looked down on by good, God-fearing people. How do you think an openly atheistic politician would fare in a presidential election?

Proselytization through coercive methods by either group is absolutely unacceptable. If persuasive presentations of one's beliefs are not enough to convince another, just back off and go in peace. A life well lived is perhaps the best way to demonstrate the validity of your most cherished feelings and beliefs. (2020)

Anti-Semitism

James Carroll, in his book *Constantine's Sword,* quotes Rabbi Hershel regarding the greatness of God compared to religion and the greatness of faith compared to dogma. It is a lengthy book dealing with the relationship between the Catholic Church and the Jews from the time of Christ to the modern era. A central thought of this book is that Christians maltreated Jews in the name of Jesus under the sign of the cross. At times, Christians have tried, over the centuries, to proselytize peoples throughout the world without recognizing or respecting the value and worth of their beliefs. Christians have sometimes failed to see the deep and meaningful relationship existing between God and these peoples.

Over the course of history, the Jews have been blamed and persecuted by Christians for the death of Christ. However, Christian theology, for a long time, has put the responsibility for the death of Jesus squarely on the backs of all people, for all people are sinners. Jesus, for Christians, is the Son of God and, therefore, a unique individual with a special role in history. If Christians believe that sin is the cause of Christ's death, then we are all equally guilty.

Through his life, death, and resurrection, he has atoned for our sins, the sins of all people. He has given us the ability to be one with God. The very word *atonement* ("at-one-ment") means bringing together. He has given us the ability to live at one with God. In him, God and man have been reconciled.

Although this is the Christian belief, living out of this doctrine often falls short of the ideal. Often, very strong beliefs of different religions are a cause of tensions. Sometimes beliefs of one religion are condescending and belittling of another religion. This is why respect, tolerance, and understanding are essential to peaceful coexistence.

In an ideal world, Jews of today should not be linked to the death of Jesus, just as Germans of today should not be linked to the Holocaust. The same could be said of whites with regard to slavery in the USA. It seems as if we all have a responsibility for these events because we all participate in evil. It is only when we participate in the goodness that we diminish evil. God asks each one of us, as individuals and as a society, to be responsible for each other. We cannot respond as Cain did when God asked about Abel. *"I do not know; am I my brother's keeper?"* (Gen. 4:9). We are all our brothers' keepers. Christ endured this passion out of love for all people. Paul, in Galatians 3:28, tells us, *"There is no longer Jew or Greek, there is no longer slave or free, there is no longer male or female, for all of you are one in Christ Jesus."*

Anti-Semitism highlights the chasm that exists between people of similar faiths. It emphasizes how at odds we can be with each other and underlines the political and religious divisions that exist in this country.

Division and further separation seem to be the direction this debate is taking at the moment. It would be a shame if we squander opportunities to better understand each other and further advance the messages of the Jewish Scriptures and the Gospels. If we are going to come together in peace and harmony, we have the responsibility to listen with open minds and hearts to one another. (2006)

True Religion

What is true religion? For some, it might be plumbing the depths of the mysteries of God. For others, it may be the sure knowledge that they are members of the one "true religion." Others may perceive true religion to be theological or dogmatic correctness. The question is, what does God consider true religion to be? James 1:27 tells us, *"What God the Father considers to be pure and genuine religion is this to take care of orphans and widows in their suffering and to keep oneself from being corrupted by the world."*

    Christian churches traditionally translated this admonition into the physical works of mercy: feed the hungry, shelter the homeless, clothe the naked, visit the sick and imprisoned, give relief to the poor, and bury the dead. These mandates are certainly in the spirit of James's admonition concerning true religion. If we look within our own circle of family and friends, we may even find examples of true religion. The practitioners of true religion are people who are not perfect. They are people who, in some way or other, give of themselves in ordinary but spectacular ways. How can something be ordinary and at the same time be spectacular? A paradox! I would like to give an example from my own life.

When my mother turned sixty-nine years of age, she began to manifest signs of Alzheimer's disease. It began with memory loss, first short-term memory and then long-term memory. As anyone who is familiar with Alzheimer's knows, it just gets worse as time goes on. However, this story is not about my mother; it is about my father. He was just an ordinary guy—a good man, a family man, a hard worker, a faithful husband, and a good father! I guess that is quite a lot. But his greatest lesson to me was his loving and caring service to my mother.

My father's heart ached, and his spirit sagged on occasion, but he was always there for my mother. As difficult as this situation was, it brought into sharp focus what true love is all about. My father was a human being, just like all of us, with his own problems and idiosyncrasies, but in the final analysis, he was a man of true religion. He was not a man who wore his religion on his shirtsleeve, not a man of high honors or position, just a loving, caring guy who, for ten years, cared for his disabled wife, washed her, dressed her, fed her, kissed her, held her, comforted her, and cared for her every need. He made enormous personal sacrifices and thought nothing of it. He expressed only love and affection for this woman who was his partner for over fifty years.

Here was a man doing common, ordinary activities in a spectacular way. Part of what made it spectacular was the fact that he performed these acts of love and kindness for ten years—day in and day out, year in and year out—and almost never showed any sign of aggravation or frustration. He was and still is, for me, the personification and model of true religion. I am sure you won't have to look too far for a model of true religion in your own life. (2003)

Thank God I Am Not Like the Rest of Men

You have heard all the reasons for and against homosexuality and same-sex marriages. I won't bore you with a rehash of these arguments. Because of my religious and family background, I have ambivalent feelings regarding homosexuality and same-sex marriage. However, it is hard for me to imagine that same-sex marriage would ever become the norm when it becomes legal. I would like to discuss these issues from a slightly different perspective. I do have ambivalent feelings, but they flow more from a concern with Christian charity rather than moral precept.

After all is said and done, I find myself aligning emotionally with those who are homosexuals and proponents of same-sex marriages. Although I have reservations engendered by religion and upbringing, I do essentially agree with them. I believe I am in an evolutionary process regarding questions of sexuality and reproduction. I find many of our brothers and sisters who view sexuality, marriage, reproduction, and identity in a nontraditional way to be loving, faithful, committed, compassionate human beings.

Promiscuity, for me, is morally unacceptable in committed relationships whether they are heterosexual or homosexual. I find myself feeling very uncomfortable when Christian people display hatred, bigotry, intolerance, and self-righteousness regardless of what side of the issue they take. We see similar attitudes displayed on both sides of the abortion issue. The real issue for me is not whether we ultimately accept same-sex marriages, etc. but rather how we are going to treat each other in the process of this debate. Jesus admonished and instructed but never resorted to disrespect and hatred. He stood strong and clear but never forced anyone to act in accord with his will.

How certain are we that two people of the same sex can't raise a healthy, happy, and holy child? How certain are we that unmarried people living together can't truly love each other? How certain are we that society will come to a bad end if people of the same sex marry? How certain are we that same-sex marriage is worse than divorce? How certain are we that a bad heterosexual marriage is better than same-sex marriage? The questions in this area go on and on. Asking important questions like these might help us to remain open to the possibility that although we reject the concept of same-sex unions or same-sex marriages, people who are in them are genuinely good and loving people.

Some of us seem to be so concerned about the nature of love and truth that we run the risk of condemning people who are real live persons in our attempt to preserve and protect abstract principles that we believe in but are difficult to prove. To say that there can be no true love between people in a homosexual relationship is to contradict reality. Because a relationship is seen as illicit in some people's eyes, it is not automatically without love. Reality is more complicated and nuanced than our conceptual constructs.

Church and society sometimes use sexuality to assign goodness or badness to an entire relationship or to all relationships that fall into a particular category (e.g., sexual relationships without the benefit of marriage). Some people feel that love between two people of the same sex becomes totally inauthentic when sex is introduced. The fact that people of same-sex relationships have been faithful to each other, have shared pain and suffering for each other, have sacrificed for each other, and have loved each other, in similar ways to heterosexuals, must count for something. When we isolate sexuality and make it the condition without which a relationship can have value, we tend to relegate all the other values of the relationship to unimportant entities. Have we reduced relationships to black and white, right or wrong, good or evil based on one's sexual orientation?

We should be careful that our zeal for our position does not put us in the same posture as those who wanted to stone the woman caught in adultery. We have often heard the saying "*Love the sinner, hate the sin*," and in our hearts, we may feel that this is our attitude. The truth is that it is hard for human beings to separate the sinner from the sin. If you don't think so, try it. Let me give you a few examples: the 9/11 hijackers, Palestinian suicide bombers, Bill Clinton, and George Bush.

Our emotions and feelings sometimes overpower our will to do what is right. Care must be taken when interacting with people who practice what we don't like or agree with. These people can become the object of our displeasure and ill-treatment. We need only to look to Jesus, who disobeyed the laws of his day and blasphemed in the eyes of religious leaders. I am not comparing the righteousness of these two causes but only the end results. Jesus was killed because some people didn't like his stance on many sensitive issues.

You might think it can't happen today, but it can. It has, and it will. Past history shows us that loving people who disagree with us is no mean task. This, however, is the task that falls to true Christians. When we fail to try to achieve this ideal, we may become greater sinners than those we feel are engaged in immoral activity. Remember the story of the Pharisee and the tax collector. The Pharisee prayed, "*God, I thank you that I am not like other people,*" while the tax collector prayed, "*God, be merciful to me, a sinner!*" Jesus tells us that the tax collector went home justified rather than the Pharisee.

Homosexuality and same-sex marriages are not now normative, but if society chooses to accept these realities as part of the fabric of life, just as they have with divorce, then we at least need to respect and treat with dignity those who differ from us even as we work to preserve what some see as Christian values. (2006)

Religious Freedom and Love

I often thank God that I live in a country that embraces religious freedom. Sometimes we fail to recognize the significance of this right. The freedom to choose the God we worship and the right to practice that worship in any fashion we choose, as long as it doesn't cause harm to others, is an awesome freedom. As part of that freedom, we have the right not to profess, practice, or even believe in a divine being.

I fear people and groups, Christian or otherwise, who present their views and opinions with certitude and conviction that coerce people into viewing things their way. In the extreme, this becomes a violation of religious freedom and a violation of God's first law, the law of love. Love has freedom as its heart and foundation. Real religion is rooted in the love of God and the love of man. Religion that engages in oppression and violence in the name of God is a distortion.

When a state tries to force its citizens to follow a particular religion or any religion or to practice no religion at all, it becomes an agent of repression and a servant of evil. When a church coerces people to act against their will and conscience, it no longer stands for the law of love. When individuals try to convert or proselytize by intimidation, force, or subtle pressure, they undermine and destroy the meaning of real religion. We should keep foremost in our minds and hearts that real religion is based on love and freedom, and without these fundamentals, we will always miss the mark.

In John 4:19–21, we are told:

> *We love because God first loved us. If someone says he loves God, but hates his brother, he is a liar. For he cannot love God, whom he has not seen, if he does not love his brother, whom he has seen. The command that Christ*

has given us is this: whoever loves God must love his brother also.

No matter what religion we practice, no matter what sect or denomination we belong to, no matter whether we believe in God or not, we should never let other people's beliefs intimidate us or make us feel inferior or less valuable to God. The passage from Luke 18:9–14 (the Pharisee and the tax collector) can help us understand that the way God sees things is oftentimes different from the way people see them. This parable is a lesson to those who are sure of their own goodness and despise everyone else.

We are all unique. We should not compare ourselves to others. In the final analysis, God is the only one who knows where we stand. And in fact, where we stand with God is the only measure that counts. How we go about practicing or living the law of love is singular to us as individuals. Just as every person's fingerprints are different, so too will be each person's execution of God's law of love. This should bring us peace and relieve any tension or pressure we might feel to compare ourselves to others.

We all have our individual way of expressing love. For some, like St. Paul, Gandhi, or John XXIII, the expression of love can be outwardly very powerful, but for most of us, it will be rather common and ordinary. No spotlight will shine, no large crowds will gather, and no publicity will ensue; just the day-in and day-out contact with our family, friends, coworkers, and fellow churchgoers will endure. We should never underestimate the enormous influence we can have on others when we live the law of love to the best of our ability. The example of good-living people goes farther than coercive activity.

At the core of religion are love and freedom. In fact, they are two sides of the same coin. Without freedom, there is no love, and without love, freedom is an empty shell. Freedom to practice the faith we profess is a gift and a right to be cherished and appreciated. (2002)

Fix the Children

In this day and age of teenage gangs and school massacres, people are searching for answers. In this era of drive-by shootings and post-office slaughters, people are searching for causes. To be sure, the causes and answers are complex and inextricably bound together. If we know the causes, perhaps one day we will figure out the answers.

Are the causes and answers we come up with correct? Some say there are too many guns available. Others say guns do not kill people; people kill people. Some experts say there is too much violence on television, in the movies, and in video games. Other experts say some of the media violence is a good outlet for pent-up aggression. Many think it is the press writing, exploiting, and promoting violence for the sake of the almighty buck. Still, others say we need to report these incidents so that we are informed. They say it is our right and obligation to know what is going on. Some say it is because we don't pray in schools and in public places. Others say we cannot pray in schools and public places because it is a violation of the separation of church and state.

The arguments regarding the causes and solutions of violence go on and on. No matter which way we turn, some group or other objects that the answers are either too liberal or too conservative too superficial or too complicated. They say it limits my rights or it gives too much freedom, and indeed, in a country devoted to and founded on freedom and majority rule, we should have the right to agree or disagree with each other. Only when enough people agree on something can we come together, as it were, and legislate for the common good. This is how the system works, but even when we come up with a legal solution, it is not always the right one, nor does it always work well.

As Christians, we think we have the solution, but perhaps so do the Jews, Muslims, Buddhists, and every other religious sect. Will we continue to pass laws that do not really work, that conservatives and liberals disagree on while the killing goes on?

I personally don't have the solutions, nor am I sure of the causes. The other day, I was listening to the radio and heard an advertisement for a program called "Fix the Children." How strange. Who broke the children in the first place? Do the children really need fixing? A better name for the program might be "Fix the Parents." If we could fix the parents, the children wouldn't get broken in the first place.

One thing I feel strongly about, and it seems basic: if the parents are emotionally healthy, loving, compassionate, and just people, the children will be basically healthy and well-adjusted and later healthy and well-adjusted adults. If the parents are emotionally unhealthy, unloving, cruel, and unjust people, the children will be basically unhealthy and maladjusted and later unhealthy and maladjusted adults. There are exceptions to this rule, of course; and at times, there will come from a healthy family an unhealthy child and from an unhealthy family a healthy child. But this is the exception, not the rule.

You are perhaps thinking, *That's too simple. There are too many other influences in this world for that to work.* Indeed, there are other influences in this life that can lead children astray; however, those other influences are not the primary and essential ones. Those other influences are accidental to a child's formation and usually only exacerbate an unhealthy situation. If the adults in a child's life teach by word and example that love is at the heart of their relationships, that tolerance and understanding are essential to good relationships, that justice and compassion are at the center of human living, then we will begin to see a change not only in our children but in our society as a whole. This is not simple to do. It is hard and complex, but so is the problem.

Introducing prayer into schools and public places is a simplistic solution. Taking violence and sex off the television is a simplistic solution. Banning guns and hiring more police are important but are not at the core of the issue. All these solutions and many others strike at the accidentals surrounding the problem rather than dealing with the heart of the problem. They do little to really cure the problem at its root or foundation. Making some of these changes probably wouldn't hurt, but they are not at the essence of the problem.

St. Paul has a suggestion for us, as do many of the other major religions—a plan, a solution, but it is not an easy one. It is one that is not new, and it requires tremendous effort, but it is one that works.

> *"Love is patient and kind; it is not jealous or conceited or proud; love is not ill mannered or selfish or irritable; love does not keep a record of wrongs; love is not happy with evil, but is happy with the truth; love never gives up; and its faith hope and patience never fail"* (1 Cor. 13:4–7) (2005).

Sharing

> *The group of believers was one in mind and heart. No one said that any of his belongings was his own, but they all shared with one another everything they had. With great power the apostles gave witness to the resurrection of the Lord Jesus, and God poured rich blessings on them all. There was no one in the group who was in need. Those who owned fields or houses would sell them, bring the money received from the sale, and turn it over to the apostles; and the money was distributed to each one according to his need.* (Acts 4:32–37)

It is certainly impressive that the early Christians shared all their belongings and no one was in need. In light of our present-day economic structure, it might seem a little strange that people who owned property or houses sold them and gave the money to the apostles to be distributed according to the needs of the community. This type of activity seems almost impossible in our society and would come with risks. Would this work in our social and economic system? Did this work only because the church was a cohesive small community whose leaders were directly appointed by Jesus? Did the fact that they believed that the end days had arrived also influence their activity?

This way of living in the apostolic era is, for us, a challenge; but this way of relating to other people is the heart of religious belief. We may not be able to replicate the socioeconomic community of the early Christian days; however, this early Christian attitude is essential.

We need to realize that we are all one. In Corinthians 12:12–26, all people are characterized as part of Christ's body and must be concerned for each other regardless of sex, race, religion, or class. If some are endowed with talent or money, we need to realize that these are gifts, and gifts are not earned. Even if these assets have been worked for, they are still gifts. For this reason, they are not "*mine.*"

We may not be able to provide for others in the same way as the early Christians; nonetheless, there remains an obligation to provide for those in need. This isn't just charitable work but an act of justice and equality, an obligation as brothers and sisters to share and provide for one another. Everyone is needy in many ways, and those who seem less fortunate are, in some ways, the more greatly blessed.

The physically poor have riches to share also. Sometimes these riches are hidden from sight because our pride and materialism obscure them. Although the exact details of the early Christian community may be impossible to duplicate, the spirit of sharing is a real possibility, and all will be richer for the experience. (April 2001)

The Truth Will Set You Free

There is a possibility that when we fill our minds with only that which reinforces what we believe, we could become narrow-minded, closed to possibilities, and rigid in our approach to life and its important questions. Most religions, governmental bodies, and basic belief systems don't encourage truly critical thinking, but asking questions and challenging the status quo is an integral part of truth-seeking. Beliefs long held as true are difficult to question. It is daunting for us to question these things in our own minds, let alone in a public forum.

In the seventeenth century, people in general and the scientific and religious community in particular found it difficult to accept and assimilate Galileo's revolutionary view of the universe. Facts about the relationship of the sun to Earth, which contradicted a literal interpretation of the Bible and altered perceptions of the centrality of the earth in the universe, were threatening to most of the religious and scientific world. Many religious leaders claimed these new ideas were contrary to what the Bible taught and, therefore, could not be true.

Jesus challenged and questioned many of the long-held beliefs of the establishment of his day. He said holiness came from an internal source, not from external practices. He claimed that sacrifice and oblation could not take the place of caring for widows and orphans. Keeping holy the Sabbath had little to do with keeping external rituals. He explained in the Sermon on the Mount that being powerful, healthy, and wealthy were not the signs of God's favor. Service was something to be rendered to others, not sought after for oneself. The chosen ones of God were the simple people like Mary and Joseph, a country maiden and a carpenter. His friends were simple fishermen and sinners.

The Christian church, in the beginning, was composed of all classes of people; but the majority were the poor of God, the lowly, and the uneducated. As time went on, the leadership of the church often became more identified with those who wished to be served rather than to serve. At times along the way, the church lost contact with the meaning of God's Word, which is the touchstone of its existence. During these periods, truth seekers brought about many renewals and eventually the Reformation.

To some degree, traditions and commonly held beliefs can seem more important than the bedrock of truth. This is not to belittle traditions and commonly held beliefs, but when they are substituted for truth, they become detrimental to individuals and the common good.

Viewing reality only in a traditional or orthodox way can limit the potential for new and important insights. Slavery, war, capital punishment, uncontrolled consumption of natural resources, and suppression of women have all been seen, at times, as moral activities. Although sometimes uncomfortable, seeking truth by questioning the status quo can help lead us to true freedom.

It is ultimately more beneficial to seek the truth rather than accept things because they have always been that way. Every human being has to answer to God; to live and act as Jesus lived and acted. If what we say and do is infused with love, we share in the redemptive work of God. The goal is not to be blind sheep led by blind leaders. We are all children of God with minds and hearts endowed with the Spirit of God. It is our responsibility as stewards of these gifts to respect and honor those who have gone before us but also to take up the challenge that lies ahead. Being open to ideas, traditions, and beliefs that are different from ours can encourage spiritual growth. No one should ever be intimidated by closed minds. *"The truth will set you free"* (John 8:31). (2002)

War

The prisoner abuse scandal in Iraq and the brutal killing of Nick Berg came together so powerfully that I felt compelled to write this reflection. These two events, experienced together, threw me into an uncharacteristic depression. Usually, I am a very optimistic person, full of hope and trust regarding life and the future. For the first time in a long time, I got the feeling that there is no way out of the mess we find ourselves in, not only in Iraq but also throughout the world. It is as if we have lost our minds and souls, and our hearts and wills are in an abyss out of which they cannot escape unassisted.

War is a horrible affair, which brings about horrible events that seem to take on a life of their own, usually spiraling out of control. As I grow older, war seems to be less and less of a solution to the world's problems. It sometimes becomes the avenue by which our beloved soldiers are sacrificed for reasons that do not justify this horrific loss.

Defending ourselves from terrorism and evil people of this world is a necessity, but we must be careful that we don't become what we fear and despise. War should be a last-ditch measure. Unfortunately, war usually says that we have given up hope. It should mean that we have explored all possible remedies and solutions. There should be no options, no paths or routes that cannot be investigated. It means that we have come to the point where we admit that killing and being killed is the only alternative, that the death and destruction of our loved ones and our enemy are the only remaining viable solution. How insane is that? Is war ever justified?

It also strikes me that political leaders, without full disclosure and proper discussion and input on the part of the general population, justify wars. How could parents in their right minds approve of their sons and daughters going off to fight an unjustified or immoral war? Past wars (Vietnam) show us that we have not always been informed as to the real reasons we go to war.

In Iraq, it seems that we have moved from what appeared to some as a noble cause to a situation of reciprocal violence and hatred. I fear that we, along with the Muslim world, will find ourselves in a similar situation to Israel and Palestine, not because of land but because we will be trading violent and murderous acts, not knowing exactly how we got to this state of affairs and without any clue to a solution because we are so intent on seeking revenge for what we see as injustices perpetrated against us.

Politicians in this country and elsewhere are so entangled in partisan politics that they cannot see beyond their own partisan agendas. The nations of the world seem to be at a loss to solve these conflicts. For this reason and the reasons stated above, I have fallen into a depression. It is perhaps time to recognize that we alone cannot solve this dilemma. Is it a problem beyond our human solutions? It is time for us to recognize that only by looking to the collective wisdom of the religions of the world is a solution possible. Is this irrepressible optimism or a viable option? The world religions tell us that by seeking our own self-interest, we cut ourselves off from the transcendent and each other.

Many times, we hear that by war, we are protecting American interests abroad. Perhaps it is time to be concerned about everyone's interests. Until we follow wisdom as set forth in all the great religions of the world and begin to change as individuals and as a nation, concerned not for ourselves but for those in the world community, we will continue to be at war without much hope for true peace. We cannot possibly go to war with everyone we disagree with. It is time to try something different. As Christians, we should try the Gospel! Active pursuit of peace through adherence to positive religious principles seems to me to be worth a try. (2007)

Nonnegotiable Beliefs

Larry King, a famous TV talk show host, on the night before the first presidential debate of 2004, hosted five guests, all of whom were religious leaders of one type or another. The gentlemen represented Islam, Catholicism, Judaism, Protestantism (Southern Baptist), and Eastern Spiritualism.* Part of the program centered on God and religion and their relationship to war, anger, hatred, terrorism, and politics. The Jewish author and the Baptist minister were less able to dialogue and communicate with the

---

* Reverend R. Albert Mohler Jr., president of the Southern Baptist Theological Seminary; Deepak Chopra, a world-renowned spiritual adviser and author; Fr. Michael Manning, host of *The Word and The World*; Dennis Prager, author of *Why the Jews*; Maher Hathout, scholar and senior advisor to the Muslim Public Affairs Council.

rest of the panel because of their strongly held religious and political beliefs.

To be perfectly honest, personality played a role, as it always does, in the way their religious beliefs and opinions were presented. These two men, although wanting to appear as much as possible to be open, were so convinced of their beliefs that it left little room for the respect of the other panelists' beliefs. This is not to say that both of these men were not cordial or did not have valuable insights and many creditable positions.

The Judeo-Christian tradition has made some truly remarkable contributions to mankind. It is also obvious that in many ways, other religions have paralleled many of the tenets of these two faiths. If we were to live according to the Ten Commandments, the Beatitudes, and the Golden Rule, a panel discussion of this type might not be necessary.

For many Christians, beliefs regarding scripture are held as if they were facts. Not only are they held as facts but also as nonnegotiable facts or beliefs, admitting no possibility of error. These beliefs are usually interpreted in the most literal and fundamental sense. This is, in and of itself, not a problem, but when joined with the idea that every other religion, in some sense, is erroneous, then danger lurks around the corner. When Christians assume they have an obligation or mission, beyond living an exemplary life, to spread the true and correct message of God, it is on the way to becoming a big problem. This mindset is one additional step toward what could result in serious negative consequences. These observations apply not only to Christians and Jews but also to all religions that assume that their sacred writings are the Word of God while all the rest are something less.

In a civilized society with checks and balances, some of the more serious consequences can sometimes, but not always, be avoided. Examples of these consequences are evident in our recent history. Muslims are slaughtering Christians in Darfur, Jews and Palestinians massacre each other on a daily basis, and Christians butchered Muslims in Bosnia. If we look to the distant past, we see Christians persecuting Jews in the Inquisition and Muslims and Christians killing each other during the Crusades. Some of these conflicts are not purely religious but have been or are being waged by people who consider themselves to be good Christians, Muslims, or other religious representatives. These are the kinds of consequences we can have when beliefs are nonnegotiable or considered irreconcilable among parties.

Beliefs about Christian scriptures can fall into the nonnegotiable category. When the belief that Scripture is the Word of God inspired and revealed, is interpreted in the strictest and most fundamental way, it becomes a non-negotiable belief and is the cause of untold hardship. There is no discussion with someone who claims that Scripture is the Word of God because the Scripture says it is the Word of God. This kind of statement excludes any possibility of dialogue or discussion. God said it is so, and that is that.

When one reaches this point, one's vision becomes myopic, and the thought process becomes circular. These assumed truths become so rigid that we fail to see that they are indeed flexible enough for us to hold that Scripture is sacred, inspired, and revealed without detracting from our beliefs or what others believe. When we use Scripture as a weapon or an apologetic tool instead of a road map to God, truth, and holiness, it becomes a vehicle that leads away from God rather than to God.

Reverend Mohler, when asked about capital punishment, endorsed it because he said God not only approves it but also mandated it in both the Old Testament (the Jewish scriptures) and the New Testament (Christian scriptures). Using this type of reasoning, we could surely support slavery, for it is at least tacitly endorsed in the Jewish scriptures and the New Testament. In fact, some of our Founding Fathers did indeed use scripture to support their arguments in favor of slavery.

Whether you are for or against the death penalty is not the point. Using the Bible literally and equating God's Word with what it says instead of what it means is an abomination. To most thinking and open-minded people, it should be obvious that the scriptures are a living document whose moral, religious, and spiritual message are not static and stagnant but alive and vibrant, always challenging mankind's conscience and moral sensibilities.

When beliefs become nonnegotiable, it is not God speaking but rather men who have replaced humility and openness with pride and arrogance. They use God's Word to hide behind, all the while claiming to be promoting God's agenda. It is at this point that the Word of God is used to divide rather than unify, to support their position rather than seek common ground, to belittle rather than to uplift.

Because we do not agree on every detail about God's Word does not mean that we are exempt from the commandment of love. Jesus tells us that we will be recognized as his disciples, not by how nonnegotiable our beliefs are but by our love for one another (John 13:35). (2004)

The Morality of War

We often hear the USA described as a Christian nation, but it is not. It is a nation made up of mostly Christians. The USA is a representative democracy, not a theocracy. With this in mind, I address this letter to most Christians in the context of what I believe is Jesus's gospel message on war.

> *Do unto others as you would have them do unto you.* (Luke 6:31)

> *You have heard it said love your neighbor and hate your enemy. But I say to you love your enemies and pray for those who persecute you.* (Matt. 5:43)

No matter how you interpret these words (literally, figuratively, or metaphorically), it is pretty hard to justify war under any circumstances. There are many other sayings of Jesus that support his stance against violence of any sort against anybody.

Jesus is the great exemplar as demonstrated in the washing of the apostles' feet at the Last Supper noted in John 13:12–15. His agony in the garden and his death on the cross are examples to us of the kind of love he seeks from us who call ourselves Christians. In the agony in the garden, Peter cuts off the ear of the high priest's servant, Malchus, John 18:9–11. Jesus then says to Peter, "*Put your sword back in its place; for all who take up the sword will perish by the sword. Do you think that I cannot appeal to my Father, and he will at once send me more than twelve legions of angels?*" (Matt. 26:52–55). Even with this power, Jesus chose to die at the hands of his "enemies." He chose nonviolence over violence, peace over war, and sacrifice over self-interest.

Jesus the exemplar gave us these examples and many others such as turn the other cheek; if one wants to take your coat, give your cloak as well (Matt. 5:39); and of course, the story of the Good Samaritan in Luke 10:25–37. There is no doubt that the implications of these scripture passages are difficult, but their message is at the heart of Christianity. These implications are so hard, we and many other nations, made up of mostly Christians, have failed miserably in their practice.

Once the war starts, the question of the morality of war is moot. All wars once begun are immoral. Collateral damage, a euphuism for countless lost lives of civilians, is an afterthought in most news stories. This alone is reason enough not to go to war but rather to investigate, with vigor, ways to avoid this un-Christian and immoral activity. I think Jesus has made a strong case for the immorality of war. (2005)

Groundhog Day

Perhaps you have seen the movie *Groundhog Day* in which Bill Murray plays Phil, a TV weatherman, who is assigned to cover the groundhog festivities in Punxsutawney, Pennsylvania. This is a deeply spiritual movie masquerading as a comedy.

Phil is a totally self-absorbed, self-centered, egotistical individual with no regard for self-improvement, except to advance his status and career. He has no real interest in other people except for his own gratification and career advancement. He treats people with disdain and disrespect, communicating with them only by means of negativity and sarcasm.

Phil, along with Rita, the show's producer, and their cameraman, arrive in Punxsutawney on Groundhog Day. After a thoroughly uninspiring day, Phil goes to bed waking the next day at 6:00 a.m. on February 2 to Sonny & Cher's "I Got You Babe." This day repeats itself over and over and over again.

As the days progress, Phil realizes that no matter what he does, he will awake again on February 2 at 6:00 a.m. to "I Got You Babe." At first, he is in a panic, desperate to get out of the hellish situation. When he realizes that this is not going to happen, he treats people with more hostility and disrespect than before. His disposition soon changes to apathy, depression, and self-destructive behavior. It really doesn't matter because whatever he does, no matter how despicable or destructive, it is all undone by 6:00 a.m. the next day.

He decides to learn French and obtain personal information about Rita in the hope of impressing her. He actually has an interest in her, but as usual, it is only in relation to his self-interest. After a few very clever but failed attempts to seduce her, he begins to realize slowly—consciously or subconsciously—that life and happiness are not about self-importance and self-satisfaction.

Phil studies ice sculpture, takes piano lessons, and genuinely tries to improve himself. Each day, he becomes more conscious and aware of other people. He starts to have real concern and affection for people and especially for his would-be girlfriend Rita. He has a wonderful day with Rita in which he shows real interest and concern about her as a person and a human being. At the end of the day, they find themselves in Phil's bedroom, but he does not take advantage of the situation. However, nothing changes, the next day arrives at 6:00 a.m. to "I Got You Babe." He begins the new day with real joy because of yesterday's authenticity and meaningfulness.

Phil spends the day doing good for other people. He catches a boy falling out of a tree, he performs the Heimlich maneuver on a choking man, and he saves a homeless man from death by giving him food and shelter.

At a town party celebrating Groundhog Day, he meets Rita, who is impressed with the relationships Phil has achieved with the townsfolk. Again, they return to Phil's room where they lie in bed, and he tells Rita how much he loves and cares for her. She falls asleep, and he lovingly kisses her good night.

The next morning arrives again at 6:00 a.m. to "I Got You Babe," but there is something different. Rita is lying in bed next to Phil, and a genuine day has dawned.

This is a really funny movie that teaches a profound truth. Although the movie does not speak of God, Christ, or religion, it is a truly spiritual work. *"For whoever wishes to save his life will lose it, but whoever loses his life for my sake and that of the gospel will save it"* (Mark 8:35). Phil, after what feels like years of trying, finally got it right. It was not about him; it was about others. It is not about us; it is about others. Hopefully, we will get it right. (2003)

Black Lives Matter

Those who respond to the BLM movement by saying, "White lives matter," or "All lives matter," seem to miss the point. Are white lives under threat? Have white lives been ripped from their homeland and placed in slavery under cruel white rule? Have white lives been diminished by laws, customs, and prejudices put in place for the purpose of subjugation? Are innocent white people shot and killed by law enforcement at the same rate as innocent black people, and if so, what do you think the reaction would be?

It seems strange to me that any human being would have a problem with the BLM movement. Perhaps black lives do matter less to some of us. The lives most in jeopardy today are the lives of people of color. This is where our attention should be. It is important to realize if we diminish the lives of people of color, we diminish our lives as well. Hate destroys and tears down; love creates and builds up.

To suppose that BLM means that white lives don't matter is just a supposition used by some to cast the BLM movement in a negative light. Why do we have this crisis in our country today? Because black lives have never mattered in the same way white lives matter. It started with slavery, which at its root, saw the black race exclusively as an economic tool. Personhood was not a consideration.

Even after the demise of slavery, attitudes and behaviors toward people of color changed very little. Practices such as lynching, mutilations, beatings, segregation, and all sorts of mistreatments are evidence of deeply rooted attitudes and feelings of hatred and prejudice.

Although things have changed for the better, these changes have come slowly and at a great price for the black race. The murder and abuse of civil rights leaders because they fought for those rights is a dark-red stain on our country, which, ideally speaking, is devoted to freedom and justice for all. Because of gains made over the last fifty years, some people claim we are beyond racism in this country; nothing could be further from the truth.

Looking at the justice meted out to men of color makes one think perhaps the system is defective. The system seems to lean in favor of the haves over the have-nots. What does this mean? It means the system of justice needs to be viewed in a more critical fashion, to be sure the large majority of law enforcement is trying their best to act with fairness and justice. Those at the top of the justice system have a need for real wisdom, leadership, and responsibility. The tenor and direction of any institution should flow, and usually does, from the top down. Better procedures, attitudes, treatment, and training should emanate from our leaders.

At this time, the recipients of our flawed justice system are disproportionately people of color. Unless we make a concerted effort to reevaluate and correct what is wrong with our institutions and systems, we are destined to repeat, time and time again, violence and injustice against people of color.

The most effective way to change the systems and institutions of government and law enforcement is to vote for candidates whom we know will honestly and tirelessly fight for the rights of *all* people.

—Letter to the Editor, *Coast Star*,
Manasquan, New Jersey (2017)

CHAPTER 2

Christian Attitudes

Service

Luke 22:14–20 (The Last Supper) and John 13:4–17 (The Washing of the Feet)

Does the Eucharist still have some relevance in our own time? Can we find meaning for the modern world in an ancient ritual?

These two readings from Scripture taken together give us an insight into the connection between Eucharist and service. Luke's account of the Last Supper emphasizes the relationship between the passion and death of Jesus and the gift of the Eucharist. John's account stresses the importance of service to each other, symbolized in Jesus's washing of the apostles' feet.

The Eucharist is the supreme act of service for mankind. It is a commemoration of Jesus's life, which culminates in his suffering, death, and resurrection. The Eucharist is about love that is so strong that God humbled himself to accept death and humiliation at the hands of his creatures. His life and death are acts of love beyond our comprehension. Through his death, Jesus gave us an example of how life should be lived and just how far our love should go. Because his passion and death are beyond our understanding, He gave us another simpler, possibly less-threatening example of service. Jesus washed the feet of his disciples to illustrate to them and us, by example, what service means.

When Peter failed to understand, Jesus said, "*Do you understand what I have just done to you? I have set an example for you, so that you will do [for others] just what I have done for you*" (John 13:12–15). Here, Jesus shared with his apostles and all of us his priesthood of service. Jesus told his disciples (and us) that we should try to become the least important and the servants of all, even to the point of the ultimate sacrifice.

This is what Eucharist and priesthood are about: love, service, and sacrifice. The message is simple but profoundly difficult. Service need not be spectacular, but it needs to be rendered in a spirit of humility and love. The needy can be family, friends, coworkers, members of the local church and community, or possibly our enemies. The lesson Jesus gave to mankind on the night before he died is a lesson we must learn over and over again. If the essence of Christianity is love, then the human embodiment of that love translates into service. (March 2001)

Image

In a TV commercial, tennis star Andre Agassi proclaims, *"Image is everything!"* At times, religion seems to be a question of an image rather than substance. Image is hardly ever what true reality is about. Jesus called the Pharisees whitened sepulchers because they were washed and clean on the outside but full of decay and rot on the inside. Jesus condemns the hypocrisy of all kinds in the strongest terms.

Christianity, in some of its dimensions, is a private matter, something that, if real, need not be worn on one's shirtsleeve. Christianity is best exemplified, not by preaching to one another but by living the gospel. We all have enough spiritual flaws of our own that we need not go poking around uninvited into someone else's religious affairs. Those who wear their spirituality on their shirtsleeves sometimes have an agenda that has to do more with their will rather than God's will. We should heed Jesus advice in Matthew 6:6: *"But when you pray, go to your room, close the door, and pray to your Father, who is unseen. And your Father who sees what you do in private will reward you."*

Keeping rules and regulations, going through rituals without investing ourselves, blindly following traditions that have lost meaning only give the appearance of real religion. We have a good image, but we miss the heart and soul of true faith. The external must be a manifestation of the internal conversion of the heart, or it is so much smoke and mirrors. Jesus says in Matthew 12:34, "*You brood of vipers! How can you speak good things, when you are evil?*"

Real spirituality is becoming loving, just, and merciful. It is becoming a caring, optimistic, faithful person. It is becoming positive instead of negative, encouraging instead of discouraging, forgiving instead of condemning, open and loving instead of closed and hateful. Christianity is becoming or living up to the potential God has given us. These are the essentials; these are the characteristics of our faith, on which we should concentrate. The accidentals of life and religion are just that, accidental and inconsequential.

If we are pure in language (don't curse or tell off-color jokes) but verbally abuse our children or spouse, of what value is it? If we give money to the Salvation Army but treat minorities with contempt, of what value is it? If we go to church on Sunday but trash our coworkers on Monday, of what value is it? If we read the Bible but treat the less fortunate as less important than the wealthy and powerful, of what value is it? If we attend charitable organizations but abuse alcohol or drugs in private, of what value is it?

These qualities of pure language, almsgiving, church-going, Bible reading, and participation in community organizations can be a sham, especially when the image is more important than the spirit of love. These actions become authentic and dynamic only when we invest in them in a loving, relational way. We fool ourselves if we get lost in trappings and façade. If dogma and ritual do not lead to inner goodness, which is expressed in actions that direct us to God and help our fellow human beings, then it is all image and no substance. (2004)

Worry and Christian Hope

As we get older, some of us tend to worry more than we did when we were young; at least this has been my experience. We worry about our kids, about their health, about their education, and about their future. There are many worries besides the ones related to our kids. Actually, some of us do not have children and are not even adults, but there is no shortage of worries. We all have our own reservoir full of concerns.

We worry about getting sick or about those we love who are sick. We are apprehensive about flying in planes or taking trips away from home. We worry about hurting other people's feelings or about not being loved. Anxiety prevents us from getting a good night's sleep, and we sometimes worry about dying or about our loved ones dying. We worry about just about everything and anything. I am sure you can come up with your own litany of worries.

For all of us who worry, there is Matthew 6:25–34: "*Instead [of worrying] be concerned above everything else with the kingdom of God and with what He requires of you and He will provide you with all these other things.*" No matter how well we receive these words of Scripture, we will always worry, but if we learn to rest in God with a hopeful attitude, much of this anxiety can be relieved. "*Therefore, do not worry about tomorrow for tomorrow will worry about itself. Each day has enough trouble of its own*" (Matt. 6:34).

An enormous amount of energy goes into worrying about all sorts of things. God reminds us, however, that we cannot add one minute to our lives by worrying about it. We are Christians; we are people of hope who have trust and confidence in God. God tells us in Matthew 6:25–34 that we are of vast importance to him and that he will work with us to provide for us in every way. We need only to have trust and confidence in him.

Worry comes from relying on ourselves. Subconsciously and sometimes even consciously, we realize that if our hope rests on our own shoulders, we have a great deal to worry about. However, if we realize that our hopes and our expectations rest ultimately with a loving, just, and merciful God, then our worries can turn to peace and serenity. This does not mean that all will be just as we want it to be, but it does mean that in the final analysis, we are in God's hands, and what better hands could we be in? (2010)

Patience

As I waited at Newark Airport to board a plane to Florida, I observed an interpersonal transaction that caused me to reflect on the quality of patience. There was a little stand in the middle of the concourse next to our gate, which was selling an assortment of fast foods. A small gathering of passengers, waiting in turn, lined up to buy snacks for the trip to Florida.

On line in front of me was a middle-aged woman who was becoming more and more frustrated and impatient with an elderly woman who was having a hard time holding her ice cream cone and paying her bill. The middle-aged woman was alternately shaking her head and shifting her weight from one foot to the other, impatient over the elderly woman's inability to move along in a timely fashion. Her lack of patience seemed inappropriate, considering we couldn't take off for at least an hour. It made me stop and think about the many times I exhibited the exact same type of behavior.

St. Paul, in his hymn to love, lists patience as the first attribute of love. Patience is often overlooked as a significant quality of a loving attitude. Paul saw patience as an important ingredient of love. Without patience, we tend to see and treat people as objects rather than real live human beings with feelings who desire and deserve respect.

In our fast-paced society with its emphasis on achievement and productivity, it is easy to lose patience with those who don't measure up to our expectations or inconvenience us in one way or another. Time is money! Don't waste my time or interfere with my ability to produce, achieve, or accomplish whatever it is that I have on my mind at that particular moment.

This attitude of impatience is not limited only to the workplace. It can be manifested in our relations with our families and friends or even the clerk at the food store or the gas station attendant. Road rage, so common today, is often the result of our impatience, our need to get where we want to go on our terms. It is a lack of patience that boils over into hostility, which dehumanizes the other. Impatience can be a sign of thoughtlessness or at times an external expression of a deeper problem.

Patience has little to do with what other people are about. Patience is a quality that emanates from inside and is controlled by us and not by circumstances outside ourselves. It is an attitude of the heart, mind, and will that can be manifested in care and respect for others. True patience is expressed without regard for position or station in life. It is a virtue that looks at and deals with others as unique individuals with characteristics and attributes who deserve to be respected just as much as we wish to be respected.

Patience can be expressed in a multitude of ways. It is really listening to what people have to say. It is not losing our composure with our husband or wife because we had a bad day. Patience is spending time with our children, although we have a number of excuses not to. It is being kind to the elderly and the somewhat slow tollbooth attendant. Patience is sincerely trying to see things from the other person's point of view.

Patience is an integral part of love and presupposes a loving, caring attitude toward all. It is not always easy. It demands effort and concentration. With practice, as with many other virtues, it can become habitual.

As stated earlier, patience is a virtue that we control. It comes from within, and in almost all situations and with almost all people, it has a transforming and enriching effect. Patience enriches both the giver and receiver. People are never seen as nonpersons but rather as individuals of real worth and value. It transforms our perception of situations as negative and degrading to positive and uplifting. Scripture tells us that patience is a virtue to be desired and practiced. *"Be completely humble and gentle; be patient bearing with one another in love"* (Eph. 4:2). (2005)

Poor in Spirit

"Happy are those who are poor in spirit for theirs is the kingdom of heaven" (Matt. 5:3).

How strange it sounds to say someone is blessed or happy because they are poor in spirit. If given the option, most people would rather be rich than poor. What does it mean to be poor in spirit? There are perhaps many ways to understand this state of being. Physical poverty that crushes people and deprives them of human dignity is never good. Poverty of spirit and physical poverty are not the same thing. On the other hand, if we are rich in the material things of this world, is it possible to be poor in spirit? I think the answer to this question can be yes.

A line from the play *Fiddler on the Roof* will help explain the meaning of being poor in spirit. "*Besides having everything I know what everything is for.*" This simple line helps put *"things"* into perspective. Possessions, talents, resources, attributes, relationships, fame, and physical well-being are all positive and good in themselves. It is only when we lose sight of what these things are for that we begin to go astray. To be poor in spirit is to recognize that these positives in our lives come from God and are not to be clung to but to be shared in a way that will benefit all of us.

Paul, in Philippians 4:10–19, says, "*I am experienced in being brought low, yet I know what it is to have an abundance. I have learned how to cope with every circumstance; how to eat well or go hungry, to be well provided for or do without. In Him who is the source of my strength I have strength for everything.*" Paul is telling us that to be poor in spirit is to be able to live with abundance or to live modestly. With God as our strength, we have strength for everything. Riches and poverty can lead us to God or away from God. In fact, it is not riches or poverty that leads us to or away from God but rather our attitude toward these things. How we choose to view these gifts and knowing what they are for is what leads us to God.

The scriptures are full of warnings about the downfall of riches. Luke 12:15 tells us, *"Take care to guard against all greed, for though one may be rich, one's life does not consist of possessions."* In Luke 12:33–34, Jesus says, *"Sell your belongings and give alms. Provide moneybags for yourselves that do not wear out, an inexhaustible treasure in heaven that no thief can reach nor moth destroy. For where your treasure is there also will your heart be."*

"For theirs is the kingdom of heaven." This is not only a promise of heaven to come at the end of time but it is also God's kingdom that comes here and now. This is why, if we are poor in spirit, we are blessed. This is why we are happy. In some way, because of our attitude, because of our spirit, God has allowed his kingdom to be made present here and now.

Another way of looking at this beatitude is to recognize our own poverty of power and control. This is why it is sometimes easier for the poor and downtrodden to understand their relationship to God and his material world. They know that without God, they have no real strength or power, but with God, they can transcend poverty and misfortune.

We who are well off, on the other hand, can easily deceive ourselves into thinking that we are responsible for our wealth and power. It is often only when sickness or death strikes, which is out of our control, that we begin to realize our true position or relationship to God. We become poor in spirit when our relationship with God comes into sharper focus. Jesus says to us in Matthew 19:23–29 that it will be very hard for rich people to enter the kingdom of heaven. He goes on to say that it would be easier for a camel to pass through the eye of a needle than for a rich person to enter the kingdom of God. At this, the disciples were shocked. For them, being rich was a blessing from God. It was a sign of God's approval for a life well lived. Jesus is teaching us that riches and possessions do not mean we are right with God; in fact, he is telling us that riches can be a hindrance to our relationship with God. For his disciples, this was a turning of the tables: "*Who, then, can be saved*" (Luke 18:26–27)?

Jesus's response was "*This is impossible for man, but for God everything is possible.*"

Here again, we see that all is dependent not on us but on God. To recognize our true helplessness and dependence upon God is to be poor in spirit. Putting ourselves and what we possess in proper relationship to God is possessing the kingdom of heaven. (2005)

Obedience

My sister-in-law Liz Edelstein, who comes from a somewhat different religious perspective than I, suggested that I might consider writing about the topic of obedience. At first, this subject seemed to be somewhat strange and certainly outside of my religious comfort zone. I began to think about it, and some questions came to mind. What is the nature of obedience, and to whom should we be obedient?

I remember a film I saw at Seton Hall University when I was taking some graduate courses. In this film, they used a prestigious university setting to lend import and authority to the experiment. The people running the program wore white lab jackets and were addressed as doctors. The whole idea was to create an atmosphere of authority and prestige. A by-product of this established format was fear and intimidation. The experiment was set up to have the test subject inflict pain on an individual at the behest of an authority figure.

It was incredible to see how far the test subject would go in this process. Many went to the point of inflicting severe pain on the individual involved. This film suggests that some people, in the name of obedience to authority, will act without questioning or evaluating what is being asked of them. I began to realize that regarding the question of obedience, obligations fall on both parties. Those who exercise power and authority are obliged to seek obedience in an equitable fashion characterized by justice and concern. There is also an obligation on those who obey to exercise good judgment concerning to whom and to what they are being obedient.

Obedience in the Bible is often equated with conformity to rules, laws, and commandments or acting in accordance with God's will. At times in the Jewish scriptures, it appears that the motivation is couched in fear and trepidation. This, however, is not always the case. Oftentimes, obedience is motivated by love and respect. It is interesting that the word *loyalty*, which connotes allegiance, devotion, and faithfulness, is often substituted for *obedience* (2 Chron. 31:21, 2 Cor. 9:13). In the Christian scriptures, it is almost self-evident that obedience is motivated by love and respect. Trust is at the root of authentic obedience and loyalty. Obedience, in its purest form, is based on faith. It is the belief that the one trusted has our best interest at heart. This is obvious in Jesus's relationship to his Father.

True obedience seems to be related more to love and respect than fear and intimidation. On the night before Jesus died, he asked his Father to spare him the impending anguish and pain. Although his prayer was not granted,

Jesus was obedient unto death. Jesus acted obediently, not out of fear but out of love and respect. He believed that his Father had his best interest at heart. As we mature into spiritual adulthood, obedience is motivated more and more by love and respect and less and less by fear and intimidation.

I have to thank my sister-in-law, one of my favorite people, for motivating me to reflect a little more deeply on the nature of obedience. Thanks, Liz. (2006)

Peacemaker

"Happy are those who work for peace; God will call them His children" (Matt. 5:9). Who are the peacemakers? Are they people who negotiate for peace in Ireland, the Middle East, or Yugoslavia? These people, of course, are peacemakers in a very real sense. However, the peace they usually achieve is a peace that is characterized by a lack of external violence or war. This is a good thing, but real peace is not just a cessation of violent behavior but something that emanates from internal core values. What does it mean to be a peacemaker in the most basic and fundamental sense of the word?

How ironic that a gun, the Colt 45, is called *the Peacemaker*. This is a testament to how badly we have failed to understand the meaning of peacemaker in the Gospel.

True peace issues from the heart, not from the end of a gun. The use of violence, intimidation, or brute force to bring about peace is far from the ideal set forth in Scripture. The Sermon on the Mount tells us that those who work for peace are the children of God. Although each person's role in creating peace can be different, we are all called to be peacemakers.

Parents are the first teachers of peace, which is expressed in love, freedom, and mutual respect. This doesn't mean that there is never conflict or disagreement, that there is never tension or bad feelings. On the contrary, all this is part of the peace process. Being human and being in a relationship means working at peace. The lives of those who love and respect each other stand in stark opposition to verbal, physical, and psychological violence. This type of living requires give and take, compromise and concession, but in the end, it is the only authentic way to attain peace.

Peace is an expression of love and justice and is a quality that must be acquired. How we accomplish peace with our mates has a significant influence on how our children will make peace with their mates, their children, and the world at large. If we teach them that violence is the answer or solution to conflicts among family members, we fail to bring peace, not only to our families but also to the larger community. Violent behavior (physical or emotional) begets violent behavior. Loving, respectful behavior begets loving, respectful behavior.

When we look at the multitude of conflicts around the world that have lasted from generation to generation, from age to age, we begin to realize that these hostilities have been fueled by parents' passing on to their children, violent attitudes toward other people. This is not to say that a great deal of violence within families does not come from systemic problems and inequities inherent in the nature of society. When parents encourage prejudice in their children—for example, with regard to peoples' color, religion, or national origin—they are promoting attitudes that can ultimately lead to violence.

In our own country, we tend to blame violence in our literature, movies, newscasts, and other media for violence in our society. While these things can, in many cases, be contributing factors, they are not the root cause of violence. Sometimes we don't want to admit that violence in the family can be the source of violence directed toward individuals and society. To a great extent, violence stems from parents who have failed to be peacemakers within their own families.

In the Gospel stories, Jesus gives us examples of how we should relate to each other. "*Do unto others as you would have them do unto you,*" "*Love your enemies and pray for those who persecute you*" (Matt. 5:44). The motivation is always love and respect, openness and understanding. If we model ourselves on these attitudes of Jesus, we will demonstrate to our children and to the world that the resolution of differences comes not through violence or conflict but through love and peace. (2009)

Being Perfect

In 1 Corinthians 12:12–31, Paul speaks about the body of Christ. He says it is one body, although it is made up of many parts. He notes that all the parts of the body are important, yet all the parts are different. The hand is not the foot, and yet the body cannot do without either of these parts. If a part of the body suffers, the whole body suffers. If one part of the body is praised, the whole body feels good. St. Paul says that all people make up the body of Christ. There are no exceptions!

This passage from 1 Corinthians is followed immediately by Paul's hymn to love. This is no accident. Paul wants us to see the connection between love and our role as members of the body of Christ. He speaks about having all kinds of gifts and about doing all manner of good works but sees them as nothing without love. We can be apostles, but if we don't have love, we are nothing. Love binds the body of Christ together. It sustains and supports it. Paul wants members of the one body to treat each other with love.

On the night before Jesus died, he prayed that all would be one. More than being one in faith, he desires us to be one in love, for faith without love is nothing more than a noisy gong. This unity achieved through love is the coming of God's kingdom.

Paul describes love in human everyday terms. What Paul is describing, in a sense, is God. God is patient and kind, not jealous, not boastful, not rude, not selfish or irritable. God does not keep a record of wrongs. He is unhappy with evil but happy with the truth. God never gives up on us. His faith, hope, and love for us endure forever. He is eternal. God possesses these qualities in an infinite and mysterious way that is beyond our comprehension.

In Matthew 5:43–48, Jesus talks to us about the love of one's enemies. The last line of this paragraph is *"You must be perfect—just as your Father in heaven is perfect."* Here again, it is no accident that Matthew uses this sentence to follow Jesus's teaching on love of enemies, for St. John tells us God is love.

What does being perfect mean? Being perfect as our heavenly Father is perfect means attempting to be perfect in love. We must endeavor to love our enemies as we love ourselves. We must strive to be patient and kind. Matthew and Paul have given us the benchmark. They have made clear what we must do to be perfect. We must see all people as members of one body. Even our enemies are sacred to God and an important part of the one body of Christ. We must comfort and care for them just as we comfort and care for ourselves.

As God has treated us, we should treat others. Sinners though we are, God has not kept a record of our wrongs but has wiped them out with the love of Christ. Paul tells us in the first line of 1 Corinthians 14, *"It is love then that you should strive for."* (2006)

Tez
Giving Is Receiving

The following is a letter I wrote in 2014 to Tez, who was a boy at St. Peter's Orphanage who came into my life when I was newly ordained. Tez was sixteen at the time and is now sixty-nine years old. Little did we know, this would be a lifelong relationship. To say the least, his future "success" was not assured based on his precarious past.

Hey, Tez:

I would like to thank you and Donna for hospitality above and beyond anything I could have expected. My visit with you guys was a real joy. It was great to meet Donna, Adam, and Alex for the first time. I felt bad that Alex was under the weather but maybe on another visit I will be able to get to know him a little better. Adam is a great kid; I know I don't have to tell you that but it is always nice to hear it from someone outside the family. You guys have done a terrific job with your boys. Your life together has yielded abundant fruit. You and Donna have much to be proud of a special family with lots of love and a handsome home in a beautiful neighborhood. How wonderful you and Donna are!

On the trip home, I went over in my mind many of the things we talked about, and I reflected on our relationship over the years. The first thing that came to mind was how I have always felt you were part of my life and family. I have considered you to be a son to me practically from day one. I still feel the same way. You are very special to me. I love you and I always have. I also thought that over the years, I had a positive influence on your life, but I realize it is a two-way street, and as much as I might have given to you, you have graced my life in just as many ways.

The fact that you appreciated some of the things I said and did for you over the years touched me deeply. As I journeyed home, the idea that you kept the treasure box, I brought back for you from Puerto Rico, moved me to tears. I could go on but I think you get the point. The last thing I would like to note is that I am very proud of how you handled all the challenges of your life and there have been many. Against great odds, you have been a real success in all the important things in life. Give my love to Donna and the boys.

Peace and hope,
Your friend Joe

The point here is that in our giving, we at times, without realizing, receive abundantly. This is what can happen when we reach out to others. (2013)

Forgiveness

On the way to Vermont to go skiing with a good friend of mine, we were searching the airways, hoping to listen to something interesting. Lo and behold, we tuned into a Christian radio station, so we listened for a short while. A young woman with a very sweet, caring voice was giving a talk about God as the "good shepherd" in very soft, warm tones. However, to our shock, she described a horrible and terrifying scene. She said in order for the "good shepherd" to keep his lamb from straying and perhaps being separated from him, he would break the little lamb's legs. We looked at each other in disbelief. How could such a sweet, comforting voice suggest such a distorted and sadistic image of a loving, caring God? Indeed, there must be many other ways for a good shepherd to keep his sheep from wandering.

I think some Christians justify this image of God from their incorrect perception of God in the Hebrew scriptures. The people of the Hebrew scriptures had only a partial vision of God, which was evolving and moving slowly toward a fuller and clearer revelation of the God of history.

Christian scriptures see God as the good shepherd who extends only love and compassion to his sheep. God is a good shepherd who invites but does not coerce. He is a God who lovingly invites but leaves us in freedom, for he knows that forced love is no love at all. If this is how God acts, then he is guilty of violating the very prohibitions he enjoins on us. Only love given freely is true love. Acts of violence and coercion end in resentment and hostility. The example of his life and death are the tools by which he helps us to keep from straying—no broken legs and no force, just sacrifice and love. The good shepherd possesses nothing but love for us, and he shows this by laying down his life for his sheep.

Forgiveness is at the heart of Jesus's ministry. In fact, an essential part of his coming is tied to forgiveness. The gospel is filled with accounts of Jesus's forgiving people. In John 8:3–11, Jesus forgives, without hesitation, the woman caught in adultery. In Luke 15:11–32, God is portrayed as a loving father who forgives his wayward son, again, without hesitation. On the cross, Jesus forgave those who actually crucified him and those who share in that guilt throughout history. The stories of Jesus's healing those afflicted with both physical and spiritual ailments are numerous indeed.

These are all stories of forgiveness. As Paul tells us, the wages of sin is death, possibly physical but certainly spiritual (Roman 6:23).

Jesus has no interest in condemning sinners. His parable of the Lost Sheep shows us that his only interest is in saving us, forgiving us, and bringing us back into his loving care. He shows us that anger and harshness are not part of his approach, but mercy and love are. He extends these gifts to us no matter what we have done or how badly we have acted. Jesus seeks out sinners. He tells us that he has not come for the righteous but for the sinner. He is found in the company of tax collectors, prostitutes, and those who have, in one way or another, separated themselves from God. Jesus calls us back from death to life. He invites us gently and lovingly to come into his forgiving light and life.

No matter how often or how badly we have sinned, God always stands at the top of the hill, looking out to the horizon, watching for his sons and daughters, whom he gently calls back to his forgiving and merciful heart.

At times, we feel that we are not worthy of God's forgiveness, that we are too evil, too worthless for God to care about us. When we feel this way, we need to realize the lengths to which God has gone in order to forgive and save us. He became man, lived, suffered, loved, and ultimately died so that all people might have life. We should realize that forgiveness is fundamental to the nature of God. We can say this with confidence because the heart of Jesus's ministry is love and forgiveness, and Jesus and the Father are one.

All men and women, no matter how serious their sins (adultery, murder, prejudice, hypocrisy, perversion) are extended forgiveness by an all-loving and merciful God. No matter what our sin might be, God actively invites us to forgiveness, waiting patiently as a loving parent waits for his child to respond. God is always at the top of the hill, watching and waiting for us to return to him. (2014)

Joy

In our lives, there are many occasions of joy: the birth of a child, the marriage of young lovers, the celebration of anniversaries, birthdays, and graduations. All these occasions bring joy because they affirm life and love in the present moment, but they also present enormous potential for the future. Joy flows from the overwhelming delight of the moment.

Our lives and spirits are also renewed through the recollection of these joyous moments. So the church returns year after year to seasons of joy such as Easter and Christmas. By annually revisiting these joyful events, the church nourishes and sustains us spiritually.

Spiritual joy is founded on the fulfillment of Christ's word that not only gives joy in the moment and a promise for the future, but it sustains us through dark and desperate times. The foundation of Christian joy is hope in the Lord. It is based upon the expectation of the fulfillment of God's promises, if not at this moment, at some time in the future. Joy is an experience or emotion that happens in time but speaks of all the wonderful possibilities of a time to come. Joy is the abiding presence of God's Spirit.

Genuine joy is not predicated on success as the world measures it but rather on living life based on the gospel message. In the Sermon on the Mount, Jesus doesn't promise life without difficulty but rather tells us to rejoice and be glad when life is tough, for our reward is great. (Aug. 2001)

God's Mercy Is without End

Jesus repeatedly stressed the joy in the kingdom of heaven over a single sinner who repents and returns to God in Luke 15:1–7 (the parable of the Lost Sheep). It is clear that God's generous mercy applies to all people. Jesus gives us the following parables as a reminder: Luke 15:25–32 (the prodigal son's brother), Matthew 20:1–15 (the parable of the workers in the vineyard), Luke 18:9–14 (the parable of the Pharisee and the tax collector).

Self-righteousness doesn't look too flattering in these stories, even if the "righteous" are not "serious" sinners. It is important to remember that all human beings are in need of God's mercy and love.

The point of Matthew 20:1–15 (the parable of the workers in the vineyard) is that God's generosity and mercy far exceed man's limited view of justice. The keeper of the vineyard asked if he had the right to be generous. Perhaps we have heard this parable and possibly have felt, in our heart, that the owner was just a little bit unjust to those who had endured the full heat of the day. I know I have often had that thought.

God's mercy is without end, and there is nothing anyone can do that cannot be forgiven. If a terrible criminal asks God's forgiveness, it is extended to him. A lifelong sinner can repent at the end of his life, and God's compassion is there for him. God's forgiveness is limitless no matter how deep and dark our sinfulness may be. He asks only that we recognize our sinfulness and return to him.

In the parables of Jesus, the individuals who recognized their sinfulness and repented were a cause for great joy and happiness in the kingdom of heaven. The fate of those who thought themselves righteous and not in need of forgiveness is less clear.

The strange and scary element of these parables is the lack of love that the "righteous" folks display. A pious life can bring joy, peace, and happiness, but jealousy and self-righteousness should have no place in our relationship with God or our brothers and sisters. Emulation of God's mercy and compassion are key to our own joy and happiness. (2016)

A God beyond Mercy and Forgiveness

Before the Lord the whole universe is a grain from a balance or a drop of morning dew come down upon the earth. But you have mercy on all, because you can do all things; and you overlook people's sins that they may repent. For you love all things that are and loathe nothing that you have made; for what you hated, you would not have fashioned. And how could a thing remain, unless you willed it; or be preserved, had it not been called forth by you? But you spare all things,

> *because they are yours, O Lord and lover of souls, for your imperishable spirit is in all things! Therefore, you rebuke offenders little by little, warn them and remind them of the sins they are committing that they may abandon their wickedness and believe in you O Lord.* (Wisdom 11:23, 12:2)

In light of this passage, will not God after death still be merciful? Will he not overlook people's sins that they may repent? For he loves all things that are and loathes nothing that he has made; for what he hated, he would not have fashioned. You spare all things because they are yours. O, Lord, you are lover of souls, and your imperishable Spirit is in all things. For this, we shall shout out. All praise and glory to you, O Lord of mercy, forgiveness, and love. Your name, O Lord, is *love*.

How limited and truncated is our concept of God's mercy and forgiveness? Through categorization—moral, spiritual, and dogmatic—we have limited an infinite God to finite concepts. These words of Scripture, whether one is a believer or not, are a statement of our worth as human beings. They are also a mandate that behooves us to look at each other with the eyes of God—with eyes full of wonder and respect, with eyes full of mercy and love even for those who believe differently than we. We are all daughters and sons of God and brothers and sisters to each other.

In his book *Far from the Tree*, Andrew Solomon, with great wisdom, concern, and empathy, delves into issues of identity, disability, and love as set within the family and the surrounding society. Solomon, in great detail, deals with homosexuality, deafness, Down syndrome, autism, rape, transgender, and several other issues. He notes that fewer and fewer people are mortified by who they are, whether they be homosexual, autistic, or a member of any of the groups he writes about.

In the past, we have shamed, consciously or subconsciously, many people for what they were and assigned erroneous reasons for their conditions. These reasons were mostly negative and, in some cases, sighted as punishment by God or seen as the devil's work—in either case, a devastating and false judgment. "Hate the sin and love the sinner" was used to cover deep animosity regarding many of these conditions or identities. Oftentimes, we would wind up hating the person and not doing much to understand and assist our sisters and brothers.

What becomes very clear in *Far from the Tree* is that those who have offspring cherish and seek happiness for their children. Happiness is desired by all people. If you ask parents what they desire most for their children, happiness ranks right up there with good health and success and all that these things include.

Do we—should we—expect less from God? Religion, in many cases, has lost sight of the personal and has focused on trying to ascertain right from wrong and believing and defining dogmas. This is not to say the Catholic Church has not done tremendous work in many areas such as health, education, aid to the poor and hungry, and many other areas. However, scriptures of all faiths say little or nothing about dogmas and articles of faith. What else should religion be doing? Perhaps Jose Arregi's open letter to Pope Francis will give some insight as to the answer. "*The church is not here to define what is regular and what is irregular, but to accompany, encourage, and support each person as they are, where they are.*"

The Catholic Church and many other churches have lost touch with this mission in pursuit of patriarchalism, neglect of dialogue, being too anxious about being right, too willing to express in absolute terms or semiabsolute terms what they see as truth or making *their* truth absolute or without error. Putting rules and regulations above people with complicated problems does not address in an adequate way these problems.

The mantra of a recent pope, "Be not afraid," has been undermined by his fear to even dialogue with learned theologians of the church. The traditional paradigm is not open or flexible enough to take into account the complexities of the present time. A lack of sensitivity for individuals and the complexity of the issues is becoming a stumbling block for meaningful dialogue about the intricacy of multiple and complicated issues of modern society. The church has set itself up as the authoritative guide to right action and the enforcer of rules and regulations, many of which have come about through a priori reasoning. (2019)

Diversity and Respect

While in South Florida last week, I went scuba diving with a friend. We dove off Key Largo in the Florida Keys. When we hit the water, we knew this was going to be a great dive. The water was crystal clear and as blue as the sky. The fish were abundant and bright, and vibrant colors jumped out at us and beckoned us to come closer. The variety and diversity of the fish life were just astounding. There were sergeant majors, some with yellow-and-black stripes, others with blue-and-yellow stripes. There were needlefish and boxfish, grouper, and snook. The parrotfish came in all sizes and colors. Some were blue, some were brown, and others were green. The diversity among the parrotfish was a treat. We even saw a moray eel and a nurse shark. I could not help but think of how wonderful and diverse God's creation is. God could have made all the fish the same, but he chose this wonderful amalgamation of colors and sizes, shapes, and forms to express his creativity and love.

On this same trip to Florida, I attended the graduation ceremony of the class of 2001 on a beautiful spring day at St. Thomas University. My classmate, dive buddy, and best friend Frank Casale is the president of St. Thomas University. As much as I had been awed by our experience of God's wonderful works on the reef off Key Largo, I was even more awed and moved at this ceremony. The diversity and harmony among the students of this graduating class were marvelous to behold. What I saw was truly edifying and joyous. There were Hispanic students of Cuban descent and students from Spain, South America, and Central America.

There seemed to be people from every tribe and nation under the sun. There were Native Americans and people from Europe, India, and Asia. The color of the people ranged from dark black to white and every shade of brown in between. This scene filled me with emotion and nearly brought me to tears. How wonderful is God's creation! How diverse are God's people! What a plan! How thankful I am to be a small part of that diversity. The love, affection, and respect these students had for each other were wonderfully apparent. It became even more obvious to me how graced we are that God shares and reveals his inner being with us through the diversity of his creation and especially in the diversity of the human race.

One of the scripture readings from Mass that Sunday was from the book of Revelations 22:10–14, 22–33. The reading spoke of the temple of Jerusalem and about its twelve gates—three facing east, three facing north, three facing south, and three facing west. The church was filled with people of many different colors who spoke many different languages. In the homily, the celebrant asked the people why they thought there were twelve gates and why they were facing the four directions of the compass. Aside from the fact that there are twelve tribes of Israel and twelve apostles, it was decided that the twelve gates facing all directions were so that all peoples could enter God's temple. All the diversity of God's people would enter through the gates to be in the kingdom of God, the Father of all humankind.

A little further in the reading, there was no temple made of stone with twelve gates but only God, who is the gate and temple and who is open to all the peoples of the earth. All these thoughts and experiences came together in a very special and meaningful way for me on this short stay in Florida.

These thoughts of diversity and respect led me to reflect on my feelings regarding religious and ethnic differences. It seemed to me to be evident that religious and ethnic diversities are as much a part of God's plan as diversity among his creatures. Nicholas of Cusa, a theologian and philosopher, reflecting on the mystery and otherness of God, characterized God as a line going in opposite directions. Just when we think we are at a point where God is somewhat comprehensible, we are confronted with his utter incomprehensibility. At times, some of us are confused and unsure about our own faith and beliefs. Should we question or impugn the beliefs of our fellow human beings? Those who believe differently from us are no less committed and are no less worthy of respect and dignity than we. If we fail to realize this and act accordingly, we violate our own beliefs.

Religious fundamentalism, close-mindedness, and the pressing desire for total adherence to one set of spiritual beliefs can end in disaster. Islam, Christianity, and Judaism have all been guilty, to a greater or lesser degree, of using violence in the name of religion. Whenever religious fundamentalism and the power of the state join together, it is not good for society. Religious diversity, human freedom, and ethnic multiculturalism suffer, and at times severely.

We need not look too far into the past to see how racism in Germany devastated the Jewish population of Europe in the 1940s. In Ireland, we see how religious and political enmity has wreaked havoc on the Irish people. In the United States, the fundamental racial inequities that have lasted for more than three hundred years threaten the foundations of our democracy. In Palestine, the constant tension between Jews and Arabs is a threat to the peace of that region of the world. This is to say nothing of the conflicts in Africa, China, Afghanistan, South America, and many other parts of the world.

When we look at God's creation with open minds and hearts, we can see that diversity is part and parcel of this creation. It is at the very essence of life on all levels. It is evident in the plants and trees, fish and animals, and in the races of the human family.

The experience I had on this short vacation in Florida gave me an opportunity to reflect on God's wonderful creation, on its diversity, and on the respect God shows for each and every one of us no matter where we fall in the spectrum of color, language, ethnic background, or religious affiliation. It is up to us to show respect and reverence for the differences among races and creeds. It is up to us to appreciate different religious beliefs and national customs. Humanity is more important than race, and people are more important than national and religious boundaries. (May 11, 2001)

Enlightenment

Purgatory, a concept that is all but forgotten, was defined and decreed by the nineteenth ecumenical council, which is known as the Council of Trent (1545 to 1563). Purgatory's existence was affirmed, and certain characteristics were delineated. It was seen as a place of final purification, which is somewhat rational and sane but which is entirely different from the concept of hell (eternal punishment with no hope of redemption), which is totally irrational and insane.

For me, purgatory or a similar concept makes a great deal of sense as opposed to the concept of hell. If we truly believe God is an all-loving, all-good, all-merciful, and all-forgiving God, how do we justify hell? You might say God gave us free will; therefore, we condemn ourselves to hell. Just think for a moment, if your child or loved one committed an act that society saw as worthy of the death penalty, would you not have difficulty condemning him or her to death? You might say, "No, it would only be just." That might be so, but could you condemn your son or daughter to eternal punishment? This is what we claim God does. Remember, justice is the minimum required by all religious and moral nonreligious people. Can we expect less of God? The gospels tell us over and over again that mercy, forgiveness, and love trump justice.

When I was in the second or third grade in a Catholic school in Jersey City, a kind Sister of Charity taught us of the mercy and love of God for his creation and especially for his children. She explained that even Judas, who betrayed Jesus, was not necessarily condemned to hell. She talked of the love, forgiveness, and mercy of God. This magnificent religious insight left an indelible mark on my psyche and soul. From that point on, my feeling and belief were that God, by his nature, wills to offer forgiveness to his sons and daughters for all time. He would never have created us (being all-knowing) knowing that our fate would be eternal punishment. I believe God will offer again and again the chance and the ability to seek his love and forgiveness.

For me, hell doesn't make a great deal of sense and seems an impossible creation for a loving God. Even If one says hell is of our own creation, it still does not ring true. The concept of purgatory makes more sense than the concept of hell. I would consider purgatory as a place in which God offers his forgiveness over and over again until we ultimately come, with humble hearts, to that love that has always been there.

You might say, What about justice? If someone leads a life that is truly evil, why should they not be condemned to hell, punishment for all eternity? A state such as hell does not seem befitting or reflective of a God who is love. It would seem more just and loving if there were a process by which even the evilest person could come to redemption. Purgatory should not be a state of punishment but rather a state of enlightenment. My question again would be, how could an all-loving, all-good, all-merciful, and all-compassionate God conceive of and create a being that could be capable of committing an act that would cause himself or herself to spend all eternity in agony? Why would God bother creating an individual whom he knew would be consigned to eternal punishment? We might ask what kind of masochistic being would act in this sadistic fashion?

I would suggest that even the evilest person, let alone a loving person, would not do this to another human being. Is there something wrong with our concept of God? Perhaps our theology and our concept of God need more development? Would not a non-God be better than a God who could condemn his children or allow his children to be consigned to eternal punishment? Is our concept of God still evolving? Perhaps we still have much to learn about God?

If we take a moment to reflect on a few parables used by Jesus to enlighten us of the scope and depth of God's love, it may help us to see the heart of the gospel message, which is love that goes beyond even mercy and forgiveness. Luke 15:11–32, the parable of the forgiving father, known in the past as the parable of the prodigal son, beautifully reminds us of the unconditional love God has for each and every individual. The father said to the faithful son, "*You are here with me always; Everything I have is yours. But now we must celebrate and rejoice because your brother was dead and has come to life again; he was lost and now is found.*"

Again, the parable of the lost sheep (Matt. 18:10–14) gives us an insight into how valuable even one person is in the eyes of God.

> *If a man has one hundred sheep and one goes astray, will he not leave the ninety-nine in the hills and go in search of the stray? And if he finds it, amen I say to you, he rejoices more over it than over the ninety-nine that did not stray. In just the same way, it is not the will of your heavenly Father that one of these little ones be lost.*

And finally, for our consideration Jesus's admonition to love our enemies: "*But to you who hear I say, love your enemies, do good to those who hate you, bless those who curse you. Pray for those who mistreat you… Do to others as you would have them do to you…for he [God] himself is kind to the ungrateful and the wicked*" (Luke 6:27–36). If this is what God asks of us, how much more will he offer us infinite mercy, forgiveness, and love.

It is my contention that even with our limited knowledge of God, eternal punishment is not a believable option. (2019)

Jesus's Mission

This by no means is an orthodox view, but as I see it, Jesus's mission was religious, social, and political. He came *"that we might have life and have it more abundantly"* (John 10:10). He came for us not just for himself or the Father but for you and me. He strove to give us an example of how to achieve the fullness of life in this world and in whatever is to come. This is what I see as salvation. Jesus did this by giving us positive examples as demonstrated in his life and teaching. The gospels are replete with stories and parables illustrating this point, The Beatitudes (Matt. 5:3–11), the parable of the forgiving father (Luke 15:11–32), the parable of the judgment of the nations (Matt. 25:24–46).

For I was hungry and you gave me to eat.

*For whenever you did this for one of the least
of my brothers and sisters you did it for me.*

This is the answer to social equality and justice. Through his devotion to what he saw as the Father's will, he worked to bring men and women into relationship with the transcendent and each other by establishing a kingdom of justice, mercy, peace, and love. Throughout his life, he emphasized not hatred, not vengeance, not selfishness, not greed, not war but rather love, peace, justice, generosity, and sharing. His first commandment was and still is to love God with all our heart and with all our soul and with all our mind; this is the first commandment, but the second is similar: "*You shall love your neighbor as yourself*" (Matt. 22:39).

How do we actually love God? By doing his will? What is his will? Is it not for us to love our neighbor (our brothers and sisters, all people)? "*You shall love your neighbor as yourself*" (Matt. 22:39). It bears repeating. If this isn't Christianity, what is?

There is no other measuring rod for our love of God other than how we love and treat our brothers and sisters. All the rituals, rites, dogmas, articles of faith, rules, and regulations are not a true measuring rod of our love for God and mankind. We should also remember that those who do not believe in God but do his will are like those in the parable of the two sons (Matt. 21:29), one saying he would not work in his father's vineyard and the other saying he would. In actuality, the one who refused worked, and the one who said he would did not. Who then did the father's will? Just as Jesus said, *"Not everyone who says to me 'Lord, Lord' will enter into the kingdom of heaven; but he who does the will of my Father in Heaven"* (Matt. 7:21). We must actually practice what we say we believe if we are to have life more abundantly or salvation.

Jesus was also a figure who called religious, political, and social institutions and systems to accountability, repentance, and reform. The Gospels are again filled with condemnations of hypocrisy and injustices of the religious and political institutions of the day. In Matthew 3:7, immediately after his baptism, Jesus's first recorded act in Matthew is the condemnation of the religious leaders of his day (Pharisees and Sadducees): *"You brood of vipers."* Religious leaders tried to condemn Jesus for doing good on the Sabbath, putting rules and regulations above people and claiming it to be God's will:

> *Is it lawful to do good on the Sabbath, or to do evil or to give health to a life, or destroy it?* (Mark 3:1–6)

I desire mercy not sacrifice. (Matt. 9:13)

Shortly after Jesus's triumphal entry into Jerusalem, both the political and religious leaders came together and planned his capture and death. He had become a threat to the systems and institutions of society, religion, and politics. This could not be tolerated; death, rather than conversion and repentance, was the solution. The same conflict is being waged today. We are still at odds with the same hypocrisy and corruption that plague religious, political, and societal institutions and systems to say nothing of individuals.

We must be careful not to condemn all institutions and systems as a whole because some institutions and systems, even though flawed, do enormous good, and without them, we cannot function. We should also recognize that they are neither all good nor all bad. What we need is more transparency, honesty, accountability, and critical oversight. Looked at in this way, it is easier to see that these systems and institutions are, in fact, part and parcel of religion. For Jesus, the love of God and God's will are intimately tied to how we treat each other. (2011)

CHAPTER 3
Christian Concepts

Word of God, Bread of Life

The Eucharist is the centerpiece of Catholic worship and spiritual life. Catholics (or at least older Catholics) believe in the real presence of Christ in the Eucharist. This means that Jesus's body and blood are made present to the community of the church during the celebration of the mass in the form of bread and wine. In John 6:34–58, the people ask for the bread of life, and Jesus responds,

> *I am the bread of life; he who comes to me will never be hungry; he who believes in me will never be thirsty. I am the living bread that came down from heaven. If anyone eats this bread, he will live forever. The bread that I will give him is my flesh, which I give so that the world may live.*

Catholic theology teaches this impractical and puzzling doctrine.

For Catholics, Jesus is not only the Bread of Life, he is also the Word of life, the Word of God. Although Catholic theology has always stressed the belief in Jesus's real presence in the Eucharist, there is a vital connection between the Word of God and the Bread of Life, even if the Eucharist is only symbolic. The Eucharist never stands apart from Scripture. The link between the two cannot be emphasized too strongly. Through the centuries, the church, composed of laity and clergy, has developed a liturgy embracing God's Word and God's Eucharist. These two elements are interdependent. Without the Word of God read, preached, and absorbed during this celebration, the Bread of Life is trivialized and can become an empty symbol that has little relevance to our daily lives. When viewed this way, the scriptures come into clearer focus. It is Scripture in combination with the Bread of Life that gives Christian life vitality and meaning.

The Word of God gives power and freedom to us as Christians. In order for the Eucharist to be vital in our lives, we need to listen, to read, and to act upon the Word of God. *"Indeed, the word of God is living and active, sharper than any two-edged sword, piercing until it divides soul from spirit, joints from marrow; it is able to judge the thoughts and intentions of the heart"* (Hebrews 4:12).

A Eucharist, empowered by the Word of God, goes out into the world, renewing and recreating. The Word of God and the Bread of Life are two sides of one reality and that reality is the Word of God, Jesus Christ. (2005)

The Meaning of Creation

The story of creation found in Genesis 1:1–31 is much more than a simple creation story. These thirty-one verses of Scripture give us a deep insight into the creativity of God. The creation account tells us more than God creating the world in six days and resting on the seventh. The time and order of God's creation are not important. God being responsible for all of creation in all its multiplicity is important. Whether God created in six days or a million years, through an explosion or through a process, is not important. God creating the universe and seeing that it was good in every aspect and detail are important. Whether God created man and woman in an instant or over a long evolutionary process is not important. God creating man and woman and them being created in his image and likeness are important. God creating the fish of the sea, the birds of the air, the animals of the land, and the plants of the earth on a particular day or in a particular way is not important. All his creatures being a special and vital part of God's creation and plan is important.

God has communicated to us in the creation account, not facts about creation but the meaning of creation. He tells us about his generosity and love, about his desire to create and share. He speaks to us of his relationship to the world and all its creatures. God maps out man's relationship to the world's creatures and its Creator. He tells man of his importance in this ongoing creation and of his obligations and responsibilities. In Genesis 1:26–31, God is described as man's creator: "*They [man and woman] will have power over the fish; the birds and all the animals…your descendants will live all over the earth and bring it under their control. I am putting you in charge of the fish.*" What a privilege! How honored man should be to be in charge, to be responsible for creation.

This does not mean man is more important than creation but rather is part of creation and is charged with its care and protection. In order that man might not be prideful and miss the point, God, in Genesis 2:7, is described as creating and forming man from the soil of the earth. This was done to show man his basic and fundamental connection to the earth. It is the earth from which man is brought into existence; it is to the earth that man is bound and inextricably connected. It is to Mother Earth that man will return. It is not man who produces earth but rather earth who produces man. It is not man that nourishes Mother Earth but Mother Earth who nourishes man.

God did not want us to miss this point. On the one hand, God puts us in control, but on the other hand, God demonstrates to us how dependent we are upon the rest of his creation. Just as the chosen people were not chosen for privilege but for service, so too man has been created not to exploit the universe but to be responsible and accountable for this wonderful creation of God's.

Just as an individual cannot abuse himself or herself without severe repercussions, so too mankind cannot abuse this world and its resources without serious consequences for all mankind. We should derive pleasure and delight from the universe, but we should realize this creation does not belong to us. We are part of this creation, and only if we see ourselves as we are—a small but integral part—do we begin to understand God's plan.

If we look closely and realistically at the universe and our Earth, in particular, we begin to realize that it can exist without us. The birds, fish, animals, and plants of this Earth can exist without us. The water, air, and mountains can exist without us. We need them! We are dependent on them! God has made this abundantly clear. We are the stewards of God's creation, and as Mario Cuomo explains in *More than Words*, our survival is dependent on the survival of all God's creatures. (2006)

Sacred Scripture

Mario Cuomo, in his book *More than Words*, wrote of the constitution of the United States, "*Much of the Constitution is deliberately and unavoidably ambiguous-written in its time, its genius is that it can be stretched to fit changing realities without tearing.*" He also points out that the constitution of the United States is a wonderful governmental document based on the values of equality, individual rights, respect for the rights of others, work for the common good, respect for law, and love of country.

The Founding Fathers had a vision in which they realized that no one individual or no group of individuals could write a document that would cover all situations for all times. They gave us a set of principles to guide this country now and in the future. This human document has guided us for over two hundred years. What a tribute to our Founding Fathers and those who followed in their footsteps.

The Constitution can be used to illustrate what a living document is meant to be. If we can say this of a document written by men, how much more powerful and awesome are the scriptures that are both the work of God and men. The scriptures are a living, vital work that contains eternal truths that have been written by men under the subtle direction of God's Holy Spirit. God has revealed himself and his plan in history through these writings of men. The human authors of Scripture used many different literary devices including metaphor, myth, poetry, epics, psalms, parables, laws, fables, and more to express what God wanted to reveal to man.

The question is, in seventy-some books of Scripture, was every circumstance and situation addressed for all times? The answer to that question is yes and no. The Constitution was not meant to address all political and governmental issues for all time but to set principles to help in the present and to guide us in the future. So it is with Scripture that sets forth truths and principles that spoke to the people of yesteryear but also speak to men and women for all time. Issues of our day—such as cloning, racism, environment, slavery, war, capital punishment, sharing wealth, in vitro fertilization, sterilization, and countless other issues—are not dealt with or considered specifically in Scripture. The principles and truths found in Scripture can be used to guide us in dealing with these modern problems.

We don't take each and every word in only a literal sense since this would limit the richness and depth of God's Word. We look, above all, for the truth, the spiritual and theological meaning of Scripture, that allows us to apply these truths to our present-day problems and concerns just as people have done throughout the ages.

Raymond Brown, in his book *Reading the Gospels with the Church*, quotes Vatican II's document on Divine Revelation: "*The books of Scripture must be acknowledged as teaching firmly, faithfully and without error that truth which God wanted put into the sacred writings for the sake of our salvation.*" He also tells us, "*The Gospels are the product of considerable development-narrative, organizational and theological development. They are not simply literal accounts of the ministry of Jesus.*"

He goes on to say that this is a far cry from assuming that every statement in Scripture has to be literally accurate. In fact, there are many obvious scientific and historical errors and contradictions contained in the Bible. This, however, in no way diminishes the truths intended to be communicated. Even the four gospel accounts have some significant differences in their presentation of Jesus's life, death, and resurrection. These differences, rather than causing concern, should help us understand that God, in Scripture, is teaching us religious truth rather than science, history, or some other discipline. Through human authors, the transcendent is showing many facets of truth. Over the centuries and especially over the last two hundred years, the church has recognized the flexibility and adaptability of the scriptures. This has allowed people to be guided and inspired by the riches and depth of the Living Word. (2004)

Incarnation

"And the word became flesh and dwelt among us" (John 1:14). This is a verse from John's gospel read on Christmas Day. The incarnation: the Word of God made flesh, the Word that existed with the Father before the world began—this is the Word, without whom nothing came to be, the source of all life taking on our human life. This event described by John emphasis the transcendent, theological, and mysterious nature of the incarnation.

"And she gave birth to her first-born son and wrapped him in bands of cloth, and laid him in a manger because there was no place for them in the inn." Luke 2:7 approaches this event from an entirely different vantage point. He accentuates the humble, mundane, and human aspects of this event.

Both views, when taken together, reflect a divine-human event.

For those of us who were born and raised as Christians, the incarnation, God becoming man, is part and parcel of our faith. It is an event that we take for granted. We refer to the incarnation as a wonderful, mysterious event, an act of God's love for us, but can we indeed grasp its awesomeness? How could an infinite God, an incomprehensible being, a being without wants or needs, humble himself to become the equal of one of his worldly creatures? The difference between God and man is infinite; it cannot be measured. How can this be? Unbelievable?

The ramifications are stupendous and can only engender humility and dignity. Humility flows from the realization that humankind is truly dust, creatures totally dependent on God for everything—our being, our freedom, and our goodness. Dignity emanates from the fact that all human beings are obviously of great value to God, who humbled himself by entering history in the incarnation.

Creation and incarnation speak the same message to us: you are good, you are loved, you are responsible, and you are God's miracle. Human life, made forever sacred in creation, is reaffirmed, redeemed, and made sacred again through the incarnation. As finite as we are, God has placed a spark of the infinite in each of us, a spark that cannot be revoked, which gives us value and worth. It is this spark that shines forth in us as the image and likeness of God. The incarnation is more than the birth of Jesus; it is God and his creation being made one.

The incarnation is a special event, one that for some is understandably beyond belief. It is the birth of our Savior God as man, as one who is flesh and blood. It signals our eternal redemption coming in the person of Jesus Christ.

In Genesis, God's goodness and the goodness of his creation are made manifest. God the Father looked at his creation and found it good. Through the incarnation, God becoming flesh is a reaffirmation of the goodness and value of his original handiwork.

Although man was sinful and had lost his way, God reaffirmed both his love for mankind and the goodness of his creation. With the coming of Jesus, the world and everything in it were somehow recreated. If human nature and human flesh are good enough to be the vehicle by which God came into history, then there is sacredness, goodness, and value in this world and everything in it. God says, "All this is my gift to you."

We can value ourselves and others as God values us. Is God telling us that we and the world we live in are more precious than we can possibly imagine? God chose the vehicle of flesh and blood, astounding as that is, to make himself present to us. It is only through flesh and blood that we can make God present in the world. (2005)

The Problem of Original Sin

As a child, I had real difficulty with the whole idea of original sin. Why should I be blamed for something I did not do? Why should I have to suffer for the sin of our first parents? I must admit, even today, I struggle with the concept of original sin and its significance. On the other hand, there does seem to be a societal or community aspect to sin and evil.

The story of Adam and Eve and the first sin is a beautiful and simple literary exposition of a complex religious experience. It is an attempt on the part of the author to explain the state of the world as he or she found it. It was a world composed of sin, evil, and death but also a world full of life, beauty, and goodness.

Christians have developed the doctrine of original sin using this Scripture passage as the basis for this belief. Conclusions drawn from this story are just a starting point for the discussion regarding sin, evil, and the devil. This story is a literary form used in a time and place to give some insight into these realities. New information certainly does not support a literal interpretation of this Bible story. However, this passage does capture in a primitive way the depth and mystery associated with the nature of man, sin, death, evil, and our relationship with God. What the author communicates so successfully is that man is not in balance with himself, his fellow human beings, God, and the world around him.

Death and natural disasters existed long before human beings evolved. Physical death was part and parcel of the world's existence. In nature, there is a cycle of life and death, not only on this earth but also throughout the universe. I believe when Christianity speaks of sin as the cause of death, it refers mainly to the death of the human spirit. For the author of Scripture, Adam and Eve's choice brought death to their spirit, and along with spiritual death came the litany of evil characterized in the next few chapters of Genesis.

There is a tendency toward both good and evil within all humanity. Perhaps the story of the first sin is telling us that life is all about the fulfillment of potential and the choices to be made. While God has given us the option to choose, he has also involved himself in our destiny. All along the way, in all cultures and societies, God guides and assists humans to make choices for life. According to some, the doctrine of original sin expresses the view that life after "the fall" is a punishment for sins committed at the beginning of time. The result of original sin is sickness and death, banishment from paradise, and the loss of a perfect world. Is this true, or is life in this world meant to be a gift given by God that is filled with possibilities and potential, not perfect in the sense of being complete and incapable of being made better? Perhaps it was never meant to be a static state of perfection but rather a growing dynamic movement forward in the cycles and rhythms of life. Physical death is not exclusively the result of sin but is a part of the cycle of life, not an end but a change, a movement from one stage of life to another.

Death of the spirit, however, is brought about by choices that lead away from God and away from the fulfillment of the potential God has created in us. Each and every choice leads to either spiritual life or death, and choices can have ramifications on both spiritual and physical realities. Most of the evil in this world is clearly the result of bad choices.

The doctrines of the incarnation, salvation, and redemption do not have to be in jeopardy if we view original sin in this light; in fact, they can become richer, fuller, and more dynamic. The question of whether there was an original sin and how and if it was transmitted does not devalue or enhance the beautiful story of Genesis 3. In fact, the doctrine of original sin is an intellectual concept that does little to help us understand the mystery of this pivotal event. For Christians, the ultimate guidance and direction come in the person of Jesus—one sent to be our example, our way, our truth, and our life. Jesus empowers us to choose life, not death; to live as he lived; and to fulfill the potential for which we were created. (2008)

Image and Likeness of God

Then God said, "Let us make humankind in our image, according to our likeness... So God created humankind in His own image, in the image of God He created them, male and female He created them."

—Genesis 1:26–27

This passage from the Hebrew scriptures is quoted often, but what does it mean? As we read further in Scripture, it becomes confusing. As a matter of fact, the Jewish scriptures give a mixed message about who God is. Sometimes God seems to be compassionate, loving, just, and merciful, and at other times, he seems to be angry, jealous, partial, and vengeful. These ways of looking at God seem contradictory. There are a host of emotions and qualities attributed to God by the authors of Scripture that seem to be incompatible with each other. Since the authors of Scripture give us a conflicted message about God's qualities and man is made in God's likeness, then who is man?

Holy Scripture is all about God's slowly revealing himself to man and man coming to know God in a relational process. This experience does not happen overnight. Because God is mysterious and human experience starts with self, man learns about God by extrapolating concepts from the self. As part of this process, to some extent, man has imagined a God in his own image and likeness. Under the influence of God's Spirit, man begins to comprehend, in a limited fashion, truths about God and himself. This should be no surprise since mankind is engaged in a gradual evolutionary learning process on every level of its existence.

Many of the authors of Scripture have portrayed God as a person with infinite but humanlike powers. This anthropomorphic concept of God confines understanding of God. Words themselves are signs and symbols that can inspire and inform but, in the final analysis, are an imperfect expression of even finite concepts.

Man's perception of God tells us more about man than it does about God. The danger here is that we limit the limitless because of our limitation to conceive of a God without limits. We try to make him (her, it) fit our categories. We also understand his word in a restricted fashion.

In Romans 11:33, Paul says, "*O the depth of the riches and wisdom and knowledge of God! How unsearchable are His judgments and how inscrutable His ways!*" The study of seventy-plus books of the Hebrew and Christian Scriptures is an attempt on the part of man to understand the mystery that is beyond understanding. This does not mean that God cannot communicate with mankind. It simply means that fullness of understanding is not possible, for finite creatures cannot come to a total comprehension of the infinite.

Spiritual writers over the centuries, along with the fathers and doctors of the church, have many and varied theories regarding this mystery. Even after "the fall," despite the evil and depravity at work in the world, the authors of Scripture saw in man something of God. In Genesis 1:26–27, we see that man is a cocreator with God. God has given us the power to participate in the creation of life and the ability to exercise freedom and love. In these ways, we are the image and likeness of God.

Still, we must strive to conform more perfectly to that image and likeness. We mirror God when we are compassionate and merciful, loving and just, humble and peace-seeking. In Hebrews, Paul tells us that God has spoken to us in many and various ways, but in these last days, he has spoken through his Son. The more we resemble Jesus, the more we reflect the image and likeness of God, for *"he [Jesus] is the reflection of God's glory and the exact imprint of God's very being"* (Hebrews 1:3). (2007)

Sacrament

Sacraments are seen by some Christians and especially by Catholics as gifts of grace that flow from God and his people through which God empowers the community to celebrate the sacred moments of an individual's spiritual life and the life of his people. The reality that they represent is deeper and more mysterious than the sacraments themselves. They are signs that point to a deeper and more spiritual reality of life. In many ways, they correspond to and parallel the important moments in our physical human existence. Sacraments are not only celebrations of moments in time but are eternal mysteries played out as part of our lives and are abiding, ever-present reminders of God's saving presence among us.

Just as birth gives us physical life and places us in a particular family and community, so too baptism is a sign of spiritual birth that locates us in the family of God within a particular community. Baptism brings with it many gifts that enable us to function as spiritual creatures supported by God and his people. Just as a physical family supports and nourishes life, so also does our spiritual family. The physical and spiritual life are not only parallel but are connected and intertwined, giving us the ability to grow and prosper, one life supporting the other. Without the spirit, physical life and all it entails remain uninformed and hollow. The spiritual life, on the other hand, builds upon nature and becomes difficult to actively engage in without a sound physical platform upon which to build. Without being born, physical life does not exist; and without spiritual birth of some type, we are diminished souls without an animating principle.

As we grow and develop, we need to be nourished both physically and spiritually. Life without a sustaining principle (food, Eucharist, Scripture) leads to malnutrition and eventually, death. It is important to recognize that sacraments do not exhaust our opportunity for grace or limit our contact with the transcendent. Sacraments are just one community's way of expressing the connection between God and man.

Over time, practices that were rights of imitation and traditions began to be seen as signs of Christ's presence and assistance in the lives of God's people. Christ himself is the supreme sacrament of God and the Christian church. We should also realize that the people of God are the sacrament of Christ's presence in the world. At the same time, we should remember that no institution controls the distribution of God's grace and the salvation offered to mankind in Jesus.

In penance, we seek, in a spiritual way, the forgiveness of God but also the forgiveness of the community symbolized in the priest. Again, we should understand that God's forgiveness is in no way contingent upon or limited by an institution or a sacrament. This rite recognizes the need for human as well as divine forgiveness. It also recognizes the cumulative universal effect of good and evil in the world. It is hoped that penance will vivify and magnify the forgiveness extended to us by God and his people. The form that penance has taken over the years has become inadequate for the needs of the faithful, and therefore, reform and updating are overdue.

Confirmation marks the beginning of adulthood in the spiritual life. It corresponds to coming of age in the physical realm. As we know, no one event makes us fully adult. Confirmation is not a magic sign that brings about spiritual adulthood. This sacrament aims to strengthen and support us in our growth toward maturity.

Marriage, priesthood, and anointing of the sick highlight important aspects of adult life. Relationships and family are recognized as special gifts of God needing his grace and support to be lived in accordance with the gospel message.

Priesthood is a sacrament of service, worship, and thanksgiving. It is recognized by God's people as the instrument by which the church worships God and expresses thanks and gratitude for the gift of life with its many blessings. Through an ordained minister, the community celebrates the sacred and cherished mysteries of faith.

Anointing with oil is an ancient and multifaceted sign. It is a sign of preparation for battle and strengthening. It is a sign of sanctification and healing. As a sacramental sign, it deals with extremely significant aspects of life. Sickness and death represent great mysteries both on the spiritual and physical plain. Through anointing with oil, the community of God gives us spiritual and physical support in sickness. When the moment of death is at hand, when it is time to pass from this stage of life to the next, the anointing with oil reminds us that we are not alone even in this last journey.

The church emphasizes the sacraments as avenues of grace because these times and events are the focal points of our relationship with God and our fellow man. It is at these times that God, the individual, and the community come together in a special way to celebrate his mysteries. It is at these times that we become more conscious of our relationship to God and his community, the church, and all people. It is these sacramental moments that, like the Word of God, sustain us through a lifetime. (2005)

Christmastime

It is Christmastime again, that time of year when we Christians celebrate the birth of Christ. For Christians, it should be a time of year in which we thank God for the gift of his Son, who is *supposed* to be our way, our truth, and our life. The gifts we offer to one another should represent and symbolize the gifts of life, love, and compassion personified in God's gift of Jesus Christ.

In the USA, we are truly blessed with material gifts and more. The freedoms to speak our minds, to worship as we please, and to pursue our dreams are just a few of the many freedoms and blessings we enjoy. At Christmas, the tradition of gift giving symbolizes that desire we have to share with one another and all people the blessings, gifts, and freedoms that God has bestowed on us through no merit of our own. Perhaps not by our conscious intent, but somehow, the authentic idea of gift giving has gotten commingled with materialism and self-centeredness. All this abundance has given me cause to wonder about those who are less fortunate. Has God abandoned them? Has he forgotten millions of people who are less fortunate, or does he just not care about them? Where is the justice, love, and compassion we sometimes speak so glibly about during this Christmas season?

We can't help but see these inequities. We are not stupid people, but perhaps, deep down, we are scared, overwhelmed, and more than a touch self-centered. Surely, we cannot be completely unaware of all the suffering, poverty, hunger, and sickness that exist just beyond our doorstep. Perhaps the problems are so overwhelming that we prefer to remain in the dark, or perhaps they scare us so much that we refuse to recognize or cope with them. Are the problems of the world so large and complex that we feel incapable or impotent in our ability to confront them? Does a combination of fear and self-centeredness keep us from addressing these somewhat obvious problems? Are we afraid that we will have to sacrifice our lifestyle if we are to help others? Does our self-centeredness obstruct our desire to be compassionate, loving, and just? Conceivably, a combination of these and other reasons contribute to our failure to meet moral challenges.

Lately, I have been thinking about the disparity between my blessed life and those who are less fortunate. Although I do not feel guilty, I am beginning to recognize a lack of justice and fairness that I have done little to correct. I understand that life is not fair, but somehow, to leave it at that doesn't seem right. I have been wondering why God doesn't see this, or if he does, why he doesn't do something about it. He is all-powerful, all-loving, and all-just. It just seems a little hard to understand.

At Christmastime, I have a tendency, as many of us do, to count my blessings, but this year, I felt somewhat uneasy; counting didn't seem to be enough. Over the last thirteen months or so, there have been many natural disasters: the tsunami, Katrina, and the Pakistani earthquake. Man-made disasters seem to be without number. Because of these and many other tragedies, hundreds of thousands of lives have been lost, and millions of people continue to suffer. Social agencies tell us that thirty thousand children die each day from hunger-related diseases. At times, it seems hard to reconcile our good fortune against this devastation.

We might possibly find answers to some of the above-asked questions in the Christmas mystery. God's gift is his Savior Son, sent to show us the way. Hard as it may be to grasp at times, Jesus's life is the example of how we are to respond to the world and all its problems. Jesus challenges us, in his loving way, to put aside, as best we can, our ignorance, fear, and self-centeredness. He asks us not to allow these things to overwhelm our desire to extend the gifts of love, justice, and compassion to our loved ones and to all in need.

Jesus helps us to understand that it is our responsibility to undo the disparity that exists in the world today. He came to show us the way, to show us how to live, not to live for us. We are God's gift to the world. It is through Jesus, at this special time of year, that we recognize our unique role in the redemption of the human race. We are good people who need only to act upon Jesus's example. He is the answer to all our questions. God expects us to bring justice, love, and compassion to the world in our unique way. We must tap that goodness and generosity that lie within each one of us, that goodness and generosity that is expressed in our gift giving each Christmas. (2010)

Resurrection

Looking back over your life, I am sure that there are moments, conversations, and events from your childhood that stand out with vivid clarity over and above the not so vivid and mundane memories of years ago. I have one such memory of a conversation with my brother regarding, of all things, the resurrection. I was in the seventh grade, and he was in his third year of a Jesuit high school. He claimed that the resurrection was the most important Christian event, and I argued that Christmas (the incarnation) was more important because without the birth of Jesus, there could be no resurrection. Of course, I had a point: the incarnation in some ways is even more mysterious than the resurrection, and a good argument could be mounted in its cause; however, St. Paul sides with my brother.

The fact of the matter is that without the resurrection, our faith is nothing but foolishness. In 1 Cor. 15:17–19, Paul tells us, *"If Christ has not been raised, your faith is futile… If for this life only we have hoped in Christ we are of all people most to be pitied."* These words of St. Paul are very strong and have great ramifications.

Today is Easter Sunday, and I am contemplating the meaning and significance of the resurrection. If there is no resurrection, if there is no life after death, then the truth and validity of our faith and the Christian promises are without foundation. The resurrection is the linchpin of the Christian faith, without which, its unity and truth fall to pieces. The truth and validity of all other beliefs and events have little meaning and are just part of an elaborate religious or moral system. The crucifixion of Jesus would be foolishness, and his teachings would have earthly significance only. He would have left us a moral/ethical system of great worth but not something to which we could commit our faith and hope.

Without the resurrection as the focal point of Christianity, how we perceive all the rest of our beliefs would change. All the rest of Christianity, although not unimportant, would be subject to discussion and alteration, but the resurrection in some form must stand, or the rest is without meaning. The promises are false. The fact that God entered the world and died for us would almost seem without a point. It would require a rethinking of ideas such as the incarnation, redemption, salvation, sacraments, heaven, hell, and a host of other beliefs. With all this said, we should not take lightly the incarnation. Without the incarnation, there could be no resurrection. Within the incarnation is held the seed of eternal life. Perhaps incarnation and resurrection are two sides of the same coin? One cannot exist without the other?

Our hope is based on the resurrection and the belief in everlasting life. Leading a good and moral life is motivated, for many, by the promise of everlasting life, but the example of Jesus's life shows us how to live in the here and now. Although goodness and right living should be reward enough, the hope of eternal life is a powerful motivation for most of us. It would probably be almost impossible for us to separate the desire for goodness and justice from eternal reward or punishment as the real motivating factor for our life activity. The hope and desire for eternal life are so strong that even if life everlasting did not exist, we would be like little children who, when asked to make a wish, wish for everlasting wishes.

It goes without saying that the resurrection of Jesus is a condition without which Christianity and our hope of resurrection have limited credibility. The resurrection is not a provable fact but a belief that requires the proverbial leap of faith. Whether we believe in Jesus's resurrection as a physical resurrection or as a spiritual resurrection, it is God's promise to human beings that just as Jesus was united with the Father after his death, we will also somehow be joined to God in eternal happiness. We can accept this belief or reject it, but once accepted, it can radically change all of reality. How we live, love, work, play, and relate to each other and to God are all transformed forever. The resurrection is perhaps the most important event of all time because it gives life and truth to Christianity itself. (2009)

Communication Equals Transformation

God wants us to pray. This seems to be evident from both the Jewish and Christian scriptures. Why? God knows our every thought and desire. Aside from our natural tendency to give thanks and praise to our Creator, petitioning seems to be something we do fairly frequently. But even this aspect of prayer seems quite unnecessary. God, through Jesus and the scriptures, has told us that he knows what we need before we even ask for it. It seems that God doesn't really need our thanks and praise, and he doesn't need our petitions to know our wants and needs. What then is prayer all about?

Prayer is not just about God in a narrow sense. Prayer is not an obligation. It is, in many senses, a gift. It is a lifeline by which we stay in touch with and receive support from our Creator and sustainer. Prayer is not for God; it is for us. We may not realize it; but when we drift from truth and love, when we fail to center on God, we can lose our sense of what is right and just. Without prayer, we falter in our inner self, we lose touch with reality, and we become introverted seeking our selfish desires. We may not realize it, but we fail or neglect to reflect on the ultimate, on the things that really count.

Without communication (prayer) and reflection, we tend to lose sensitivity to God's promptings. Just as in human relationships with our loved ones, communication is the vehicle by which we come to know and understand who the other is. Without it, our relationships begin to shrivel and lose the spirit that animates them.

I have never been a fan of repetitive prayer, but one of its values can be to set a tone of prayerfulness and openness, just as respectful conversation can be the door to deeper and more meaningful communication. Time for prayer, set aside on a regular basis over a substantial duration, is, for some, important. We don't usually become close friends with someone after only one or two conversations or communications. Scripture and thoughtful books, not just spiritual books, often help place us in the presence of God or prompt questions that lead us to seek truth in God.

Let your thoughts take you into the presence and mystery of God. It is not necessary to understand everything; sometimes the questions are the prayers. Be honest with yourself and God. Don't be afraid to ask the hard questions, and be open to unconventional and unorthodox responses. God loves you and welcomes your communication no matter what the content, spiritual or otherwise. Obtaining an absolute answer or resolution is not the point of prayer. Communication or friendship is what prayer is about. In prayer, we should rejoice in the encounter with God, for we have engaged God in a special and unique way that goes beyond our reality and understanding.

Transformation takes place when we put ourselves in the presence of God. It may not be as spectacular as Jesus's transfiguration on Mt. Tabor, but little by little, we are transformed when God is present to us in prayer. Prayer is one of the ways God allows us to enter into his transforming grace. Muhammad was aware of the importance of prayer when he required prayer five times a day and made this practice one of the five pillars of the Islamic faith. Jesus tells us to pray always. The essence of this communication (prayer) is to put us in God's presence, to open us to the transforming power of love that changes our lives and our relationships both with God himself and our fellow human beings. It can be a little frightening, but it is a process that usually happens bit by bit.

Prayer is not about what God needs; it is about what we need. Ask not what you can do for God but what God can do for you. Sound selfish? It's not! There is really nothing you can do for God, except love him, but he can and wants to do all things for you. Pray; be open. Let God transform you. (2006)

CHAPTER 4
9/11/2001

September 11, 2001

Today is September 13, 2001, two days after the attack on the World Trade Center, the Pentagon, and United Airlines Flight 93. My initial feelings were probably much the same as any American citizen: absolute horror, shock, and disbelief. It was hard to believe that this horrible catastrophe actually happened. The need for information and knowledge seemed extremely important. I listened to the radio while I was in the car and at home; I spent hours in front of the television.

My predominant feeling was not one of anger but rather a feeling of sadness and deep sorrow for all the innocent people who lost their lives. There was a special sense of sadness that so many police officers and firefighters lost their lives while courageously saving those trapped in the Twin Towers. There was also a feeling of sorrow that anything as evil as this could happen. The real agony came for me when I saw the pain and sorrow in the tear-filled eyes of those who lost loved ones. The anguish and frustration of those seeking information about their relatives and friends were difficult to deal with.

Politicians, and especially Rudy Giuliani, conducted themselves as real leaders, displaying compassion and understanding. The mayor was an inspiration and support for the people of New York, and especially for all the heroic firefighters, police officers, and rescue workers. He maintained an attitude of hope, calm leadership, and optimistic determination. When people of Arabian descent were being harassed and threatened, he spoke out in their defense, exhorting citizens not to act as the terrorists had acted.

These radical fundamentalists who caused the death of thousands of innocent people are an example of the perversion of religion and in no way represent the majority of believers in Islam. Most rational people would agree that the Aryan Nation and the Ku Klux Klan, who purport to be Christian, do not represent the majority of Christians. Hate and the perversion of truth is the common denominator of all radical fundamentalist groups. From their hate and perversion emanate decay, death, and destruction.

We must take every precaution to protect ourselves from this insidious cancer both physically and psychologically. For us to respond with hatred and evil will not only put us on a par with the terrorists, but it will be the beginning of the destruction of all we hold sacred and worthwhile. We need to be on guard to protect the lives of millions of innocent, peace-loving Muslims who despise the violence and death of September 11, 2001. The fundamentalist extremists who committed these crimes are religious madmen who have substituted evil for good and call it religion. They are as much a threat to the Muslim world as they are to ours.

The dilemma we face is complex. There is no doubt that a certain percentage of the Muslim world has ill feelings toward the USA. These feelings are tied to complex religious, social, political, and economic conditions. American involvement in the Middle East, weapons sales, and oil are some of the key ingredients in this tangled web. In our war with Iraq, *collateral damage*, a euphemistic term for death and destruction of innocent human beings, was seen as nothing more than the mere casualties of war. The frustrations of people who have little or no way to defend themselves, who live with death and violence as part of their daily lives, were beyond our comprehension until a few days ago. Out of this chaos come the lunatic fringe, the radical fundamentalists who are willing to make war directly on the innocent and unprotected in the name of God.

It is folly to believe that we can take on the entire Arab world. Even if we could, how could we justify the enormity of the death and destruction? It is important as a nation that we resist the notion that patience and a measured and limited response is a sign of weakness and impotence. Strength is not measured only in power and force. We must not be coerced into thinking we are weak or ineffectual because we respect life and are careful not to trample on these beliefs. Somehow, our religious and political leaders must convince our nation to do right rather than wrong, seek justice rather than revenge, respect innocent life rather than destroy it.

An appeal to all men and women of good faith must be the first approach. The potential consequences of relying on war and violence are beyond our imagination. I think the words of Martin Luther King Jr. are words to be heeded:

> *Now we got to get this thing right. What is needed is a realization that power without love is reckless and abusive, and that love without power is sentimental and anemic.*

> *Power at its best is love implementing the demands of justice, and justice at its best is love correcting everything that stands against Love.*

God in Our Lives

On Thursday morning, I went to Mass, and the scripture readings Colossians 3:12–17 and Luke 6:27–38 could not have been more appropriate if they had been selected especially for this occasion. I have included the two passages because they seem to me to be so important to this discussion.

> *Because you are God's chosen ones, holy and beloved, clothe yourselves with the heartfelt mercy, with kindness, humility, meekness, and patience. Bear with one another; forgive whatever grievances you have against one another. Forgive as the Lord has forgiven you. Over all these virtues put on love, which binds the rest together and makes them perfect. Christ's peace must reign in your hearts, since as members of the one body you have*

been called to that peace. Dedicate yourselves to thankfulness. Let the word of Christ, rich as it is, dwell in you. In wisdom made perfect, instruct and admonish one another. Sing gratefully to God from your hearts in psalms, hymns, and inspired songs. Whatever you do, whether in speech or in action, do it in the name of the Lord Jesus. Give thanks to God the Father through him. (Col. 3:12–17)

Jesus said to his disciples:

To you who hear me, I say: Love your enemies, do good to those who hate you; bless those who curse you and pray for those who maltreat you. When someone slaps you on one cheek, turn and give him the other; when someone takes your coat, let him have your shirt as well. Give to all who beg from you. When a man takes what is yours, do not demand it back. Do to others what you would have them do to you. If you love those who love you, what credit is that to you? Even sinners love those who love them. If you do good to those who do good to you, how can you claim any credit? Sinners do as much. If you lend to those from whom you expect repayment, what merit is there in it for you? Even sinners lend to sinners, expecting to be repaid in full. Love your enemy and do good; lend without expecting repayment. Then will you recompense be great. You will rightly be called sons of the Most High, since he himself is good to the ungrateful and the wicked. Be compassionate, as your Father is compassionate. Do not judge, and you will not be judged. Do not condemn, and you will not be condemned. Pardon, and you shall be pardoned. Give and it shall be given to you. Good measure pressed down, shaken together, running over, will they pour into the fold of your garment. For the measure you measure with will be measured back to you. (Luke 6:27–38)

The priest acknowledged that at this moment, the challenge of love and forgiveness might be difficult or even impossible to hear; nevertheless, it stands as the benchmark of what Christianity and true religion are all about.

For me, the ambivalent feeling seemed to be the order of the day. Pain, sadness, and loss will not be washed away in revenge. Although I believe love and forgiveness are part of the equation, I still feel that justice and redress are needed. Although these feelings seem mutually exclusive, they exist together in my mind. Will goodness and love grow stronger and larger if we pursue love and forgiveness, or will evil grow stronger and larger if we pursue violence and retribution? I as an individual and we as a nation must grapple with these issues. We need honest, open debate with no hidden agendas and no partisan politics. The only agenda should be to bring peace and justice to all people, and it should not be at the expense of innocent life. Killing and destruction are never the appropriate answer. The Jews and Arabs have been doing it for centuries and have yet to solve their conflicts.

During this time, I prayed, mostly in the morning about 7:30 a.m., in the brilliant sunlight and clear blue skies of September. This disaster along with the beautiful days made me think how wonderful it is to be alive. In my prayer, I questioned God and my beliefs about how it all works. I was keenly aware of the presence of the transcendent. The whys and the wherefores remain a mystery just as they do in the Holocaust and the genocides committed through the ages in the name of peace and religion. Prayer put me in touch with the transcendent being we call God, and I felt united somehow with all those who were in pain and anguish.

I was a student at Seton Hall University when JFK was assassinated on November 22, 1963. I was twenty-two years old. The horror and disbelief of both of these events were very much the same. They were a personal and national trauma of tremendous magnitude. Rev. Eugene Kennedy, a famous priest-psychologist at the time, spoke to the student body shortly after the assassination. He told us that we could tell who we were and what we were by the way we reacted to this horrific event. His statement made a lasting impression on me, and it seems to be applicable today. Our response to the events of September 11, 2001, will be a defining moment that will tell us who we are and what we are as individuals and as a nation. (Sept. 11, 2001)

Where Was God on 9/11?

Where was God on September 11? Why didn't he intervene, not only at the World Trade Center but also at Oklahoma, Hiroshima, Auschwitz, and thousands of other human tragedies? It is difficult to believe that God would ignore these great atrocities and intervene on less momentous occasions.

So how is God involved in this world of ours? Is his involvement normally indirect, somewhat subtle, and more mysterious than many religious folks would have us believe? Is it a mystery beyond our comprehension?

For sure, we see God in his creation and in his gift of life. The great religions of the world, along with their sacred writings, also put us in touch with God. Religious leaders, world events, and perhaps on occasions "miracles" bring us into a relationship with God. These are just some of the ways God involves himself in our lives. God, no doubt, acts through subtle and mysterious movements of his Spirit in our daily lives. I believe, much more often than not, God's Spirit is expressed through ordinary men and women. It seems to me, in this world, it is God's preferred way of acting.

When God did not intervene on September 11 (by saving the lives of innocent people), it was not a surprise, nor was it a reason for us to lose our faith. God did not intervene (save Jesus from death) on behalf of his own Son. This should be a clue for us that God's modus operandi is not normally one of direct intervention nor one we can easily understand.

The face of God is made visible in this world through human beings just as the face of evil is made visible in this world through human beings. *"A good person brings good out of the treasure of good things in his heart; a bad person brings bad out his treasure of bad things. For the mouth speaks what the heart is full of"* (Luke 6:45). From the hearts of evil men come evil acts; from the hearts of good men come good acts.

There is a great spiritual struggle going on that has its natural end in the physical and material world. There should be no mistake about the fact that the core and essence of the battle are spiritual, and the fruits of this battle often express themselves in the physical world. We saw a vivid example of the expression of evil on September 11. However, we also saw the expression of good in all the acts of people helping one another.

Unless all of us allow the Spirit of God to enter our hearts, we will continue to see the face of evil in our world. Our battle is the same as Jesus battle. It is not physical but spiritual and is being waged constantly in our hearts and minds. This spiritual battle, of necessity, spills over into the physical world. If we lose the spiritual battle, the material consequences are devastating. Just look at September 11. The perpetrators were filled with the spirit of evil. When the Spirit of God is not in our hearts, the face of God is not made present to the world. Without the Spirit, we fail to seek justice for the oppressed, to care for the sick, to feed the hungry, and to have compassion for the downtrodden. If the Spirit of God is not in our hearts, we become self-absorbed, concerned with our own small world, and blind to the needs of others. We fail to ask questions about the sacredness of life, about the mandates of charity, about the obligation to share the earth's bounty, and about the rights of all people to simply live. We excuse ourselves through some form of denial or some sophisticated rationalization.

Without the Spirit of God in our hearts, we give evil a place to grow and show its face to the world. The spirit of evil tells us it is just to be selfish, uncaring, and unconcerned about human life and well-being. The spirit of evil tells us it is morally permissible to shrink from the hard questions raised by the World Trade Center tragedy.

The real miracle is God's Spirit present in the ordinary work-a-day lives of his people. Mysterious and inscrutable as it may be, God speaks and intervenes in our lives in a multitude of ways. We need only to be open and sensitive to his presence. (2001)

Reflections

Today is the sixth-month anniversary of the attack on the World Trade Centers and the Pentagon. On the news last night, CBS aired a special program about a rookie fireman and the World Trade Center disaster. All this prompted me to write down some reflections about prayer, worship, and our attitude toward God just after 9/11.

This morning, there is a clear blue sky and bright sunshine. It is one of those mornings that is so beautiful that it seems inconceivable that anything evil could happen, a morning not unlike 9/11. But our experience belies the feeling of well-being that bright blue skies and bright, sunshiny mornings promise. We know all too well that evil things happen even on days of great promise.

Immediately following that fateful day and for a short period thereafter, people flocked to churches, prayed unabashedly, and seemed keenly aware of the spiritual dimension of life. This change was the subject of many news articles, and more than a few news commentators took note of these changes. I thought it was strange that it would take such a disaster to bring people to worship God and to pray. I wondered how real it all could be. Here we, are six months later, and the churches are just about back to where they were before 9/11.

Those who prayed and worshipped God before 9/11 were not driven to God by this disaster. A change had occurred for me and for most people who sought God on that day and shortly thereafter. Most of us became acutely aware of our vulnerability, powerlessness, and our dependence for life on a power far beyond our comprehension. We became conscious of our inability to control and protect our lives and the lives of our loved ones. The sense of security and control in our lives was seriously damaged, if not totally gone.

Rabbi Heschel's words come to mind:

> *It is a bitter observation: Life is constant peril; moral or even physical security is myth. It is only when we suddenly come up against things obviously beyond the scope of human domination or jurisdiction, such as mountains or oceans, or uncontrollable events like sudden death, earthquakes or other catastrophes, that we are shaken out of our illusions.*

It is an event like 9/11 that shakes us to the depths of our souls and challenges our illusions. This is just what happened! We realized just how little control we had over whether we lived or died. It is a frightening and scary thing. We turned to prayer, God, and the church because we became acutely aware that things were completely out of our control. We knew that only God could save us, that only God had control of life and death. Our reactions during this time, to some extent, were rooted in fear for our lives and the lives of our loved ones and in the hope that God somehow would save us, console us, and lead us from death to life.

This response of faith and prayer, for many of us, was like the seed sown by the farmer of the parable, which fell onto rocky soil. We responded quickly in a positive fashion but soon lost sight of the real lesson to be taken from this experience. We, at first, understood; we again saw the place of God in our lives, but for many of us, the message faded into the background. Perhaps this is because part of our response was based on fear. It did not sink in, and we returned to rely on ourselves while God's place in our lives faded into the background. When the fear dissipates, human nature tends to rely on its own devices and returns to a false sense of security.

Man has been learning and relearning the lesson of his true relationship to God from the very beginning. Throughout the Jewish Scriptures, the prophets called the Israelites to return to God. They were asked to live lives of devotion to God with justice and compassion for their fellow man. This attitude of mind and heart remains strong and lasting when it is based on love and respect and not on fear and need.

For some people, the next disaster will be seen as punishment for not heeding the message that could have been taken from 9/11. To view reality in this fashion is to distort God's will for us and to misunderstand God, whose great mercy and love could never allow him to act in this way. God stands ready always to help us understand the true meaning of life. He has shown us through his Son that the only response to rejection is selfless love. God does not punish us when we reject him; he only loves more. Man has visited evil on top of evil to his fellow man, but God visits only love, mercy, compassion, and forgiveness on those who reject him and do evil to his creation.

Sometimes we misunderstand scripture and glean from it a punishing, vengeful God when, in fact, it is only man who can be punishing and vengeful. God is incapable of meting out evil and hatred, and God is not man's enemy. He seeks out and loves all, even those who break his laws. Jesus tells us that he has not come for the righteous but for the sinner. Until we learn this lesson in our own lives, we will continue to return evil for evil, and the chain of violence and hatred will go unbroken.

The mystery of God's love expressed in the incarnation is beyond our ability to understand or fathom. God can never stop loving us regardless of what we do. Even if we don't seek forgiveness, God's love for us never fades. He loves us for all eternity, whether we reject him or not. So it becomes clear that hell, which probably doesn't even exist, is not a place that God condemns us to but rather a state of being that we choose when we deny and reject God. He never denies or rejects us. It is not God who rejects us but we who reject God. We cut ourselves off from God by seeking our own selfish ends, by seeking evil instead of good, by masking our bad will for our fellow men in self-righteous judgment. It is too often easier for us to see the speck in our brother's eye while ignoring the beam in our own eye.

We come to realize that our prayer must recognize God as the only true source of life, the one who has the ability to control life and death, the one who shows us we must choose life not death. We recognize that guilt and innocence accrue to all of us. Evil and goodness exist in each one of us. When we choose evil or goodness, the entire world moves toward sin and death or toward life and redemption. This is an awesome responsibility, but it is ours. God has shown us a better way in Jesus. It is through our good deeds and good thoughts that we restore and redeem the earth and all who live here.

After each disaster, man recognizes in the depth of his soul, his need for God. As long as man insists on following his own selfish desires, he will remain lost. God's way leads to goodness and life. As long as man does not heed the Word of God, he will continually remind himself, by events like 9/11, that his way (man's way) leads to disaster, death, and evil.

Our prayer today must recognize our true dependence on God, which becomes so vividly clear at times like 9/11. In our prayer, we need to be sensitive to the unity of all men founded and rooted in God's creative love for each one of us. God has no favorites!

Without a real attempt to reconcile with our sisters and brothers, we condemn ourselves to a hell that God abhors. It is only by asking for forgiveness and offering forgiveness and reconciliation to each other, a forgiveness and reconciliation that God has extended to us, that we escape the hell that we create. (2001)

Opportunity

The Rev. Jerry Falwell and Pat Robertson alluded to God's veil of protection being lifted from the USA during the terrorist attack on September 11, 2001, as if God loves and protects us more than other people. They indicated that because of our moral lapses as individuals and as a nation, God turned away from us and through the terrorists visited punishment upon us. It was as if God were no longer loving and forgiving but punishing and unforgiving. They were, in my estimation, positing evil acts as part of God's plan and somehow blaming us.

The truth and accuracy of this proposition are certainly suspect. But more to the point, it seems to be another example of religious fundamentalism passing itself off as the authoritative interpreter of God's will. It is amazing how so-called religious leaders are willing to speak for God and explain his ways so that they fit their theological and political agenda.

God, according to Jesus, *"makes his sun to shine on bad and good people alike and gives rain to those who do evil"* (Matt. 5:45). This tragedy had little to do with who was good or bad in the eyes of God or some mythical veil that protects only the good.

In Genesis, when Joseph's brothers sold him into slavery, he spoke about God's bringing forth good from evil. The evil of today that is brought forth from the hearts of evil men can only bring forth good if we, in our hearts, choose to be open to God's love and goodness. In both these cases, evil is not a legitimate vehicle to bring about good. This is what Paul means when he says all things work for good for those who love God. It is not a justification or a condoning of evil. It is rather a positive and hopeful reaction to evil and sinfulness. It is a realization that through love and forgiveness we conquer evil and sinfulness.

Perhaps Reverend Falwell and Pat Robertson should have pointed out that this tragedy was an opportunity for all of us to condemn evil of all kinds and to take a long hard look into our own hearts and souls. What we don't need are Christian or Islamic fundamentalist condemnation and self-righteousness.

As individuals and as a nation, we have started to evaluate our priorities. We are looking at life with a new sensitivity and realizing the preciousness of this gift of God. We are showing concern for our own lives and the lives of our brothers and sisters throughout this land and throughout the world. The words of Genesis have new meaning for us. When God asked Cain, *"Where is your brother Abel?"* Cain answered, *"I do not know. Am I my brother's keeper?"* (Gen. 4:9). For us today and in the future, the answer is a resounding yes!

The pursuit of material possessions and the acquisition of material goods have lost some of their luster. If we had to choose between another September 11 and a more sharing, more spiritual, and less materialistic world, the choice would be easy. Perhaps we are at a time when we are willing to move from an economically based society toward a more morally based society. We are more ready today than ever before to make decisions based not on economics but based on moral correctness and the good of all. We should seize this opportunity. We should not let it pass.

In the Sermon on the Mount, Jesus teaches us about anger, revenge, judgment, love, and forgiveness (Matt. chapters 5, 6, and 7). In these scriptures, we see that anger must be washed away before we can approach God's altar, that revenge must be transformed into generosity, and that hatred must be changed into love. The judgment we place on others will be placed on us, and only through forgiveness will we be forgiven. (2001)

Religious Fundamentalism

> *"If we lay aside our preconceptions about these religions, seeing each as forged by people who were struggling to see something that would give help and meaning to their lives; and if we then try without prejudice to see ourselves what they saw—if we do these things, the veil that separates us from them*

can turn to gauze." Huston Smith, <u>The World's Religions</u>.

Religious fundamentalism is an almost unavoidable by-product of religion. It seems to occur when members of a particular religion irrationally purport to be in possession of the truth revealed by God himself. Of course, all religions ask members to adhere to certain beliefs and practices. However, in extreme cases, rigid adherence to these beliefs can become abusive, and devastating to human dignity. Religious fundamentalism tries to reduce a complex reality, man's relationship to God, to relatively simplistic terms, which must be adhered to at all costs. There seems to be little room for diverse interpretations of source material such as revelations, sacred writings, dogmas and human experience and tradition.

A basic principle upon which religious fundamentalism stands is the belief that one possesses the complete and absolute truth about God and his will for humankind. Because of this belief, it becomes difficult—and for some people, impossible—to regard others' beliefs as well grounded, valid, and worthy of respect. It becomes hard to admit the possibility that other religions may also hold the truth although seen from a different historical and cultural perspective.

Fear, based on an erroneous concept of God, seems to be at the heart of religious fundamentalism. God may sometimes be seen as loving and merciful but only toward those who follow him without deviation. God is seen consciously or subconsciously as a punishing being. For the extremist, the predominant attributes of God are justice and retribution. God dispenses love, mercy, and compassion in a parsimonious fashion. Fear is a natural outgrowth of this conception of God. It then becomes normal to fear and view as a threat anyone who does not believe and adhere strictly to God's laws and commandments. The more excessive the fear is, the less one trusts and loves self and others. One becomes fearful that he or she might offend God under any circumstances. Clear judgment and common sense give way to fanatical compliance with prescribed principles.

In order for religious fundamentalism to grow and prosper, it is usually necessary to have a closed system in which authority cannot be questioned. Intellectual curiosity, religious inquisitiveness, or a general thirst for knowledge is often repressed and sometimes punished. Any challenges to authority are generally forbidden and seen as a violation of God's will, which at times can be dealt with harshly. Religious fundamentalism is conspicuous by its absence of female participation and leadership. It is a male-dominated system in which specific individuals claim to be unerring in their judgments based on their own authority as God's representatives.

Religious fundamentalism takes advantage of man's propensity to seek systems that present beliefs and moral precepts in a more or less dogmatic fashion. These systems help man to negotiate life's spiritual complexities with a minimum of conflict and anxiety. Willingness to adhere blindly to questionable religious principles can lead people into a position of vulnerability. Unscrupulous leaders can take advantage of people by demanding blind obedience and strict adherence to rules and behaviors. There seem to be few questions to be puzzled over or decisions to be made, but there is also little freedom to be exercised and limited ability to seek the truth beyond what is dictated. There seems to be only black and white, only good and bad, only the righteous and the condemned.

Religious fundamentalism can be seen as a perversion of the truth. Often, it starts with truths or elements of the truth, which are then twisted and distorted. True religion might teach that there are principles and truths worth dying for while fundamentalism would teach that these truths and principles are not only worth dying for but worth killing for. True religion might teach about the dignity of women while fundamentalism would teach repression of women under the guise of modesty, respect, and tradition.

Fundamentalism can use physical, spiritual, and psychoemotional force to achieve conformity and adherence to religious beliefs and moral codes. This type of coercion and intimidation can be used in varying degrees by extremists to achieve their desired ends. These ends may consist of adherence to physical dress, maintaining proper ritual behavior, preservation of dogmatic purity, or the promotion of extreme aggressive behavior in the pursuit of religious goals or other dehumanizing requirements or activities. The end result often appears to be control and manipulation of people.

Although these are only a few of the characteristics of religious fundamentalism, these concepts seem to be the foundation and springboard for this radical and extreme behavior. Recognition of these characteristics is the first step in the process of ridding religion of this deadly malady. (2002)

Fundamentalism

Fundamentalism is always limiting and restrictive but in extreme forms is recognized by most people as a threat to freedom and physical and spiritual danger. Fundamentalism seems to flow from a religious belief system but is not completely restricted to religion. Political fundamentalism, which is usually tied to religious fundamentalism, is real and fraught with many of the same dangers and perils.

While I was listening to a radio talk show, the guest speaker, a prestigious scientist, talked about new, unexpected discoveries. Unfortunately, I cannot remember his name. He explained that data from the telescope indicated that activity seen encircling the stars mimicked the activity that occurred at the beginning of our solar system. These occurrences, which were thought to be unique to our solar system, were now being seen throughout the galaxy. This, in his opinion, sets the stage for a replication of our own solar system and the creation of life as we know it. He then made an interesting comment that I would like to paraphrase. He said the discovery of life beyond our solar system would be the removal of the last crumb of arrogance from the plate of humanity.

Most religions speak about the necessity to depart from egocentric attitudes and to move toward other-centered posture. Eastern religions suggest a departure from personal desires and expectations that lead away from the oneness of life and end in disappointment and suffering. Christianity speaks in similar terms. *"For those who want to save their life will lose it, and those who lose their life for my sake, and the sake of the gospel, will save it*" (Mark 8:35).

The sin of fundamentalism is a pride or arrogance that allows a person or group to believe they possess the only religious, social, or political truth. This attitude essentially places ego at the center. It is an arrogance that isolates and condemns. It says, "*I am right and you are wrong.*" There is no room for dialogue. One centers on what one believes to the exclusion of all other possibilities. It is an attitude that allowed Lt. General William Boykin to state that America is at war with "Satan" and that the God of Islam, Allah, is "*an idol.*"

He also stated our God is bigger than their God. The very concept of bigger and better in reference to God smacks of competitive self-righteousness. These words are frightening to those who respect others and believe in freedom of religion. It is hard to believe that John Ashcroft, the attorney general of the United States, spoke negatively of the God of Islam compared to the Christian God. This use of contentious, negative language in the relationships among religions is a sign of deep-seated rivalry and hostility, which portend a dim future for the peace and oneness so desired by many of the great religious figures of history. These attitudes belie the fact that we have missed the real message of religion.

As long as religious and political systems act arrogantly and defensively rather than humbly and openly, little change will occur in how we regard other people and their beliefs. Fundamentalism closes the door to meaningful negotiation and rejects the possibility that the other could have something of value to offer.

Unless we follow the higher road put before us by great religious leaders like Moses, Jesus, Muhammad, Buddha, and the like, we will fail to achieve the peace, justice, and unity that the world is searching for.

Jesus tells us that seeking selfishly what we think is good for us, leads only to a loss of our real life. It is when we are willing to lose our pride and arrogance and seek to be humble and open to others that we will find our true life. (2002)

Creation
The Future

Creation is not an act of God that once done is over. It is a work in progress. Creation is an ongoing process in which God has given man a significant role.

The view man takes of the world and the universe will, in large part, determine his future and the future of creation. Man's destiny is dim if he sees himself as master of a world that exists to serve his needs and desires instead of seeing himself as being an integral part of a system that is interactive and interdependent on all its creatures.

God has placed a huge responsibility on mankind. Man's role is unique and essential because he, above all the other creatures, has the ability to control, to some degree, his participation in the ongoing creation of the world. If we see ourselves as the center of creation, we are missing the point. Creation is an act of God in which he pours forth his generosity and love. For God, creation is about sharing goodness and life. Our task is to parallel God's creative activity. It has nothing to do with self-interest and exploitation. We should strive not only to conserve the treasures of creation but also to create products, processes, and systems that enhance the environment. We have an obligation to manufacture, build, and create in a way that enriches all life on this planet. This calls for a vision that sees every aspect of creation as sacred and leads us to act with respect and reverence for all God's creatures. This vision and understanding of creation can serve as a foundation and starting point for our role of cooperation with God in the continuing creation of this world.

Our responsibilities are multifaceted. They include accountability with regard to the air we breathe and the water we drink. The homes we build and the manner in which we recreate should be a positive contribution to creation. Respect for the plants and trees that give us breath and shelter should be an integral part of our environmental plan. The regard we have for the animals and the ecosystems, how we understand their roles in the universe today and in the future, will determine our course of action. Climate change should be at the top of our list. Our concerns about these issues and other issues such as poverty, overpopulation, and blatant materialism could determine the future of creation. How we deal with the problems of creation today, and how we plan today for tomorrow, will affect creation for good or evil, not only in the near future but also for generations to come.

God will not only judge us on how we cooperate with him in this ongoing creation, but the world community will also look back at us and either despise and loath us for our shortsightedness or will thank and praise us for our insight and activism in this cooperative creative effort. The earth itself will judge us, either by punishing us or by rewarding us. The punishment will take the form of an Earth that can no longer supply itself or us with the elements that support, nourish, and sustain life. Earth will reward us with its goodness and blessings. This is our choice! This is the challenge of Genesis in the twenty-first century. We can reject the challenge and decline cooperation in God's continuing creation or we can choose to continue God's creation in a fruitful, prudent, and productive manner. (2004)

CHAPTER 5
Fragile and Sinful

Hypocrisy

Hypocrisy seems to be rampant in religion and politics. These two occupations or fields of endeavor seem to have at their foundation a special connection to service to individuals and communities. A certain amount of trust is required of those who are served by religious and political leaders, and in the same way, a certain amount of honesty is required of our religious and political leaders. There is, in fact, an unwritten contract between both parties. No doubt, there are other occupations that have service to people as a fundamental part of their makeup but perhaps none to the degree of religion and politics. Some examples would be the medical field and education, which seem to require more altruism than professional sports or sales. Of course, in a perfect society, all occupations require a certain amount of trust and honesty; but in some cases, a "buyer beware" attitude makes sense. The expectations for people of religion and politics are somewhat higher and should be because the personal, spiritual, and communal well-being of all of us are at stake.

It is sad when we look at religion and see people like Jimmy Swaggart; Jerry Falwell; the Bakers; former Cardinal McCarrick, pedophile priest; and so many others who have betrayed the trust of so many people. These people of religion are spoken of by Jesus in Matthew 23:4, *"For they bind up heavy and unbearable burdens, and they impose them on men's shoulders. But they are not willing to move them with even a finger of their own."* Jesus called them hypocrites. The same goes for politicians like Richard Nixon, Rod Blagojevich, Jim McGreevey, Eliot Spitzer, and a host of other politicians who are corrupt, including some presidents who have not been held to account. They require laws to be followed by the common man, but they see themselves as above the law.

Why are there so many hypocrites in religion and politics? Did they have good intentions when choosing these walks of life? I feel the answer to the first question is, for the most part, power and money. The answer to the second question is yes for the most part. Many started with good intentions but were corrupted along the way. Of course, there were some who had questionable or mixed motives from the outset. Not that it is right, but we can understand that many people do what they do for selfish reasons. We hope for more, but as realists, we understand the dynamic.

In the case of former Cardinal McCarrick, we wonder, as we do in many cases, why one would live in hypocrisy rather than change one's situation or occupation? Why not seek help to correct the situation? Why would one instruct people how to live while he is living an inauthentic life, especially if in the beginning he had good intentions? *"Hypocrite! First remove the beam from your own eye, and then you will see clearly enough to remove the speck from your brother's eye"* (Matt. 7:5).

The issues of hypocrisy are certainly complex and complicated. It is my belief that it is a sickness, and the essence of that sickness is the inability to either see one's own deviation or the ability to extricate oneself from the dilemma. Perhaps the individual knows not what he or she is doing. This, however, does not take away accountability. My advice to anyone in this situation is, at the very least, to get help! (2020)

Truth or Consequences

The Catholic Church's reaction to the sexual abuse scandal has been defensive, limited, and inadequate. This catastrophe, and the response to it, was able to occur because more enduring and fundamental problems were not only allowed to exist but were fostered and cultivated over the history of the church. The Church's incapacity to exercise sound moral judgment has led to the present dilemma and perhaps to an inability to reform her from within.

Instead of cleaning the house and confronting her demons, she chooses to defend outdated traditions and customs such as mandatory celibacy, clerical honors, and saint-making while ignoring more vital problems. Important issues such as the ministerial function of women, married clergy, and optional celibacy are summarily dismissed. The many good works of the church cannot be used as a shield to deny problems in need of solutions. Problems of pedophilia and homosexuality have been long known within the church. The public now recognizes that these problems are not only long-standing but have been known by church officials for many years.

Many attempts to force the church to address the situation have been made over the years by priests, theologians, psychologists, and mental health experts. The church has ignored these pleas for years. The lack of concern for the victims, our youth, betrays a calloused and un-Christian attitude on the part of the hierarchy.

To be sure, there was confusion and trepidation on the part of church leaders, and legal standards were not spelled out as clearly as they are today. There is, however, no excuse for the lack of moral leadership that should be an integral part of the Christian character. Certainly, throughout the '70s, '80s, and '90s, publications like *The Atlantic, Newsweek, National Catholic Reporter*, and *Commonweal* raised a red flag regarding sexual misconduct of the Catholic clergy. Writers such as Andrew Greeley, Richard McBryan, Donald B. Cozzens, and many others warned of the growing incidents of pedophilia and the increase of homosexual priests in the ranks of the Catholic clergy.

The terrible sinfulness of this whole matter is that the last concern of the church was for the victims, the abused children. Their immediate concern was to protect the church's reputation and reduce financial damage. The thought of future victims was not or did not appear to be a primary concern.

It is time for the church to address the enduring and more fundamental issues, which have as their symptoms a myriad of problems. Power and control within a closed institution are at the heart of the dilemma. Homosexuality, pedophilia, and celibacy are tied to power and control within the church. It seems to take much of the meaning and spiritual value out of the commitment to celibacy when there is no option to serve God, as a priest, without being celibate. When an institution demands that a priest must be submissive and forfeit a fundamental human drive in order to serve God and attributes that demand to scripture, it becomes evident that more than subtle control is being exercised.

The refusal to involve women and the laity in meaningful positions of authority is another demonstration of power and control used to the detriment of the whole church. There is an air of arrogance on the part of the hierarchy revealed in this sexual scandal that fosters an environment of repression and secrecy. This needs to be exposed to the light of day. It is sad when a church dedicated to Christ's message of service cannot step back and relinquish power and control, especially in the light of such sexual dysfunction. Through sexual control, the church tries to dictate artificial living conditions and even the thought process of its clergy.

The control exercised by the church goes beyond sexuality. Free and independent thinking is discouraged, not only on the part of priests and theologians but also at Catholic colleges and universities in this country and throughout the world. Over the last three decades, innovative thinking on the part of theologians has not only been discouraged but has been repressed and silenced by the Vatican. In the final analysis, many of the problems that have come to the surface during this present crisis are symptoms of deeper, more complex issues.

There is a great lack of leadership among bishops and a lack of trust in the Holy Spirit within the church. Rather than relying on the movement of the Holy Spirit in a free and open institution, the authorities of the Catholic Church feel a need to have a closed and regulated organization. They seem to prefer power to service, control to freedom, wealth to generosity, and repression to openness. Until the official church can, in humility, confess her sins, ask the faithful for forgiveness, and resolve to change her ways, the majority of the Catholic laity will not see her as a credible representative of God.

Reform is the order of the day. Nothing less than firm resolve, bold steps, and a willingness to confront sexual misconduct and all the underlying contributing factors will be acceptable if the church wishes to again become a viable, believable representative of Christ on earth! (2004)

Where Do We Go from Here?

The sexual abuse scandal and the crisis of leadership in the clergy, especially in the hierarchy, should give the Catholic Church pause for reflection. The Word of God, through the prophet Ezekiel (34:7–11) to the shepherds of Israel, rings true to this day. These scandals give the entire church an opportunity to evaluate what true shepherding entails.

The conference of Catholic bishops was a good start. The proper course of action is for the church to act with charity and compassion for the victims and their families. Financial aid, counseling, and spiritual direction should be made readily accessible to all who seek it. The protection of our youth from future abuse is of critical importance.

The priests and bishops who have perpetrated these crimes should be removed from ministry and punished according to the law. Because this is such an emotionally charged issue, hate and contempt for the offenders would be natural, but it would continue the travesty of insensitivity and abuse. Those who stand accused must be treated with justice and Christian charity. Perhaps some who have been accused are innocent. As difficult as it may be, the gospel calls for forgiveness and compassion for all sinners. Justice must be served, but condemnation without an attempt to answer complex and complicated questions could keep us from discovering solutions. Some of these solutions could aid in the prevention of future abuse.

Where do we go from here? Some have suggested a plenary council or perhaps a Vatican Council. Still, others feel that the democratization of the church is the only answer. Self-imposed controls could be a significant step in setting the stage for renewal. However, there can be no substitute for internal conversion and renewal inspired by cooperation between the faithful and the clergy. The church must come to a deeper understanding of the essence of shepherding, which has at its heart humility and service.

When Jesus speaks of shepherding, he speaks of a complex but loving relationship between shepherd and sheep. The shepherd is a leader, and his sheep are his prized possession. The value of the flock and the obligation of the shepherd to protect the sheep are crucial to his calling. He is to seek out lost sheep and protect the sheep from ravenous wolves with little regard for personal cost. Jesus admonishes shepherds not to look down on or despise their sheep but rather to love and sacrifice for them. In John 10:1–21, Jesus outlines the relationship of sheep and shepherd. We often think of sheep as dumb animals that will follow whoever leads them. Jesus tells us this is not the case. The sheep know and recognize the voice of a true shepherd. The sheep will refuse to follow the voice of a false shepherd. Jesus goes on to tell us that he is the good shepherd, who is willing to die for his sheep. Again, Jesus gives his future shepherds an example of the cost of shepherding.

It is time for today's shepherds to rededicate themselves to the service and protection of their flock. We, as a church, must look to Jesus, who tells us, "*Call no one on earth father; you have but one father in heaven. Do not be called master; you have but one master, The Christ. The greatest among you must be your servant. Whoever exalts himself shall be humbled; but whoever humbles himself will be exalted*" (Matt. 23:9–12). Humble service in the spirit of loving sacrifice is the hallmark of Jesus life. Our shepherds and leaders should see themselves as no wiser or more important than their flock but rather as equal partners on the path of salvation history. Arrogance and power must be transformed into humility and service. Leadership without humility and service is fundamentally opposed to Christ's message.

Today's scandals should not be the occasion for our leaders to forfeit their role as shepherds, but without personal conversion and rededication, their leadership could be seriously diminished. External compliance to guidelines, commissions, and councils holds little hope for meaningful change without personal reconciliation and renewal. Our shepherds would be wise to hear and heed the words of Christ in Matthew 20:25–28:

> *You know that the rulers of the heathens have power over them and the leaders have complete authority. This however is not the way it shall be among you. If one of you wants to be great, he must be the servant of the rest; and if one of you wants to be first, he must be your slave—like the son of man, who did not come to be served, but to serve and to give his life to redeem many people.* (2004)

Final Thoughts

It is June of 2006, and I am trying to put the final touches on this book. As I was going through the final process of reading, rereading, editing, and reediting, this section on the sexual scandal in the Catholic Church seemed to lack closure. I felt uneasy without including some final words on the subject. I think my uneasiness stems from the feeling that this travesty has evoked little more than some apologies, statements of resolve by the church varying in kind and degree, and some sorely needed regulations to control this type of behavior in the future. Minor changes in the training of candidates for the priesthood have been made but no serious consideration, not even a hint, of a possible dialogue regarding married clergy or women priests. No dots have been connected between sexual misconduct and the nature of the priesthood as it exists today.

It is somewhat baffling that the church seems to lack the initiative to make this travesty an opportunity to deal with a multitude of problems, including those related to this scandal. I am also disappointed in the overall long-term reaction of the people of God. This issue cries out for attention and reform, but like so many other important issues, it has fallen by the wayside with the passage of time. There is hardly a whimper from the laity regarding reform.

It is sad to think that we and our leaders are content to have this and related issues fade into oblivion. Just as the church failed to confront sexual abuses in a responsible fashion at the outset, she seems now quite intent on avoiding a dialogue and quite content to allow an opportunity for spiritual and moral renewal to slip away. The end result seems to be business as usual.

The introduction of a married clergy and the ordination of women, although unsettling for a male-dominated institution, would revitalize the church for good beyond our wildest dreams. It would, in a most natural and healthy way, give us men and women who, as ordained ministers, could be role models of true Christian manliness and womanliness. But for this to happen, the church would have to lower her defenses, be willing to relinquish control to some degree, and allow the Spirit to freely act and direct the future of the church.

The Catholic Church, like many other religious institutions, is a mixture of both good and evil. She is capable of, and indeed has performed, great works for the benefit of mankind. Over the ages, the church has done monumental good in the fields of education, care for the sick and elderly, homelessness, feeding the poor, defense of life, health care, disaster relief, human rights, and so much more.

On the other hand, she has also been responsible for a great deal of pain and suffering over the ages. She has participated, either by active involvement or by omission, in the suffering of Jews and Muslims who have been persecuted by the church throughout history. The treatment of native and black South Americans in the name of evangelization resulted in the deaths and subjugation of millions of people. The use of church authority for political, military, and financial ends is appalling. Just as there are countless good deeds, there are misdeeds.

All this being said, there is good reason to be hopeful if we, the church, can express genuine sorrow for misdeeds and develop a spirit of humility going forward with the knowledge that we are weak and must take great care in the fulfillment of the gospel message. Although principles have been compromised, the church still holds at its core the doctrine of love and forgiveness. As long as we—the people of God, the church—strive to attain the ideal of love, there is hope.

I am optimistic because I do not believe that men and women, in the long run, can frustrate the power and movement of the Holy Spirit. There will come a day when married clergy will be the norm, and both men and women will work side by side to serve God's people. It is, however, unfortunate for the time being that this opportunity for positive change seems to have passed us by. (2006)

The Eucharist and Abortion

The implication of using the Eucharist to achieve a political solution to a moral problem is, in my opinion, a dangerous mode of operation. It seems to say that if the church had the political clout in this country, it would impose on Catholic and non-Catholic citizens alike its concept of morality. This somehow smacks of the evils of the Middle Ages. It is when this realization strikes home that we should be thankful for the separation between church and state in this country. It is frightening when any church singles out individuals and makes a (negative) judgment about the state of those individual's relationship with God.

Abortion, at its root, is a moral problem, and as such, the church should and must speak out in favor of life. But in a pluralistic society, a society of laws, the church should involve herself in the political process in a legal fashion or even through civil disobedience. The Catholic Church, in my estimation, should keep its nose out of the bedroom and reproductive rights and should never set herself up as a moral judge of an individual's worthiness to receive the Eucharist. More than that, she should speak out and engage the social and political fabric of this country. It is by being engaged and involved in dialogue, not by solemn statements or demanding sanctions, that she will convince people of the moral righteousness of her position.

It is sad to say that some polls indicate that as many as 40 percent of Catholics in this country are in favor of abortion. It seems to me that the church has her work cut out for her. Perhaps the church should concentrate less on coercing politicians who are perhaps personally against abortion but who represent people of diverse moral persuasions. She should concentrate more on instructing and educating her members regarding the sanctity of life in all circumstances and the newest methods of preventing conceptions that have a high percentage of ending in abortions.

I believe most Catholic politicians are personally against abortion but feel obligated to support other people's right to choose according to their conscience, whether or not that conscience coincides with Catholic teaching. The church does not know for sure the conscience of each Catholic politician. It is not a Catholic politician's duty to form the conscience of those people who may not even be Catholics or hold Christian principles. This would seem to be more the function of the church.

The *Catechism of the Catholic Church* states, "*Conscience is man's most secret core, and his sanctuary. There he is alone with God whose voice echoes in his depths.*" It also states that "*a human being must always obey the certain judgment of his conscience.*" Since when is the church in the business of usurping the function of man's conscience? Even US Catholic bishops and priests disagree on the use of the Eucharist as a tool in what they see as a battle concerning the right to life. This is to say nothing of the fact that some clergy disagree with the church on the issue of abortion. It is up to individual Catholics to judge whether they may properly receive communion. Many religious leaders are unwilling to presume that someone approaching the altar for communion is not in the state of grace.

Bishop J. Sheridan's statements with regard to Catholic politicians paint all of those who seem to support abortion and any number of other issues with a brush that makes no distinctions or qualifications. Bishop Sheridan said that Catholics who vote for politicians who support abortion "*place themselves outside full communion with the church and so jeopardize their salvation.*" That statement is not only arrogant and judgmental, but it is monumentally bad theology.

It is possible for one to be personally opposed to abortion and support a person's right to choose without violating any moral precepts. It is also possible to vote for a politician who supports the right to choose, not because he supports abortion but because he supports many other positive moral issues. It is also possible for a right-to-life candidate to be on the wrong side of issues such as the death penalty, war, environment, and social justice. Pope John Paul II has taken as strong a stand as possible against war. Who do we vote for? Do we vote for the war candidates or the abortion candidates? And do we risk going to hell either way? I think our conscience should be our guide without fear of some bishop or priest exercising his personal form of excommunication.

Father Peter J. Daly in an article quotes Father John Courtney Murray, a renowned expert on church and state, indicating that the church must be part of the "*civil conversation.*" Father Daly goes on to say, "*A conversation is not a monologue. The church has to listen as well as speak. A civil conversation must be carried on without threats or bullying.*" He makes the point that faith influences politicians while providing motivation and guidance. The church needs to be careful that she does not do evil in order to bring about good. (2006)

Abortion

It is somewhat strange that during the time of COVID-19 and the renewed quest for civil rights that the topic of abortion came to mind. Perhaps it is because all three issues have to do with life. Each of these issues has its own complicating aspects and questions. The issue of abortion is complex, as are the other two issues. After much thought, I realized it would be impossible to write an essay on abortion unless I limited the scope of the essay to a particular aspect of the issue. To concentrate, in a meaningful way on even one aspect might be difficult.

What I began to realize in a more conscious way was that there were, and still are, strong and deeply rooted opinions and feelings held over long periods of time, which need to be recognized and addressed before anything meaningful can be accomplished. Religion, politics, human rights, and a multitude of other factors must be considered in the equation.

This means going back to the beginning, the fundamentals. Before useful and constructive dialogue can happen, an openness to another's words, thoughts, and feelings is a sine qua non. It is vitally important that each person be sensitive to the concerns of the other. There can be no underlying anger or hostility. The whole thrust of a dialogue is not to convince the other that you are right or correct and he or she is wrong and incorrect. It is rather to seek a common ground upon which both sides can develop a sensitivity to and for the feelings and beliefs of the other. Without goodwill, trust, and the strong desire to understand the other's concerns, success is not likely.

The ideal solution to a problem would be complete agreement and the creation of effective measures to resolve the issue. However, this is just not how it works. My niece, who is a doctor, makes a good point: being pro-choice is not being proabortion. The labels *pro-choice* and *pro-life* paint individuals as a monolithic group all holding nonnuanced positions, which is just not the case. The barriers to effective dialogue start right there.

Perhaps you have heard the maxim *"Don't let the perfect be the enemy of the good."* Voltaire and Confucius may or may not have said these exact words, but both seem to ascribe to this approach in difficult issues. Within this maxim is implicit the seeds of compromise and negotiation, which to some might at first look like a sellout. However, without compromise and negotiation, we remain without a solution or amelioration of conflict. Goodwill turns to obstinancy and intransigence, leading to a breakdown in the process of dialogue.

Compromise is the art of coming to an agreement or settlement in a dispute or disagreement, which is reached by two or more parties by way of making concessions to one another in order to achieve a resolution or make progress in dispelling or resolving a disagreement. All this being said, there are at times irreconcilable differences, but if two parties embark on the process of sincere dialogue, concession and compromise can successfully obtain many seemingly unachievable results. At the least, the issues become somewhat more manageable, less contentious, and perhaps, if done properly, can lead to respect for the other. Dialogue and communication must equal long-term commitment to the process in order to achieve any type of progress in these difficult issues.

An example or two might help. Like Christianity, true dialogue has not been tried and found wanting. It has been found difficult and left untried. The following information is not new or revolutionary. But some of these possible problem-solving solutions need to be revisited in a new spirit of mutual concern if any advances are to be made. Pro-life people feel their concern for fetal life is irreconcilable with the practice of abortion. What if something could be done to lessen the number of abortions? There is great potential to accomplish this through education and science. Methods of contraception are many.

Still, there are people who feel contraception is wrong, but it is an option with far less harmful ramifications than abortion. Pro-choice people are not interested in abortions for abortion's sake. They are concerned about women's rights, the right to make personal decisions about their own bodies without the interference of male-dominated political and religious institutions. Would pro-choice people be willing to take steps to lessen the number of abortions provided their rights of self-determination were not violated? Granted there are other concerns of both the pro-life and the pro-choice people, but this is an area where dialogue could advance the cause of both concerned parties. Don't let the perfect be the enemy of the good.

Perhaps science, in the future, will supply even more effective means of lessening abortions. Would both sides be open to the intervention of science in the control of abortions? Would pro-life people accept the use of medications and the like in exchange for an abortionless society even though they have natural law objections, which seem inconsistent when applied to other unnatural medical procedures such as heart transplants? What does it mean to err on the side of life?

What about pro-choice folks? Would they give up abortions as a means of controlling unwanted offspring? Would pro-life and pro-choice come together to adopt programs of education for those individuals who are most vulnerable and for whom abortion seems to be the only option? If the answer to these questions is no or there is an unwillingness to consider the possibility that there may be some common ground upon which to build, then we need to reassess our positions, or we will be doomed to failure. There are many other areas of necessary discussion to be dealt with once a commitment to dialogue is made.

Only if both sides can come together, sincerely addressing the concerns and problems of their fellow human beings, will progress be made regarding abortion and many other thorny issues. "Don't let the perfect be the enemy of the good." (2020)

CHAPTER 6

Christian Attitudes Continued

Lessons of Christmas

Each evangelist describes the Christmas story in a unique fashion. No one of them gives us the same version of the birth of Jesus. In fact, Mark says nothing of the birth of Jesus but does speak of preparing the way for his coming. He relates Jesus's baptism and his temptations in the wilderness. For Mark and the other evangelists, the physical birth of Jesus is not the focal point. This birth is primarily a spiritual event.

Matthew, after giving us the genealogy of Jesus, tells us, "*The birth of Jesus the Messiah took place in this way*" (Matt. 1:18). Mary was found to be with child, and Joseph, in a dream, was instructed by an angel to take Mary as his wife, for the child was conceived in her by the power of the Holy Spirit. After that, Matthew skips the birth of Jesus and tells us the story of the wise men from the east, who follow a special star to Bethlehem.

Luke gives us the most elaborate and complete information about the circumstances surrounding the birth of Jesus. He tells us of the conditions circumscribing John the Baptist's birth, the announcement, by an angel, to Mary that she was to conceive a child by the Holy Spirit, Mary's visit to Elizabeth, John's birth, and Zechariah's prophecy. Luke then describes the birth of Jesus and how Mary and Joseph came to be in Bethlehem. He speaks of how the birth took place in a stable and that the first visitors to the stable were poor shepherds who were tending their flocks in a nearby field. These humble shepherds had heard the announcement of Jesus's birth from angels on high.

Last of all John, begins his gospel with what at first seems like a very un-Christmas-like account of the incarnation. He tells us that in the beginning, the Word was with God and the Word was God. *"And the Word became flesh and lived among us"* (John 1:14). In these nine words, John summed up the birth of Jesus and God's unlimited love for us.

These evangelists, each in his own way, mark the birth of Jesus. This birth, with all its marvelous and strange happenings, has a simple and consistent message, which we should not overlook. Mary and Joseph were simple people of little estate. There was no pretension or guile in them. They were people without position or power who saw themselves with no special prerogatives. Unlike the spiritually righteous, they were meek and humble. Mary and Joseph were people of meager means with little material possessions who did not complain when directed to a stable when there was no room at the inn.

This child, who is the Son of God, did not choose to be born of royalty. He chose to be born in a stable and laid in a manger. His first visitors were common shepherds, who themselves were held in little regard by those who considered themselves valued members of society. All the material surroundings of Jesus's birth speak of humility and poverty. It seemed that God put little value on what mankind saw as important and of worth. For all those who lived in arrogance and splendor, this was a tough message to understand. This message is spiritual and lasting. It is not "the good things" of this world that are of lasting value.

It was not to Herod or the self-righteous religious leaders that God revealed his Son but rather to the kings (from the east) who were called wise men. They were called wise because they were humble enough to realize that the wealth they possessed was not in the form of worldly wisdom or riches. They were wise and rich because they recognized

God in this poor helpless child. They also saw in this holy family's poverty the richness of God's kingdom.

The lessons of Jesus's birth are just as valid today as they were two thousand years ago. Among them are lessons about power and weakness, about righteousness and humility, and about wealth and poverty. What is real power? What is real righteousness? What is real wealth? (2013)

Relationship Equals Worship

Have you ever wondered why God would need worship and praise? Worship and praise seem to flow from man's natural tendency to love and appreciate the gift of existence. The ontological nature of our relationship with God dictates how we should relate to him. No amount of religious systemization can affect the internal nature of this relationship.

It seems contrary to the concept of a loving and giving God that he would expect adoration out of fear. Such a God would be incapable of endowing his creatures with the freedom necessary for true worship. The fact that we are creatures means that we should regard God with awe and thanksgiving. This is at the core of the relationship. If all religions and all churches were to disappear, if all sacred writings were to be lost forever, we would still have a relationship with God from which worship and praise would flow. It is built into us to be thankful and appreciative, not because of a fear of a self-aggrandizing God but because we have the ability as thinking creatures to recognize the tremendous gift of being.

Our motivation to act in a moral way also comes from our relationship with God. Spirituality is about grace and purity of motive. For worship, praise, goodness, and morality to be honest, they must grow out of love for God and love of others. If fear or hope of rewards to come is the motive for worship, then the intended nature of our relationship with God cannot mature. Over the years, religion and society have at times taught differently. There is no doubt that God is love and that love must be at the core of our relationship with God and our brothers and sisters. This is the ideal; this is the perfection spoken of in Christian scripture. *"Be perfect as my heavenly Father is perfect"* (Matt. 5:48).

If a child obeys a parent because of fear or a mixture of love and fear, that good behavior isn't a purely loving response. This less-than-perfect motivation is a stepping-stone. Unfortunately, religion at times seems to encourage mixed motivations. In either case, it is expedient but not right.

Religion or worship based on fear and habit may be acceptable at the beginning of a relationship with God, but as we become aware that God is love, our response naturally moves from fear to love and freedom. When the emphasis is on fear and obligation, the center of religion shifts away from love, and only a caricature of our relationship with God is left. The belief that God is watching every move, waiting to tally up our mistakes, makes it hard to act in more than fearful ways. The well of love is poisoned with fear and guilt so that it is hard to act out of love and freedom. The first thing we need to do as individuals is to recognize the process and be honest with God and ourselves.

If individuals and institutions put less emphasis on the fulfillment of the externals, they might encourage people to act in more genuine ways. Conversion to save one soul, receiving a sacrament out of obligation, or celebrating a Bar Mitzvah to uphold tradition, although not totally without merit, fail to engage God and others in the most authentic ways.

Worship and praise flow naturally from the man-God relationship once man recognizes his status as a creature. Encouraging this relationship with God in an atmosphere of service, freedom, and love is the purpose of worship. (2014)

Does God Get Off the Hook Because of Free Will?

I was about to write this essay just as COVID-19 erupted in the USA. I would be hard-pressed to ignore this ongoing event or its relationship to this topic. Who is responsible for COVID-19 or events of this catastrophic nature?

We have been told by religion that it is because of free will that our ultimate end could be eternal happiness or eternal punishment. That really seems strange to me. It is held by some that we condemn ourselves by freely choosing evil acts. Many believe that God reveals himself to us in multiple ways. The claim is that God gives us some insight into his nature through creation, scriptures, revelations, and charismatic individuals, etc. I would assume that if we possess free will, God most certainly possesses it also. Surely, God could have chosen to create the universe, and our world in particular, based on a different paradigm. Why he did not will to do so remains a mystery. But why he did create in the way he did is an even greater mystery.

All these considerations are based on the assumption that God exists. And if God is love, as religion espouses, how can he allow the existence of war, poverty, starvation, torture, slavery, abuse, hatred, suffering, and today, COVID-19, along with other natural evils? Do we let God off the hook by assigning free will to men and women? Are there evils that exist apart from the actions of men and women, or are we even responsible for natural disasters? Could God have created men and women who are loving, honest, considerate, healthy, open, holy, and without sin and still preserved free will?

Again, we are told that he did! However, Scripture then tells us men and women fell from grace and introduced sin, evil, and suffering into the world. We get the blame for screwing it up, not God who started it all. Really? Does that make sense? A God who is capable of all things could not have done better?

If God is revealed through the natural world, how do we justify God's innocents with regard to "survival of the fittest" and other harsh laws of nature? The reality of this law is violent at its core and requires one creature not only to kill another creature but to do it in the most violent way. Natural events cause much agony and suffering (e.g., COVID-19, hurricanes, tornadoes, earthquakes, fires, volcanic eruptions). Do we humans have the power or the evil intent to do all this? Disregard whether God wills this or not, why would he even allow this? Would you allow it? Are we not culpable when we allow evil to exist, especially when we have the ability to do something about it? What about God's culpability?

We seem to be constantly making excuses for God. We can quote scripture and through convoluted thinking, reasoning, and interpretation justify pretty much anything. *"For my thoughts are not your thoughts, and your ways are not my ways, says the Lord. For just as the heavens are exalted above the earth, so also are my ways exalted above your ways, and my thoughts above your thoughts"* (Isaiah 55:8–9). Does this mean that we should not recognize the subtext of this passage that says, "Accept, don't question"?

This attempt to shroud reality in mystery should not justify a surrender of critical thinking in deference to an all-knowing God. This text protects God by undermining man's ability to understand the "mysterious" thoughts and ways of God. Proverbs 9:10 tells us, *"Fear of the Lord is the beginning of wisdom."* What does that mean? Does it mean we should be afraid of God or we should respect God, or is it a warning that if we don't fear and respect God, there will be a price to pay? Have we been brainwashed into absolute submission to these ideas? How dare we question God. How audacious of us to hold God to the same rules he holds us to. These questions that challenge traditional beliefs about God and religion seem atheistic, blasphemous, and threatening to many people when, in fact, they are questions of sincere and honest people. It, in a way, casts all atheists as evil people. They are not evil! The vilification of any group is evil; the very things religion says it is against, it engages in.

It seems that religion gives us mixed messages. On the one hand, we say God is good, but on the other hand, he will punish us eternally if we transgress his laws. But it is he who gave us free will, knowing we would transgress. Why would a God who knows everything give us free will if he knew we would transgress? God is all-merciful and expects us to be merciful, but if we aren't, then his judgment of us will be merciless (James 2:12–13). These mixed messages are numerous throughout Scripture and religion.

We defend God by saying, "Look at all the good in the world," and there is an abundance. However, it is like defending a man who is a good husband, father, breadwinner, and philanthropist but is also a cold-blooded, premeditated murderer (e.g., a mob boss). The good does not justify the evil; in fact, the evil nullifies the good. This really sounds like blasphemy, but it is rather a striving for truth and honesty.

Just imagine if God had created a world or universe in which love and goodness could coexist with substantial free will, a world where men and women could make free choices among infinite possibilities with one restriction, an inability to choose evil and suffering of any kind. It is no wonder that churches and religions react negatively to questions that challenged the irrational or nonsensical notions about religion and God. It took thousands of years for these beliefs to evolve. Along with these beliefs, structures have developed and been put in place to promote and defend traditional beliefs and ideas. If after all is said and done, the truth is that God actually exists and is all-loving, merciful, and forgiving, then we have to change our perception of God, religion, and reality.

It seems to me that suffering, sacrifice, and vulnerability are the hallmarks of love and true religion, but why? The answer to this question is tied to God's nature and will. Unanswerable? Perhaps, but we should never stop questioning. (2020)

It's About Time

John Denver, in his song "It's About Time," sings, "*Who's to say you have to lose for someone else to win.*" It is certainly about time we realize when one of us wins, we (should) all win. The whole idea is that we are all in this together. What does that mean?

It just so happened that today—Friday, October 2, 2020—the White House announced that the president and first lady tested positive for COVID-19. It does seem quite serendipitous that I would be writing an essay on it being about time we realized that we are all in this together. I had just started this essay when the news was announced. My initial thought was *Boy, we are all really in this thing together.* No one is exempt or invincible.

My next thought was for the health and well-being of the president and first lady. I also thought that perhaps this might help all of us to refocus on the importance of all lives. Being in this all together not only applies to coronavirus but to the everyday life we share with all our brothers and sisters; we should all be pulling for each other.

This is one of those opportunities to reevaluate and recognize that we are not so different from each other. No one wants to get sick; no one wants to have a family member or friend get sick; no one wants to get sick and die. We are all on the same page. This is a chance to be more sensitive to the reality of our situation. We share a common humanity with common hopes and dreams. We should realize when something positive happens to our neighbor, we lose nothing and should rejoice in his or her good fortune. In the same way, when something positive happens to us, our neighbor loses nothing and should rejoice in our good fortune. This attitude has the potential for something optimistic and constructive to happen. It is by multiplication of these positive moments that authentic change can take place.

There will always be difficult times and situations, but at least we will be headed in the right direction. The diagnosis of the president can engender empathy toward the president and others who have contracted COVID-19 and help us to see, as a nation, that we are truly all in this together.

My hope for the president, the first lady, and their son is a speedy and complete recovery in as short a time as possible. I also hope Mr. Trump gains greater insight and understanding of the human drama being played out in this great country of ours. He is the president of all the people of the USA—the good, the bad, and the ugly. Please listen to us all, Mr. President. (2020)

Desires of the Heart

Last night, I watched the Barbara Walters special "Heaven: Where Is It? How Do We Get There?" Two things impressed me about the show. The first was the fact that all faiths believe in a *place* where people will spend their afterlife. The second was that the representatives of the different faiths all had their own peculiar (strange) slant on the nature of heaven. The different descriptions of who would be there and what it was like, of how one spent his or her time, or whether there was sex or not, or how much one could eat without gaining weight gave me the distinct impression that no one among all these religious experts had given the nature of heaven any really serious thought. They never mentioned the notion of relationship to God or our fellow human beings. This was disturbing, for if they understood so little about heaven, what did they really know about religion in general?

The fact is these religious leaders seemed to *know* very little of God, heaven, and hell. Faith and belief go hand in hand. Religion is not about knowledge but about belief, faith, and relationship. The silliness of some of the views expressed on last night's show would have been funny if it weren't so serious.

Since religious leaders do not possess divine authority, they use tradition and sacred writings, such as the Koran, the Bible, and the Upanishads, etc. to bolster their positions. There is no doubt that these traditions and sacred writings have significant religious value, but to use them apologetically is to distort the message contained within them. These books and traditions can be used to learn religious and moral truth to guide the lives of men and women in their relationship with God, nature, and each other. The importance of these writings and traditions is derived not from claims that God inspired them but from the values and meaning they give to life.

Perhaps the important notion about heaven is that almost all religious people believe in its existence even if they can't agree on the details. This is not science but rather the realities of the spirit. This seems to indicate that there is a deep-rooted ontological dimension at work here.

Lorenzo Albacete puts it another way in his wonderful little book *God at the Ritz*. He speaks of the "*desires of the heart*." Because man has a deep-rooted longing for a *place* like heaven, it seems to testify to its existence. We know from our own human experience that man's longing to love and be loved is indicative of the existence of love. The desire for God, for love, for justice, and for hope of salvation may be more important than specific beliefs that are simply attempts to categorize these yearnings of the soul.

The cravings of the heart do not prove beyond a doubt that spiritual *realities* exist, but they bring these beliefs within the realm of reason. Basic universal religious desires that have their foundation in the heart allow us to separate magic and superstition from our religious beliefs without denying the mysterious nature of religion. Religion is not about knowing in a scientific way but about realities that are neither provable nor measurable but nonetheless real.

The differences amongst religious peoples regarding specific spiritual matters seem to testify to the possibility that diversity of belief is part of the nature of religion. Most religions have these deep-rooted longings at their core. Each religion develops these desires of the heart within its own culture, yet when we strip away the nonessential, we find some basic beliefs common to almost all men and women. (2014)

Hope and Consolation

Yesterday, I attended the funeral of a thirty-three-year-old woman who had suffered from a debilitating disease all her life. The liturgy, prayers, songs, and scripture all spoke of hope and consolation—the hope of everlasting life, the hope of being reunited with loved ones, the hope of conquering sickness and death, the hope of overcoming man's faults and sinfulness, the hope that evil will eventually be overcome.

I thought that without hope and consolation, mankind could not deal with the harshness of reality. Without these attributes, men and women would find it almost impossible to grapple with suffering, war, sickness, injustice, and death.

I sat there thinking about the times I had doubted my faith. The doubts I have had and still have are not without good reason. How does a merciful, just, and compassionate God even think of allowing the evil and inhumanity of this world? Is religion, faith, or myth, which offers hope and consolation, an unconscious or conscious invention of men and women to get through these otherwise hopeless situations? Does hope exist outside the realm of faith?

As the liturgy progressed, my spirit was moved, and in my heart, I experienced an overwhelming feeling of comfort and encouragement. Is it possible this type of response could be the source of myth, faith, and religion? Man, for the most part, cannot endure the overwhelming evil encountered in this world without some type of hope and consolation.

The very next day, I received one of those e-mails that blamed all our problems on people who believed differently from what the author saw as orthodox religions. It appeared to me the article was filled with half-truths and intolerance cloaked in a narrow belief system. It seemed to blame people who held a nuanced position with regard to faith and religion for all the problems in our society. He felt he was being persecuted by people who disagreed with him. It is always easier to blame the other guy. In this way, no self-examination is necessary.

I have been exposed to religion and religious beliefs all my life. I have lived it, studied it, and practiced it for over sixty years, and I have found that hope and consolation along with a touch of fear and guilt drive a good part of religious belief. This is not an indictment of faith and religion but only an insight into something of a mysterious and complex nature.

A touch of humility wouldn't hurt any of us when it comes to discussing religious beliefs. I realize trying to make sense of reality, truth, and belief is in many ways beyond our intellectual capability. It is my personal choice not to reject the possibility of God and belief, but it is also not within my power or purview to judge others who choose a different faith or no faith at all.

So as I reflect on these important issues, I take solace in the belief in God's existence even though at times it seems irrational and unbelievable. For me, it is still something I hold fast to in my heart and soul. It does give me hope and consolation to think that perhaps evil and death will be overcome someday. I do believe that this hope based on faith is not necessarily some sort of human fabrication that came about because without it the alternative is despair and meaninglessness. So in the end, many, like me, believe at the very core of their being, there is a God of justice and compassion, and yet there are many difficult questions.

Respect and consideration for those who feel otherwise are important, realizing they, perhaps, have more courage, understanding, and insight than we give them credit for. Remember, the virtue of humility is the antidote for self-righteous judgmentalism.

In this season of peace, no matter what we believe, there is always room for hope and consolation. (2010)

Happy, Healthy, and Holy

As our kids were growing up, I used to tell them life is about being happy, healthy, and holy. Looking back, I wondered if I ever really explained in any formal or concrete way what that means to me. Hopefully, I taught them by example. While in Vermont last weekend with our youngest of three sons, James (thirty-two years old, not a kid anymore), I began to think about putting on paper just how I feel about these three concepts.

Happy means being satisfied wherever you are in life. You should not necessarily accept where you are, but you should always strive for maximum satisfaction with whoever and wherever you are. It means being upbeat and optimistic without being unrealistic. Happiness does not mean complacency. For sure, there are things that can make us unhappy, but we should strive to limit the depth and duration of unhappiness. We do have much to be happy about. We can find happiness in all sorts of places: our families, our friends, our work, our relaxation, our hobbies, our spiritual life, our intellectual pursuits, our marriage, and our children. The list goes on and on.

Holy means being in a state of thankfulness and gratitude to whoever or whatever (God, the universe, nature, etc.) for the blessings in our lives, for life itself. We will find that this attitude of holiness will add to and enrich our happiness and the health we have. Holiness comes to us through our concern for others. We know in our hearts that the more we give of ourselves to others, the happier and healthier we are.

Healthy is between happy and holy. Health is almost always bolstered by happiness and holiness. It is not just about physical health, although physical health is important. As we learn over time, nothing is quite as simple as it may first appear. Being happy, healthy, and holy is not always easily achieved. Age, physical and mental health, circumstances, experience, and a multitude of other factors can be strong influences on the achievement of these qualities. Healthy is about attitude. A positive attitude about life, in general, can lessen the anguish we may experience. A good attitude can, at times, transform a bad situation into a learning experience and turn a negative into a positive in the long run.

As you can see, these concepts or virtues dovetail with each other. The same things that make us happy are the same things that make us healthier and holier. These three concepts are inextricably interconnected. It is difficult to achieve one without the other. As you know, if you have read any of my essays, the Jewish and Christian scriptures are vital to my life. They are the touchstone of reality to me. The feelings I have with regard to happiness, healthiness, and holiness are directly connected to these scriptures.

You may have a different touchstone, but whatever that may be, cherish it and depend on it as a guide for life. You may also surmise from my essays that at times, the hard questions of life lead me to reflect on the existence of God. Many times, God's existence and presence are overwhelming, and at other times, it is truly hard to believe there is a God. Whether God exists or not, the scriptures, understood and read properly, are still my guide to a loving, compassionate, merciful, empathetic, and just life. (2020)

Interchangeability

The book of Genesis tells us we are created in the image and likeness of God. "*And God created man to his own image; to the image of God he created him; male and female he created them*" (Gen. 1:27). This does not, in any way, completely or definitely tell us who or what God is. Scripture, over time, gives us varied pictures of God. These pictures are at times contrasting and contradicting conceptions of God. Both Hebrew and Christian scriptures share these misconceptions; however, we should understand an evolutionary process is at work here. The message here is that humankind throughout history has struggled in its quest to understand the nature of God. In 1 Corinthians 2:9, Paul tells us, "*Eye has not seen, and the ear has not heard, nor had entered the heart of man, what things God has prepared for those who love him.*" If we cannot even imagine what God has in store for us, how can we imagine what God is in actuality? Richard Rohr tells us, "*Any God worthy of the name must transcend creed and denominations, time and place, nations and ethnicities and all the vagaries of gender and sexual orientation extending to the limits of all we can see, suffer and enjoy.*" This is because we are God's children, and love is his name.

James tells us, "*For judgment is without mercy towards him who has not shown mercy but mercy exalts itself above judgment"* (James 2:13). Throughout Scripture, we see man's evolving notion of God, which helps us to better understand our relationship with him. It is only slowly, over time, that we grow in our understanding of God and expand our insight into his nature.

We should always recognize our own limited nature and the inadequacy of our ability to understand God. Because we are finite, we can only understand in a finite way. Is God a he, she, or it? Is God a being? Is God being? Is God? Philosophers, theologians, scientists, and people in general down through the ages have been grappling with this question and are still without adequate answers. This issue, without a doubt, has an unattainable answer for us who are mere mortals and are limited in time, space, and intellect. All our answers are only attempts. One answer has been given to us by the apostle John in 1 John 4:8: "*God is love.*" This is a major insight into the nature of God. This insight is over two thousand years old. yet it is still not understood. We have failed to grasp the relationship between God and love. and we have failed to see or understand the imperative it asks of us.

At this point, I would say the terms *love* and *God* are somewhat interchangeable. If we substitute love for God, we achieve a unique insight into the nature of God. God is patient, God is kind, God is not jealous, God is not pompous, God is not inflated, God is not rude, God does not seek his own interests, God is not quick-tempered. Do these words sound familiar? For Christians, they should! This is Paul's hymn to charity or love found in 1 Corinthians 13:4–7. I have substituted the word *God* for the word *love*. Viewing this passage in this way gives us insight into who God is and is not.

"*Whoever does not love, does not know God. For God is love*" (1 John 4:8). John is mystical. John tells us in the most positive way what God is. Paul is more practical and enumerates what God is and is not. Both, however, make the same point: God is love, and love is God. If we view these attributes, even in our limited way, we begin to understand that God and love are equal in value and have no limits. Paul seems to be saying that love is unconditional, given freely without reservation. One conclusion we can make about love and God is that they are limitless and coequal.

As I stated in the essay "A God beyond Mercy and Forgiveness," there is no limit to God's mercy and forgiveness, and that would seem to be love. God's love is beyond what the Bible tells us. It is beyond what churches tell us. It is simply beyond our expectations and comprehension. God's love is God.

This essay seems to beg the question, Why would God create? Perhaps it has something to do with the idea that love, at its core, is creative and sacrificial, that God/love is expressed in sharing and emptying oneself for another and becoming vulnerable for another. Christianity seems to have lost this message somewhere along the way. There is nothing we can say or do that can separate us from love/God.

> *Neither life nor death nor angels, nor principalities, nor powers, nor present things, nor the future things, nor strength nor the heights, nor the depths, not any other created thing, will be able to separate us from the love of God.* (Rom. 8:38–39)

Mysterious? Yes! Hard to believe? Yes! Impossible for us to fathom or comprehend? Yes! But somehow, we want to believe in love/God.

Somewhere deep down in our being, this seems to ring true even in the face of contradictions and proof in opposition to this real-but-unbelievable-and-unknowable intuition or instinct. We really don't know the nature of God. We don't know if he is a person let alone a he or she. We don't know if he is a spirit or a being or being itself. But if John and Paul are on the right track, then God and love are the same reality.

Because we are so limited in our ability to identify just who or what God is, we tend to apply to the concept of God anthropomorphic categories. That is, we assign human characteristics to God. We are limited human beings, so our concept of God is limited. Paul and John described in words what God is and what love is, but people like Jesus, Martin Luther King Jr., Pope John XXIII, and many others flesh out in human terms what God/love actually means in day-to-day life. Those who die for their fellow human beings like Jesus and Martin Luther King Jr. demonstrate the extreme generosity of love as men and women know it. Besides being creative, God/love has shown itself to be sacrificial in the deepest sense of the word. No greater love does a person have than to give his or her life for another human being. Jesus, whether we believe him to be the Son of God or not, makes this clear by his life and death. It is the Christian belief that God entered this world and submitted to the worst we had to offer and did not reject us but embraced us all the more. (2020)

What Do You Treasure?

"Where your treasure is there also will be your heart" (Matt. 6:21). All of us have conscious or unconscious

beliefs, thoughts, and feelings that can be somewhat paradoxical or confusing. We human beings are complex. Nothing is black or white, totally right or totally wrong. That being said, Jesus, in Matthew's gospel account, tells us that where our treasure is, there also will be our heart. The things we really value are our treasures. We can measure who we are through what we value.

Our values and what we value are not exactly the same. It can be confusing because values and what we value are so closely related that it is sometimes difficult to differentiate between the two. Core values are fundamental beliefs. They are guiding principles or concepts that direct or dictate behavior and can help people understand the difference between right and wrong. Values are not always positive, and thus, our treasure may not always be positive. Values and what we value are inextricably connected and intertwined.

Some of the things we value are family and friends that flow from the values of love and affection. Without the values of love and affection, the family becomes less meaningful and is valued less. Love, affection, and family are inextricably tied together; this is our treasure; this is where our hearts reside. Honesty is a value that is transformed into something valued when it is exercised for personal good or the good of others. In this way, it becomes our treasure; this is where our heart resides.

We should be sure of what our treasure is. The heart represents who we really are. Thus, it becomes imperative that we get in touch with or determine what is truly valuable because that is our treasure, and that is where our heart resides. If our values are negative, then what we hold as valued is negative and pessimistic. Unfortunately, that becomes one's treasure. It is only by knowing and understanding what we value that we can reinforce, adjust, change, improve, and strengthen our values. This is the way we get in touch with our authentic selves. The hearts of men and women will be on what they treasure or value most. This should give us pause to think, pray, and contemplate on what we feel is valuable.

While writing this essay, I thought of at least twenty things I value. Many of these would be seen by most people as positive in nature: family, freedom, justice, liberty, safety, the pursuit of happiness, etc. Other things we might value or cherish are not so clearly positive: money, power, control, fame, and acquisition of material goods. There are, to a greater or lesser degree, some real differences in these two groups we value. The first group seems, to some extent, to flow from the positive nature of human beings. The things we value like love, honesty, mercy, open-mindedness, and the like seem to be almost intrinsically good while the second set, although not intrinsically bad, can be corrupted more easily.

Why we seek, how we achieve, and how we use the second set of valued things are critical. Proper motivation, a moral means, and proper use regarding these things of value are important if they are to be positive and self-improving. The possibility of their corruption is ever present. It is incumbent upon each one of us to examine all the things we value using conscience and honest self-questioning, along with some type of fundamentally objective external guide (e.g., sacred Scripture or ethical guidelines and the like) in order to come to an awareness of those things that are really valuable to us. We should seek, as far as possible, these things of value not only for ourselves but for others.

Through this self-examination, we can come to see, in an honest way, what we treasure and thus where our hearts rest. Do our hearts have, at their center, generosity or selfishness, compassion or hard-heartedness, empathy or indifference? If we see ourselves as moral or ethical or as people of faith, then using these systems as a measuring rod might lead us in the direction of positive good. Our treasure should grow more and more in the direction of generosity, toward compassion and empathy for others. Once we have consciously and firmly established what our treasure is, we should try to live by that treasure because there is where our heart resides; it is who we are!

CHAPTER 7
COVID-19

For Just Such a Time as This

The 2004 presidential election is over, and the people have spoken. We will have four more years of George W. Bush. This will make a lot of people inside and outside the USA happy or unhappy, depending on their point of view. The campaign was quite bitter, and the differences between the two candidates were striking. The exit polls indicated that moral issues played a strong role in this election. Both candidates and parties felt they held the moral high ground. On the one side abortion, stem cell research, same-sex marriages, euthanasia, and like issues were condemned in the strongest fashion. The other side saw preemptive war, unequal health care in the richest society in the world, economic elitism, nation-building, and the death of innocent bystanders in war as the premiere moral issues of the day.

In the book of Esther, when the Jewish people were about to be slaughtered, Mordecai, the uncle of Esther's father, warns Esther that she must intercede on behalf of her people. *"For if you keep silence at such a time as this, relief and deliverance will rise for the Jews from another quarter, but you and your father's family will perish. Who knows? Perhaps you have come to royal dignity" for just such a time as this"* (Esther 4:13–14).

If we keep silent today and in the future, we may find our world and ourselves in grave jeopardy. Perhaps God has placed us here to speak the truth *"for just such a time as this."* Two questions come to mind: What is it that we need to speak out about? And in what manner should we speak? Religion and politics seem to have come together in this time and place in a more critical way than usual. The first question is a long and complex list of moral issues. Some of these moral questions take the form of issues that seem to be irreconcilable or to have solutions that are mutually exclusive. They range from terrorism to political emasculation, from abortion to capital punishment, from materialism to economic deprivation, from preemptive war to self-defense. They also concern issues that range from overabundance to starvation, racism to self-responsibility, medical care for all to survival of the fittest, same-sex marriages to healthy relationships, environmental concerns to sustainable growth, and so much more. These and many other moral issues must be recognized and addressed. They are questions that are at the same time moral and political in nature. If we fail to ask these questions, we will make no progress toward a meaningful solution that benefits all parties.

The second important question concerns *how* we speak about these issues. Are we going to dialogue seriously amongst the many sides and recognize people on all sides of an issue as real human beings? Are we going to recognize all sides as having legitimate points of view and respect the depth of feelings that others have for their beliefs? Are we going to come together with a sincere hope of making progress, believing that real gains can be made for all concerned? Are we going to dispense with an attitude of our way or no way?

If the answer to any of these questions is no, then we are in extremely deep trouble. Recognizing the difficulty of these problems, it may seem to be naive and unrealistic to think we can solve these moral dilemmas. However, maintaining the status quo is just not an acceptable course of action. To actively agitate or exacerbate the situation—as do many politicians, religious leaders, and talk show hosts of both sides—is the immorality of the hypocrite spoken of in the gospels. If any side, because of their strength, decides to vanquish their enemies and revel in their victories rather than reach out in a spirit of understanding and compassion, they will have chosen the road of darkness and falsehood rather than the road of truth and light.

The solution to these types of moral/political conflicts can only come through sincere and honest bipartisan dialogue based on a willingness to negotiate some meaningful form of compromise. If we hold to our beliefs so strongly that we cannot move one centimeter to the right or left, we are in actuality dooming our fellow human beings and ourselves to an immorality more detrimental than the potential immorality of compromise. Our beliefs concerning religions and forms of government can be obstacles that, in the end, contradict the very truths and beliefs we are trying to share. We are building walls around our hearts and minds, which cut us off from each other, walls that our political and religious leaders at times seem to encourage.

God, however, asks us to tear down these walls that cannot protect us but only isolate us from each other. It is *"for just such a time as this"* that God has called each one of us to do our part to bring down these walls that separate us and enter into a dialogue that can move us forward in the effort to see with the eyes of our adversaries.

Our political and religious leaders have failed to be the prophets of our times. They have not called us to come together to meet the challenges of these opposing moral positions but rather have called us to partisanship and closed-mindedness, preferring to stake out their own narrow moral agenda. They have led us in directions that alienate and estrange us from each other, all the while trying to increase their power and control. It is time to cast off the admonitions of blind leaders and come together in the spirit of the gospel, which calls us to be one.

Our call may or may not be as spectacular as Esther's, but we are all called to advance the cause of peace, harmony, and oneness in our own unique way. Mordecai's words that God's purpose would be fulfilled whether Ester cooperated or not was both a warning and an invitation by God to Esther to participate in the salvation of the Jews. We too have been both warned and invited to take part in God's salvation, which, if we reject, will come from another quarter, for God's plans will not be frustrated, but sadly, we will have missed a chance to participate in God's plan for man's salvation. (2005)

Render to Caesar

The heated debate between the left and the right in this country over evolution and intelligent design reminds me of the Gospel story recounting the scribes' and chief priests' efforts to trap Jesus. Through deceitful means, his enemies hoped to trick Jesus into making a choice by which they could either hand him over to the authorities or discredit him with the people. Jesus offended neither the emperor nor the people. He simply said, *"Then give to the emperor the things that are the emperor's, and to God the things that are God's"* (Luke 20:25). Through this simple yet valid distinction, Jesus instructs and outwits those who would harm him.

Perhaps we should take a lesson from the Gospel and render to science the things of science and render to religion the things of religion. Is there a need to choose one or the other? There seem to be lots of hidden agendas and surreptitious motivations on both sides of this issue. Two extremes are involved at the heart of this debate: those who believe in scientism, individuals who have an exaggerated trust in science's ability to answer all questions, and religious fundamentalists, individuals who emphasize a literal interpretation of the Bible. A possible answer to this debate is to recognize the fact that science and religion are two different disciplines with two distinct and different areas and methods of study.

Intelligent design—the belief that the universe, life, and its beginnings are too complicated to be explained without an intelligent designer—seems, for the most part, to be a reasonable explanation, but is it science? Evolution on the other hand uses observation and experimentation and scientific methods to explain the universe, life, and its beginnings, but can any amount of observation and experimentation prove or establish the underlying cause of it all? Since neither science nor religion had a representative be present at our beginnings, it may be presumptuous of either side to claim an exclusive on this story.

A short analogy might be helpful. For centuries, men and women watched the sun rise each morning and set each evening. They even called it sunrise and sunset. Joshua 10:12–14 was used by fundamentalist Christians of that day as an argument to combat Galileo's theory that the sun did not rise and set but Earth instead rotated around the sun. To hold that the sun did not rotate around Earth was heresy and a potential death sentence.

It should be noted that Galileo's theory eventually became scientific fact. It should also be noted that Galileo never claimed that God was not responsible for the sun and Earth and all the laws that govern them. He was simply trying to understand how it all worked. Galileo's work did not exclude God from the process; it just informs us that God's role is different than first believed.

People of faith should be humble enough to be guided by reason and science. The Bible is not a book of science, thank God, and should not be used as such by believers. Science is not always right, but neither are our beliefs. Believers need to realize that if they truly trust and believe in God, it is possible that there is a system in place in the universe that is not explainable through the Bible, and science has the ability to give us some insight into that fact.

People of science should be humble enough to recognize the existence of realities they cannot plumb. There are realities that we cannot touch or measure. Can science prove or disprove the existence of God? Can science explain why a person gives his life for a cause? Can science explain the nature of love? These realities are beyond the purview of science.

The reason the debate exists and will continue is because of extremist views on both sides. If we render to science the things of science and to religion the things of religion, we would not have a debate. Christians need not defend God's role with regard to the universe, life, and its beginnings. They need only realize that God is responsible for all that was is and will be. This is the realm of religious belief. Science is concerned with the universe, life, and its beginnings with regard to what is measurable and demonstrable. Someday, science will give us the why and how of it on one level, and religion will give us the why and Who of it on another level. (2017)

An Opportunity Missed?

Today is May 6, 2020. We are still firmly in the grip of COVID-19. In fact, it feels as if we are entering a critical stage that suggests serious questions that will have long-lasting consequences. What will be our modus operandi as we go forward? How will we approach the difficult decisions that are before us? Can we as a nation come together in a united fashion to consider the needs of all concerned? What has this virus revealed about us as individuals and as a society? Are we taking the advice of the scientific community regarding testing? How do we save the economy, and how do we, at least in the short run, care for the economic needs of our people? Are we prepared for a possible rebound? These are just a few critical questions we and our political and scientific leaders need to address as quickly as possible. Lives and jobs hang in the balance.

So far, although not perfect, our response has been, for the most part, one of concern and care for the sick and the vulnerable. The first responders—nurses, doctors, medical workers, maintenance workers, and a host of others—have sacrificed and, in some cases, given their lives in service to others.

This is not to say we have not made some missteps and could not have done better. It seemed, at least in the beginning, that we had been, for the most part, heading in the right direction. Assigning blame was not front and center, nor should it now be the task at hand; working together for the benefit of all should be our driving concern.

However, there is in this country a great divide, which is a severe fault line that, if not corrected, will take this country down. Lincoln correctly stated that a house divided against itself cannot stand. This fault line stretches back to our Founding Fathers. They somehow believed that all men are created equal and endowed with certain inalienable rights while at the same time, black people were held in slavery and subjugation. This is the original sin of our nation (along with the genocide of the indigenous people), and we must deal with it today and in the days to come. We can say the rights and freedoms stated in the Declaration of Independence and the Constitution were aspirational, but that would be false. Black men were held in slavery and subjugation by white men for economic power and privilege. This fault line or crack in our foundational beliefs is, to this day, the Achilles' heel of our constitutional republic.

The coronavirus has brought into stark relief the continuing effects of these inequalities. Since the beginning of time, the poor and vulnerable have been on the backburner. The poor and people of color in this country are disproportionately suffering in terms of having health risks directly related to racial and economic inequities. In many cases, these people are being put in harm's way through frontline exposure. They are asked to work without proper personal protective equipment. Would we like to be put in that position? I hardly think so!

It turns out that these workers are of great value to society and are vital for the survival of all. We should not let people go unprotected, and their compensation should be reflective of their now recognized true value. Are these so-called necessary workers seen only as expendable, or will they be recognized in the future for their real worth? A few examples of these important people are as follows: food workers, hospital workers who clean and disinfect hospital spaces, sanitation workers, postal workers, gas station attendants, drugstore workers, restaurant workers, and a host of others. It is clear poor people and people of color are put at a greater risk for, in many cases, less than a living wage. I am not talking about $15 an hour. You try to live on $15 an hour. Lots of luck!

These are the fruits of a system that too often neglects to ask us if we care about our disenfranchised sisters and brothers. This is the fruit of a system that values things more than people, a system that values our rights and privileges over the rights and privileges of others. Hopefully, the system is not so morally bankrupt that it willfully ignores these blatantly obvious disparities. We also hope that the system does not lack the will and ingenuity or know-how to effectively address these problems. For sure, we are a strong and powerful nation, but if we lack wisdom, compassion, empathy, foresight, and leadership, we will be listed among the ranks of failed nations, and we will have missed an opportunity to save our country and be a true leader among nations. We should be looking not to make the well-off less well-off but rather to make the less well-off more well-off, to make the vulnerable less vulnerable. Understanding and responding correctly to these issues is a complicated task but is necessary for a just, equitable, and sustainable future. The opportunity is now; the time is now!

Navigating a health crisis of gigantic proportion is difficult enough, but the added economic ramifications severely complicate the task at hand. Political considerations further complicate the matter. Recalling Lincoln's comment about a house divided being unable to stand should cause us to consider some type of unified action. This is difficult to come by when cable news stations are guilty of, if not "fake news," at least news that provokes division. Instead of trying to understand the whys and wherefores of opposing positions in an effort to compromise and reconcile views, the goal seems to be promotion and exacerbation of these differences. Carrying guns at demonstrations seems hardly the way to foster cooperation. With a presidential election coming in the fall, it is even more difficult to modulate the vitriol.

The conflict between those who want to contain the spread and those who want to open the economy is at a fever pitch. What should we do? The answer to this question is going to tell us what kind of country we are going to be. What is of value to us? There are people of good faith on both sides of this issue, and it is incumbent upon them to work to achieve the necessary safeguards to protect the health of all while endeavoring to support financially all those folks that need necessary financial help to get through this crisis and beyond. It is with care and concern for all, with humility and dialogue, with good planning, working together, and building capacity to respond quickly to an uptick that we will be able to get through this crisis and sustain a viable society and nation.

None of this will happen quickly or easily, but it must continue to be an ongoing process. We need to act in good faith, remembering the words of Martin Luther King Jr.: "*Let us realize the arc of the moral universe is long, but it bends toward justice.*" Hopefully, this will not be an opportunity missed but rather a chance to come together to form a more perfect union. (2020)

Common Sense Not So Common

My wife and I are in Vermont since Wednesday, June 24. While in Vermont, we have lost the ability to get news at will 24-7. We have no TV, no Internet, no radio, and limited cell phone service, but through conversations with friends and relatives, we get a truncated version of the news.

One thing we do get is COVID-19 updates pretty much every day. We know things are not getting better. Today is Friday, July 17, and reported cases of coronavirus are increasing. Yesterday, seventy-seven thousand cases were reported. Thirty-eight states show increases in reported cases. Eighteen states are considering reclosing, and the death toll is at 136,000 and is expected to reach 220,000 sometime in November. Thirty states report infections are going up. None of this is good news.

There are conflicting reports and information regarding the best practices to protect oneself and others. Our son James, thirty-two years old, has been very careful with regard to the guidelines put out by the White House. He wears a mask and social distances, etc. However, because he is young, healthy, strong, and in a low-risk category, he is beginning to engage in behaviors that could put him at a slightly higher risk. My wife and I have talked to him about it, not from concern about ourselves but out of concern for his health and well-being. He is very respectful of us and keeps a substantial distance from us, and he never enters our home. Given the fact that there is some contradictory information out there, it would seem prudent to err on the side of caution by observing life-protecting and lifesaving behaviors. Common sense tells us the virus will end, the economy will come back, and life will return to some type of normal. All this will happen, but if you are dead, it makes little difference.

Because the coronavirus has become such a political issue, we have diminished our ability to deal effectively with this threat. Our ability to act in a unified, coordinated, scientific, and cooperative way has been drastically reduced by a disregard for an honest and nonpartisan approach to the pandemic. First and foremost, there should be respect for life even if it is inconvenient or difficult. Remember, many first responders and frontline medical professionals gave their lives for you and me. Regardless of our political persuasion, I can't believe that all of us are not on the same page when the health of our kids, parents, grandparents, grandchildren, sisters, brothers, and other relatives and friends' lives are at stake. Life and the protection of life should be the first rule of the pandemic.

In addition to social distancing, masks, and washing of hands, not gathering in close proximity and outside is better than inside. What would be things common sense folks can do to support health and well-being? In my view, there are at least four common-sense steps we could take that would make a significant difference.

1. Put life (all lives) first above all else; err on the side of life.
2. Use caution with regard to self and others; consider comorbidities; err on the side of safety.
3. Patience with the process—it will take time, at least through the winter; err on the side of long-suffering.
4. Use self-control; err on the side of respect for others.

Masks have become a major problem. They are now signs and symbols for political posturing. At this point, I would like to recount part of an interview of Stan Van Gundy that I heard on the car radio today. In a response to a question, he told a story about England during World War II. During the blitz, people were required to shut off the lights at night so that the Germans could not locate the homes of British citizens. No one objected because common sense prevailed. Everyone understood that this practice was not only good for the neighbor but also protected the self. Pretty obvious common sense.

Perhaps we should take a lesson from the Brits and apply this story to the face mask issue and other safeguards. Life-protecting mechanisms that benefit all should not be a partisan issue. Masks are good for your neighbor and protect the self. Masks should be a sign of respect and caring for our fellow citizens. What was and is intended to be protection for all has become a symbol of division and disrespect. How difficult is it for us to err on the side of life? Even if masks are not the be-all and end-all, there is a possibility that they are protective in some ways. Why would considerate people choose not to wear one? The sacrifice is small and temporary. Let life and common sense rule the day. (2020)

Herman Cain

Sad to say, Herman Cain, like tens of thousands of people, died of COVID-19. He was a human being. He had a life, a family, friends, business associates, and so much more. He was not just a Republican, a conservative, and a presidential want to be, he was an author, a businessman, a friend, and a person who was loved and will be missed by friends and family. He shared humanity with each and every one of us. In the process of living, we sometimes forget this. It is for this reason I am pausing to remember Mr. Cain and the thousands of others who have died of COVID-19. Each of those who died had a life, loved ones, friends, and a very personal story.

The COVID-19 virus is and continues to be a devastating health crisis. That alone would be difficult enough to deal with, but we have, on top of that, complicated the issue by also making it a political crisis. Because of the political ramifications, we have been unable to deal effectively with the health questions that affect all Americans.

I can't help but feel that perhaps Mr. Cain would never have contracted COVID-19 had not the political atmosphere been so contentious. Refusal to distance, refusal to wear a mask, refusal to follow the White House guidelines were seen as more of a statement of political loyalty rather than health measures to save lives.

On the other hand, the more progressive group seemed closed in many ways to listening to, in a thoughtful way, some of the reasoning from the right that may have been an option with merit. The Tulsa Rally became a test of loyalty to the president, as were so many other activities. The longer we are enmeshed in this virus, the more we learn and the more we realize how little we knew or understood about it at the outset. Had it not become so political, maybe we could have worked together in a constructive way and avoided the deaths of thousands of people. Both right and left, because of their noncooperation, have extended the life and ferocity of this virus. It is sad that possibly because of political motivations, Mr. Cain contracted and died of COVID-19. Obviously, many others have died because of misplaced loyalty.

A few days after Mr. Cain's death, at a congressional hearing on COVID-19, a Democratic congresswoman took time to express what I hope was sincere condolence to Mr. Cain's family and loved ones. Because of the political atmosphere, it was suggested that this may have been a backhanded way of saying Mr. Cain got what he asked for. Because of his lack of compliance with health guidelines (masks, social distancing, and avoiding large indoor gatherings), he made himself more vulnerable. My hope is the latter possibility is not what the congresswoman had in mind. Isn't it a shame that because of political differences, we are sometimes prone to think along those lines?

I am sure Mr. Cain's family and friends are supporting each other in this time of grief. I extend my sincere concern and best wishes to Mr. Cain's family and loved ones. Perhaps in Mr. Cain's honor, we could try a little harder to act in the best interests of the people of the United States and not in the interests of political posturing. We should be bigger than that. We should wish for the well-being and health of all people. All lives matter: Republican or Democrat, conservative or liberal, black or white. It should make no difference; life is more valuable than party, beliefs, skin color, power, or position. (2020)

Thanksgiving 2020 / John Fitzgerald

Today is the day after Thanksgiving, and even though I have much to be thankful for, it became a bittersweet Thanksgiving Day when I received news of the death of a longtime college friend of mine. He, like me, was almost eighty years old with underlying health problems. He had, as do I, heart problems for more than a few years. I think he believed COVID-19 was real but perhaps because of his political beliefs did not pay enough attention to the recommended precautions.

All that being said, he was a good person; a good husband and father; and a good provider who loved life, family, and friends. He loved golf, basketball, and skiing and had a great sense of humor. During one of our political disagreements, he said to me, "Give a Democrat $5 and he'll become a Republican." He liked to use humor to defuse tense situations. In our younger days, we did some wild and crazy things.

Fitzie's death caused me, again, to reflect on the value and frailty of life and existence in general and my life in particular. It caused me to focus on life and relationships over and above questions and issues.

We disagreed on many political issues, but even with these differences, we never became enemies. Sad to say, this has not been the same throughout this country. We have learned to hate each other, or perhaps we have never learned to stop hating each other. Our relationship never became divisive enough to destroy our friendship. Fitzie and I would get together with three other college buddies as often as our busy schedules would allow. Bill Garrett, Andy Smith, Vince Murray, Fitzie, and I would discuss political and religious issues just about every time we got together. Fitzie and Bill were the conservatives; and Andy, Vince, and I were the progressives. We didn't often agree, but there was something in our relationships that allowed us to come together in peace and good faith.

I am sure there were many contributing factors, but the most important of these seemed to me to be trust and mutual respect. We trusted that each of us had the best interest of the others at heart. Mutual respect allowed us to come together, argue and disagree with each other, and yet remain friends. This ability not to dismiss, belittle, or make light of each other's feelings and opinions was a necessary ingredient of mutual respect and the ability to coexist in friendship. Could an effort to achieve trust and mutual respect be a formula moving forward toward resolving some of our national problems?

It seems that we have been a nation led in the opposite direction. Lack of trust and disrespect for others are not seen as negative but rather are encouraged and promoted by "leaders" on both sides. Is it any wonder that we are where we are today? The emphasis is on our political and religious differences—that is, on things that divide us rather than bring us together. Instead of trying to develop trust and mutual respect, we are encouraged to emphasize and exacerbate differences that cause division and hatred.

This is a formula for continued anger, hatred, violence, and eventual destruction of the social order. Individual attitudes and behaviors, along with systemic attitudes and behaviors, must be oriented to the common good if we are to make any progress. It is not beyond belief or imagining that if we continue on the present trajectory, the end of our civilization is in sight. A change in administrations only will not make the USA a moral nation; a change of attitudes, hard work, personal internal change, and institutional reform are just the beginning of a long arduous process. Without some modicum of trust and mutual respect, we will continue to be in deep trouble as individuals and as a society.

Fitzie, thanks for trusting and respecting me. Today, I am thankful we were part of each other's lives. Fitzie, *requiescat in pace*!

CHAPTER 8

Faith

Faith and Salvation

"*Outside the church there is no salvation*" was the mantra of Fr. Finney, a Catholic priest, of the early to mid-1900s. The essence of his belief was that if one was not baptized by water and the Spirit, one could not be saved. The Catholic Church strongly opposed this doctrine. This is a belief not very different from that held by many Christians and especially Christian fundamentalists of today. The Catholic Church's approach to the salvation of mankind is a rational and fundamentally Christian approach. Scripture is quite clear about Jesus's life, death, and resurrection being offered for *all* mankind. Is this all-embracing view compatible with the belief that some Christians hold that only those who have faith and are baptized will be saved? These two views seem to be mutually exclusive. As Christians, we should be careful about an exclusionary attitude, or we could find ourselves in the same position as the chosen people of the Jewish scriptures in relation to the Gentiles. If Christ's life was offered for *all* men and women, there can be no doubt that God desires *all* people to be saved.

As Christians, we make up a limited percentage of the human race. Wouldn't it be very un-Christian of God to exclude all the rest of mankind from salvation because of theological and ritual technicalities? The church has understood the fundamental flaw in this type of thinking. The Catholic Church, with her need to categorize and dogmatize what the faithful sense and know intuitively, has created theological constructs to give meaning to its belief. Besides baptism of water and Spirit, a fundamental of Christian belief, she uses the terms *baptism of blood* and *baptism of desire* to flesh out the doctrine of salvation. Although these constructs may be somewhat awkward and artificial, they can help clarify what we know intuitively. These basic categories explain how the church applies God's salvific will, as stated in the Bible, to *all* people.[*] The church has tenaciously defended the principle that outside the church, there is salvation. Baptism of water and the Spirit is the normal prerequisite for salvation within the church. Baptism of blood, to die for what one believes, is martyrdom and

---

[*] Isaiah 49:6, Luke 3:6, Acts 13:47, Isaiah 56, Hebrews 2:9, Luke 24:45–47, Romans 5:18–19, Romans 10:12–13, and Ephesians 3:5–6

an extraordinary means to achieve salvation. Baptism of desire, the earnest seeking of God, represents a thoughtful, just, and rational approach to the salvation of all men and is compatible with God's salvific will as found in the scripture.

Perhaps this doctrine has not been expressed in the most elegant terms, but the reality supporting the words is certainly in the Christian spirit. It seems easy for some Christians to exclude great masses of people through a harsh and erroneous interpretation of God's Word. These Christians seem to be doing what the Pharisees did in Jesus's day. In Matthew 23:4, Jesus points out that the Pharisees, who were the interpreters of the laws, were placing burdens on the people that distort religion. We do the same thing when we place the burden of damnation on those who do not know or believe in Jesus. Their destiny, thank God, will be in the hands of a loving, merciful, and just God, who is concerned as much about their salvation as he is about ours.

How can one who calls himself a Christian casually write off Jews, Muslims, Hindus, Buddhists, and countless millions of other religious persuasions? Denial of salvation, in the name of Christianity, because one has not been baptized or because one believes strongly in the God of their fathers, is just not acceptable or morally justifiable.

We Christians believe in the God of our fathers and would be insulted and outraged if someone of another faith suggested that because of our strongly held faith, we would not be saved. The church understands that those who do not believe in God as we do are nonetheless encompassed in his saving will. There are great numbers of people who, just like us, sincerely seek and desire truth. They are sincere good and loving people who respect what others believe, but who have not, and probably never will, believe as we do. They are no more or less important to God than we are. Who is to say that any person, regardless of their religious persuasion, who lives a just, loving, and compassionate life, will not enter the kingdom of God before a baptized Christian who is lukewarm and self-righteous?

In Matthew 21:28–32, Jesus tells the story of a father and his two sons. The father asks both sons to work in his vineyard. The older son agrees but fails to make good on his word. The younger son refuses but, in fact, works in the vineyard. Jesus asks which one did his father's will. (2005)

Thankful for Life

Some of my questionings are the direct result of thankfulness for the gift of life. For me, joy, gratitude, and thankfulness are a natural response to life and, in particular, my life and all the good "things" that make up my life. The idea of existence is almost overwhelming. What are the chances that any of us would exist? According to Google and most scientists, the chances are 400,000,000,000,000 to 1—that is, 400 *billion* to *one*. This makes the odds of our existence basically *zero*. Some say we can't speak of odds regarding life and existence. Life just is! Believers would say, God, in a unique act, decided to create you and me. Odds were not a factor. This, however, reopens questions. This creation could seem like a cruel gift, especially if God knew some lives would be miserable.

If our being and life are only the result of purely natural causes, then odds would be relevant. One second in time could have altered our actual existence. How many circumstances had to come together for us to come into being? What were the chances of our parents actually meeting each other? One little circumstance could have denied us being and life. Parents, grandparents, great-grandparents, and great-great-grandparents had to come together in exact moments of history with almost infinite possible scenarios to bring about our existence and lives. It's almost impossible to believe—absolutely amazing!

Let's not get sidetracked; the point here is the gratitude and thankfulness we express and share. For my life, I am overwhelmingly grateful and thankful; it has been marvelous. There is no superlative super enough to describe such a gift. I have been graced with these blessings by God, by nature, or something beyond my comprehension. This causes me to have a feeling or need to thank someone or something for my existence and life, and that need or feeling seems to be appropriate.

Beyond that, I have been graced with a multitude of gifts that I have not earned or merited. I have been gifted with an optimistic personality and nature that has been enhanced by all the good and wonderful people, events, and experiences of my life. I had and have no right to this happiness. It was neither earned nor merited. It seems in many ways to be the luck of the draw, but perhaps not. Being and life may be the strongest argument for the existence of God since forever, or it may be the best argument for shit happens or the luck of the draw theory. At times, I hold both theories simultaneously. It's a paradox!

That brings me back to the beginning of this essay and my questioning. Why should I be so blessed while others are not as blessed? Where is justice? Where is equality? Why should some be more blessed than others? These questions beg more questions. "Am I my brother's keeper?" (Gen. 4:1–13). This is a haunting question? The answer is obvious and absolute! Yes! None of us really deserve more than the next guy, but the next guy deserves at least our respect, understanding, and a helping hand. It may be an assumption. However, it seems apparent to me that our calling—whether God-based, scripture-based, or nature-based—is in this life to share and foster what I have been so blessed to be a part. To help another does not take away or subtract from us but rather enriches our lives and the lives of our sisters and brothers. This is another paradox. We should not squander or contribute to the squandering of even one of these miraculous lives. We should uplift!

"There was no one in the group who was in need... No one said that any of his belongings was his own, but they all shared with one another everything they had" (Acts 4:32–37). Sounds like some kind of communism to me—perhaps Christian communism? It is an attempt to give our brothers and sisters reason to be grateful for being and life just as hopefully you are and I am. There is great suffering and mistreatment of our brothers and sisters in this world, and it falls to us to try to transform it into joy, thankfulness, and gratitude issuing from life lived fully by all. This great gift of life should not become a life so miserable that it is not worth living. I know solutions are complicated and not easy, but not to try is just not right. The solutions start with us and how we treat others on a daily basis.

As I grow closer to my end, I realize on a deeper level the magnitude of the gifts of being and life and all the other gifts along the way that make life worth living. These gifts are not just meant for me and you but for all people. It is our job, our calling, an expression of our deepest and truest self to see that this vision is fulfilled for humankind. The sooner the better! (2020)

Give God Permission

When John Cardinal O'Connor, the archbishop of New York, passed away, there were many stories about him on the news. The one I like most was told by the cardinal himself on a previously taped interview. As he was processing from the cathedral after his ordination as bishop, he saw Mother Theresa at a short distance. Cardinal O'Connor went over to speak with her and recalled one piece of advice Mother Theresa offered him: "*Give God permission.*" These words, like Mother Theresa, were simple yet had a profound message. God, in his providence, chooses to make himself present through us. In a sense, he has put his work in our hands. God comes to us only if we allow him to do so. Our hearts and minds are doors that can only be opened from inside. God never forces himself on us. The ways in which God approaches us are infinite, but he needs to be invited. In Luke 1:38, when the angel Gabriel announced to Mary that she was to become the mother of God through the power of the Holy Spirit, she responded, "*I am the Lord's servant; may it happen to me as you have said.*" At that moment, Mary, through her faith, in a sense, gave God permission to become man.

God has approached us first and foremost through the person of Jesus. God sent his Son into the world to give us the good news of salvation and show us the way by his example. Jesus has enlightened us about the nature of God and the nature of religion. Love is at the very heart of God and religion. The presence of Jesus in history makes God's love for us apparent. Jesus makes clear to us that religion is about loving God and loving man. All religion rests upon these two truths. It is by his example that we have learned how to give God permission to come into our lives. Jesus has taught us that it is through other people that he makes himself real and present to us today. His love can be, and often is, made present to us through our family and friends, fellow citizens, churchgoers, and all those people we have related to throughout our lives. My wife's favorite saying from *Les Misérables* sums it up nicely: "*To love another person is to see the face of God.*"

When we allow God into our hearts, we receive and share the ability to see ourselves and others as unique and special. When we come to value all life and appreciate the importance of quality of life, we begin to understand that sharing and giving, rather than acquiring and hoarding, bring happiness and joy. We see that the love of God encourages us to share our unique talents and skills, recognizing that in the process, we will benefit from the gifts and talents of others.

If we look at the apostle Paul, we see another example of giving God permission. (Paul's door needed to be knocked on in a little more dramatic way.) Paul, however, made God present to thousands of people in his own time and countless thousands of people through the ages.

It is through our kindness and thoughtfulness to others that God's Spirit is manifested in the world. As Christians, if we don't act in a loving, just, and merciful way, we will fail to make God present. God is giving us an opportunity to share in his work. However, our failure to cooperate with God will not prevent or frustrate his plan. Our openness and cooperation will mark, in a unique fashion, those people we encounter along the way. Paul, Mary, and Mother Theresa, acting in unison with God's hand, marked this world in a distinct and singular manner. Although God's work through us may not be as spectacular as theirs, our giving God permission is, nonetheless, of vital importance to us and to those people God has allowed to cross the paths of our lives. (2003)

Religion, Where Is Your Focus?

St. John and Confucius have rightly asked us a very important question. How can we love God, whom we do not see, and not love our sisters and brothers, whom we do see? John simply says in 1 John 4:20, *"If anyone says he loves God, but hates his brother, then he is a liar. For he who does not love his brother, whom he does see, in what way can he love God, whom he does not see?"*

Confucius, when asked how one can minister to the gods replied: *"Till you have learned to serve men, how can you serve spirits?"* He also said about the afterlife, *"Till you know about the living, how are you to know about the dead?"* Karen Armstrong, in her book *The Great Transformation*, tells us that for Confucius, there were no abstruse metaphysics or complicated liturgical speculations; everything always came back to the importance of treating other people with absolute sacred respect. Even Jesus, who was most definitely God-centered, tells us that the Golden Rule is the sum of the law and the prophets: *"Therefore, all things whatsoever that you wish that men would do to you, do so also to them. For this is the law and the prophets*" (Matt. 7:12). If we could focus on this almost universally held truth, we might do better than we thought possible. This is not meant to take the focus off God but rather to focus more intently on the here-and-now problems of relationships amongst ourselves and our brothers and sisters.

God, for many of us, can be a way out—that is, a way of limiting or disregarding our obligations to one another. We can focus our attention on a God we do not see and don't really know while neglecting men and women, whom we do see and know. It is so much easier to pray, go to church, develop theologies and dogmas, create liturgies and rules and regulations that can distract us from the real, true, and difficult obligations to our sisters and brothers.

Much of religious practice today is about feeling good about ourselves, about believing certain articles of faith and morals, about personal salvation, about furthering our political agenda but also about many good and noble things but are not the heart of the matter. The problem is the focus should be not only or exclusively on God but what God wants for us and our brothers and sisters. Remember, Jesus came into the world not for himself or God but for us, men and women, who needed and still need an exemplar—one who shows us how to live, one who shows us the way, the truth, and the life. Jesus tells us in Mark 10:41–49:

> *You know that among the Gentiles those they recognize as their rulers lord it over them, and their great ones are tyrants over them. But it is not so among you: whoever wishes to become great among you must be your servant, and whoever wishes to be first among you must be slave of all. For the son of man came not to be served but to serve. And to give his life as a ransom for many.*

How sad it is that we (all of us) are still so far from achieving this goal. God's love is all-encompassing; God loves all of us, no exceptions. That includes Blacks, Whites, Mexicans, Africans, Americans, Russians, Asians, and Chinese. His love is universal and without exception, so if you want to be on God's side, you need to follow his example. *"Love your enemies. Do good to those who hate you"* (Matt. 5:44). This is God's focus; where is your focus? (2020)

Faith: Not So Simple

In the Gospel according to Matthew, immediately following the Sermon on the Mount, there are a series of gospel stories concerning faith (Matt. 9:18–38). In almost all these stories, faith plays an important role.

At first glance, it would seem that faith cured these people. This might indicate that if our faith is strong enough, then we will be cured, or if we ask in faith, it will be done for us. But is this an accurate picture? It is important for us to realize that our faith alone does not cure us or make us whole. It is Jesus who cures us and makes us whole. This seems a rather simple point, but we often get confused about faith and its results. Because of our faith, we do not dictate to God when, how, or even if he will choose to cure us. Because of our faith, we are open to God, and it is he who answers our prayer and makes us whole. We should remember, although we have faith, it is God who is in control. God's reasons and purposes are often hidden from us.

The strength of our faith should not be seen as a special badge used to lord it over those who differ from us in faith or those who have no faith at all. Faith is a gift offered by God to whom he sees fit and in whatever way he sees fit. There is no doubt a special relationship known only by God exists between faith and healing. Remember, in the Gospels, Jesus chose to heal only a small number of people for the purpose of building faith and proclaiming the kingdom of God. Healing and, ultimately, resurrection are signs of the power of life over death and good over evil. Perhaps it is simply meant that God's purposes were served through these limited encounters. Because he did not cure all the people did not imply that their faith was wanting. The many people who sought to be cured but were not were no more or less loved, no more or less important to God than those who were cured. It is our role to accept and grow whatever measure of faith we have been given by God. Is it perhaps by the degree of our acceptance of faith that we will be judged? Sometimes we think the greater our faith, the more God will do for us. This is not a direct equation. God treats each one of us as a unique individual who is in a special relationship with him.

What is faith? Is it believing the truths of Christianity? Is it believing in Jesus's message? Is it believing in Jesus the person? Is it taking Jesus's word on it? Faith is a complicated reality. It is all of the above and more. It is a living reality that grows and diminishes, strengthens and weakens, and has its moments of great joy and depression. It is a wonderful gift that is extended to all of us in one fashion or another. Faith is a relationship with God. To think of faith quantitatively as something that we possess in an amount that will somehow enhance our position with God over those who possess less is to misunderstand the reality of faith. It is not a commodity that, if stored, will bestow upon us more influence with God.

When we look at the Gospel, we see moments in Jesus's life when his faith in his Father differed in feeling and intensity. There were moments of exultation (the transfiguration and the triumphal entry into Jerusalem) and moments of dark depression (in the garden of Gethsemane and on the cross) when he felt abandoned by his Father. On the cross, in one moment, Jesus felt despair, and in the next moment, he commends his spirit into his Father's hands. Through all the highs and lows of his life (the approval of his Father, the joy of sharing friendship, the rejection of the people, and the denial of his disciples), there was an underlying reality, which was his knowledge that his Father's word to him would be fulfilled whatever hardships were endured.

Abraham, our Father in faith, against all odds, acted upon God's promise and departed from his home, unaware of his destination. Does this mean Abraham never had a doubt that his spirits were always high, that his faith did not flag? No! It meant that in spite of the temptation and disbelief, he continued to forge ahead in the service of his God. So it is with us. Even when our faith falters, our prayer should be that of the father of the boy with an evil spirit. "*I do believe; help me overcome my unbelief!*" (Mark 9:14–29). Like Jesus, we need to rest in the knowledge that the Father's word to us will be fulfilled whatever the hardship. (2004)

God's Will

Thomas Merton, in his book *No Man Is an Island*, tells us that we must be careful not to assign meaning to signs whose significance may be closed to us. If we do, we may fall into superstitious interpretations of commonplace experiences and events. He concludes that God's will is not so pedestrian a mystery as to be accessed through frivolous interpretations. It is true that God's will and how he achieves it are mysterious. There are signs that lead us to God. This usually happens within the context of a balanced spirituality, signs that if interpreted correctly can help us in our quest for God's will. These signs themselves are not necessarily extraordinary but are of value in a rational approach to spirituality. Superstition and fantastic explanations do little and can harm our quest for God.

Merton sees God's will tied to what he believes is the twofold end of man, his perfection as a part of a universal whole and his perfection in himself as an individual who is made in God's image and likeness. For man to achieve this perfection or holiness, the formation of a conscience that is capable of seeing God's will is essential. If man does not recognize this twofold end, he can lose sight of the forest, which is God's will, because of the trees, which are signs that are misinterpreted. We need signs that lead us to God and others rather than those that inflate self-absorption. In other words, we can get stuck on the incidentals and irrelevancies that lead us away from God and cause us to lose interest in the overall goal and meaning of life.

Isaiah speaks to the nation of Israel in the following passage in Isaiah 58:3–4:

> *Why do we fast, but you do not see? Why humble ourselves, but you do not notice? Look you serve your own interests on your fast-days, and oppress all your workers. Such fasting as you do today will not make your voice heard on high.*

Isaiah's message is loud and clear; we are a long way from the will of God when we serve our own self-interest.

We can be fairly sure that God does not seek things from us. He doesn't need our possessions, prayers, and sacrifices. He doesn't need our fasting and monetary offerings.

God loves us. Just as in human relationships we desire the love of the other person, so too God desires the love of us in return. God wants us, not our stuff. He desires to be in a relationship with us, to share our very being, to share our inmost thoughts and feelings, to share all that matters to us.

In Jesus, God has shown us that emptying ourselves in love for another is the way to true life that God wills for each one of us. It is only in developing ourselves to become the persons God wants us to be that we find holiness and fulfillment as human beings. But his will for us never stops with ourselves. God's will for us involves a multitude of relationships, each of which is connected to our own fulfillment and the perfection of the world. Jesus tells us to be perfect as his heavenly Father is perfect. God the Father sent his son in an outpouring of his divine love, and this gesture demonstrates his will in reaching out to others. Sharing in God's love is creative, redemptive work. This demands that we go beyond our own self-interest. Only service and love lead to God and true self-fulfillment.

The will of God is ultimately a mystery. What we do know is that God's will for us demands the perfection of ourselves and the world, which can only be achieved through loving involvement with our brothers and sisters. (2012)

Faith and Good Works

"Lazarus and the Rich Man," a beautiful gospel story from Luke 16:19–31, tells us how sometimes rich people deal with the poor and what consequences may issue from that treatment. Ultimately, Lazarus has his reward of eternal happiness, and the rich man endures damnation.

From hades, the rich man views Lazarus from afar, resting in Abraham's bosom. He begs Abraham to send Lazarus to visit his five brothers so that they can alter their behavior and be saved. This is a story about the obligations of the rich toward the poor, but there is also a lesson about faith to be learned here.

> *Abraham's response to the rich man is "Your brothers have Moses and the prophets to warn them; your brothers should listen to what they say." The rich man answered, "that is not enough father Abraham! But if someone were to rise from the dead and go to them, then they would turn from their sins." But Abraham said, "if they will not listen to Moses and the prophets, they will not be convinced even if someone were to be raised from the dead." (Luke 16:29–31)*

These words cut to the heart of the matter and ring true to this very day. Our faith in Jesus places demands on us. We cannot simply believe in Jesus. When Paul speaks of mankind being justified by faith in Jesus, he is stating a fundamental religious reality. Apart from Jesus, there is no salvation. What does that mean? It simply means that Jesus is the cause of our salvation and the salvation of all people. Without Jesus, there is no justification. Man is powerless to bring about his own redemption before God.

This is the truth, but given this truth, there is more. Just as for the rich man, who no doubt believed in Moses and the prophets, belief or faith even in one who might return from the dead was not enough to bring him to Abraham's bosom. Although the rich man's salvation and justification had already been secured through the merits of Jesus, it was not guaranteed to him. The same is true for us. Our redemption has been secured through the merits (life, suffering, death, and resurrection) of Jesus Christ. There is, however, more required of us. St. James tells us very clearly and succinctly:

> *My brothers, what good is it for someone to say that he has faith if his actions do not prove it? Can that faith save him? Suppose there are brothers or sisters that need clothes*

and do not have enough to eat. What good is there in your saying to them, "God bless you! Keep warm and eat well!"-if you don't give them the necessities of life? So, it is with faith: if it is alone and includes no actions, then it is dead. (James 2:14–17)

This is the point of the story about Lazarus and the rich man: all the faith in the world will not get you into heaven. From faith flows love and from love actions, which are an integral part of authentic faith. It is important that we don't confuse our actions with the cause of our salvation. According to Christian theology, all the actions and good works we perform cannot win us justification. Only Jesus can do this! He has done his part; now we must do ours.

Just believing and having faith in Jesus is not enough. Acting upon that faith in accordance with the gospel message is required. If we lack good works, Jesus's life, death, and resurrection are empty and devoid of power for us. If we believe and act upon that belief, we bring richness and quality to our lives and to the lives of others here and now and in the process, gain an eternal reward. Believing in the resurrection is not enough; good works must be added for us to be true to the gospel message. *"Not everyone who says to me 'Lord, Lord' will enter the kingdom of heaven, but only the one who does the will of My Father in heaven"* (Matt. 7:21). (2004)

Belief versus Unbelief

The universe just is. It sits out there, and the only explanation it needs is, it is. There is no other proof necessary. Basically, it is a self-evident truth that only a fool would deny. God on the other hand, and Christianity even more so, demand certain assumptions or suppositions. An assumption or supposition can be defined as an uncertain belief, a theory, or a view. Neither could be considered a fact. The first assumption is God exists—not necessarily a self-evident fact. The second assumption is the existence of a being that has always existed and is the creator and sustainer of the universe.

For Christians, the following assumptions also apply. The first assumption is this being is personal. The second and third assumptions, revelation, and inspiration are additional suppositions upon which the existence of God and belief in Jesus as God are based. There may be other suppositions, but the above will suffice for the sake of this essay. It follows that in order to be a Christian, you must believe, in faith, that there is a God and that Jesus is his Son and also God. Faith is the key word here.

Ockham's razor, a philosophical principle, simply states that all things being equal simplicity is preferred over complexity. It says of any given set of explanations for an event occurring, the simplest one is most likely the correct one. Entities should not be multiplied without necessity. When considering the universe and how it came about, a God as creator and sustainer seems to violate this principle. It would seem then that we would have to ascribe to some form of atheistic concept of reality. Which is more fantastic or difficult to believe, a universe that just is and always was, or a God who is and always was and is the creator and sustainer of all that exists?

I personally have found, in contrast to Ockham's razor, that most things are more complicated than they first appear. On the other hand, some things are simpler than they first appear. A difficult question to answer, I am referring to the question of belief and unbelief. You make the choice.

In years past when science was even more limited than it is today, believers would use a mechanism called "God of the gaps." It was the supplying of God as a cause of things that were seemingly unexplainable. We now know that many of these explanations can be ascertained through science and experimentation. Is religion still using "God of the gaps" when it is at a loss for a credible explanation for a reality that, in fact, may be just not yet understood? The rationale would be, if we can't explain it at this time, then God must be the explanation or cause. It is a logical fallacy of the nonscientific age.

This "God of the gaps" mechanism is less prevalent today because of education and science but is still in some ways a go-to explanation for some people of religion. If we accept that God does exist, we still have to grapple with the question of evil and suffering. The question of God's existence and the existence of suffering and evil has been asked throughout the centuries with little resolution of the issue.

Epicurus, a Greek philosopher, asked this series of questions and came to some conclusions regarding evil in the world: Is God willing to prevent evil but not able? Then he is impotent. Is God able but not willing? Then he is malevolent. Is God both able and willing? If so, why is there evil? He reasoned if God knows about our suffering (all-knowing) and cares about our suffering (all-loving), if he has the power to do something about it (all-powerful), then there shouldn't be suffering and evil.

Pierre Bayle, a French philosopher, proposed that although natural evil is undeniable, that doesn't challenge faith in God's love, power, and wisdom. All that is challenged is human reason and knowledge. Bayle contends we just do not have the ability to understand the complexity of God and his plan.

Nietzsche, a German philosopher known for his "God is dead" philosophy can be used to support, I believe, two distinct and opposing views regarding the existence of God suffering and evil. Nietzsche believed that the world is full of suffering and evil and that it lacks any overall purpose or meaning. However, he thought that our ability to deal with this suffering, to endure hardships and overcome them, is an important and valuable exercise of our power and character. In fact, in summoning the strength to overcome the darkness of the world, we find a way to overcome its meaninglessness according to Nietzsche. Some philosophers have drawn on similar ideas to defend theism. They have argued that God put suffering and evil in the world in order to allow us to learn something valuable from it. People challenge both sides of this argument with justification.

Schopenhauer, a German philosopher, said we would have been better never to have been born. For some, this may be the case, but by and large, for most people, this would not be true. But even Schopenhauer felt life could have some valuable experiences such as art, beauty, selfless compassion, and humane self-denial. Perhaps he was on to something spiritual.

Karl Rahner, a German theologian, does not pretend to have all the answers, nor does he take the position of an apologist of Christian faith or even of the traditional concept of God. There is no absolutism here but only a quest for truth no matter how open-ended and mysterious. He is an honest broker of truth-seeking. Rahner was committed to critical dialogue with the Enlightenment and its legacy.

With regard to the questions of God and his existence, Rahner believed we had, in the past, a primitive and childish approach to this vital subject. It just didn't stand up to critical thinking. He sought a quest for truth independent of authority, orthodoxy, and tradition. Rahner thought that some people refer to God as someone whom we can calculate into our formula of how things work, thus replacing the incomprehensibility of God with an idol. He indicated that the struggle against atheism is, for the most part and of necessity, a struggle against the inadequacy of our own theism.

Paraphrasing Rahner, the quest is a quest of never-ending questions. The answer becomes the basis of the next question. Could this condition of unending questioning mean that the human spirit is characterized by an unrestricted drive for truth, which is ultimately boundless? In every aspect, human freedom, like reason, is a dynamism that keeps on transcending beyond everything it grasps. Undergirding all personal existential moments is an immense and driving longing, which, at its root, we experience an orientation to something more. We experience ourselves as beings who constantly reach out beyond ourselves toward something ineffable. This orientation is what constitutes us as spiritual beings.

Rahner calls this orientation self-transcendence. He does not try to prove the existence of God. He feels such proof is not possible. He rather questions what supports the dynamic orientation of human nature. Our self-transcending minds and hearts are forever reaching for the good and the true. When we think we have reached the goal, we realize it has not actually been reached, and we must go forward, questioning more, seeking more, continuing the search, continuing the journey. That which we seek is forever unbounded, infinite, undefinable, forever beyond our grasp. Rahner calls it holy mystery. *Mystery* here signifies the idea that the holy is so radically different from the world, so completely other, that human beings can never form an adequate idea nor arrive at total possession. The goal of human self-transcendence is and must remain incomprehensible in depth and breadth forever. It is a mistake to think of God as an element within a larger world, as a part of the whole of reality. Holy mystery escapes all categories. Rahner contends that the incomprehensibility of the holy mystery is of the essence of God and always was and always will be. God would not be God if he were not incomprehensible.

The case for and against belief seems to be one that will extend into the future for some time to come. In fact, as long as human beings exist, the tension between belief and unbelief will continue as it should. (2014)

A Family of Faith

In October of 2002, my brother-in-law, my wife's twin sister's husband, Dan was diagnosed with colon cancer that had metastasized to his liver, involving more than twenty nodes. He was given six months to live. I am writing this essay in May of 2004. Thank God, Dan is still here, waging a monumental battle against a devastating disease.

For almost two years, both our families have been preoccupied with this new way of life. Our families have always been close—cousins like brothers and sisters and nieces and nephews like sons and daughters. Our family has tried to be as supportive as possible through prayer, weekend visits, phone calls, and my wife's continual contact with Liz and Dan. Because of the difficulty in concentrating on anything but Dan and Liz and their four kids

(Dan, twenty-four; Elizabeth, twenty-two; Rachael, seventeen; and Matt, eleven) and our visits to Maryland, I was unable to write anything for this book for the better part of a year.

Theirs is a story of faith, prayer, immediate family support, and extended family support through extremely difficult and painful times. All through this ordeal, Dan has suffered physically, emotionally, and spiritually without complaint. He has had a sense of humor beyond any reasonable expectation. He has experienced surgery after surgery and chemo treatment after chemo treatment without complaint. All this has occurred while Dan has been in constant prayer.

Liz, his wife, has been nothing short of a saint throughout. Through her constant companionship, her empathetic love, her countless hours in the kitchen preparing special organic meals, and hours of prayer, she has supported Dan in a fashion that is beyond the merely human.

Dan's oldest son, Dan, has devoted the last year and three quarters to reading, researching, and developing a regimen of dietary supplements and organic foods for his father. He has dedicated his life to these pursuits in the hope of contributing to a cure for his father. Little Dan grows wheat grass and organic foods in the basement in the winter and has a large organic garden outside during the summer.

Dan's oldest daughter, Elizabeth is graduating from the University of Maryland this May. She has been a huge support to her father, expressing her care and concern through her love and affection, which give Dan untold strength. She has been there for her father during his chemo treatments and his numerous hospital visits.

Rachel, Dan's youngest daughter, a junior in high school, has been there for her dad and mom without reservation. Her loving obedience and unflagging concern have been a cause of joy for both Dan and Liz. Rachel's love, support, and prayers have been, and continue to be, a constant consolation and blessing to her father.

Matt, Dan's youngest son, a young boy who knows what is going on but does not always fathom the gravity of the situation, is always there supporting and loving his dad. He has been on his best behavior for the last year and three quarters. Just the vision of young Matt is a joy to his father's heart.

Each and every member of this family is an integral part of Dan's ability to keep this disease at bay. But the thing that impresses me most is their faith that God can bring good out of this difficult situation. I am sure that at times, it is confusing for them. Why should God even allow this good family to go through this suffering? God and his will are mysterious and beyond our mortal comprehension. Their faith and love of God and their family devotion are true miracles. This family is God's miracle. The love, joy, and support this family gives to each other, especially when the chips are down, help them transcend the most difficult times in their lives. The Edelsteins are truly a family of faith, who, through their support of one another, give hope and inspiration to their extended family and to all who are privileged to experience this time with them. (2004)

PS: Dan died on March 18, 2005. His oldest daughter gave birth to a little girl, Lilly, on March 18, 2017. God bless the cycle of life.

A Man of God

Last night, I went to dinner with a priest who was ordained fifty-two years ago. He was my parish priest in my formative years. During those years, he lived through the tail end of the immigrant church, the Vatican II era, the clergy exodus, and the return to a pre–Vatican II church, and he did it with dedication and faithfulness. As we talked, I realized that this man was and still is a living example of what the priesthood is all about. Over the years, he has remained faithful to his commitment to his God and to the people entrusted to his service.

At eighty-two years of age, his conversation was about the great opportunities that still exist for priests to serve God's people. He spoke of the need for priests to be available to the people. His vision is optimistic and hopeful in spite of his keen awareness that the church and the world are in serious trouble. His attitude toward people is one of affirmation and support. He saw a need, today more than ever, for priests and the church to engage people on a level deeper than ritual and regulation.

I have heard people talk about our society's lacking heroes for our youth to look up to but never really gave it much thought. I realize now that as my parish priest in Our Lady of Victories Parish, he was my hero. He had influenced my life in many ways. When struggling with my psychosexual development, he was patient, supportive, and understanding. He influenced my choice of high school and priesthood because of his realistic living of the gospel in a secular society. Because of his positive influence, I had enough courage to resign from the priesthood when it became an inauthentic life choice for me.

To this day, he possesses the ability to separate what really matters in religion from that which is pious nonsense and political machinations. He is not perfect—none of us are—but he has never lost sight of the gospel message. At the heart of his ministry is a loving, compassionate concern for God's people. It is very clear that he has had a loving relationship with God that is unencumbered by hypocrisy or political ambition.

Unlike some other priests, he never became a caricature of himself. He never retreated into stifling self-centeredness or chose impersonal, materialistic interest over interpersonal relationships. To many people, he has been a close and loyal friend. It is unfortunate that today, the priesthood has a shortage of men of his caliber. His priesthood has been marked by a deep concern for the welfare of God's people without an unhealthy adherence to rules and regulations that have little or no relationship to the gospel. Over the years, his sense of compassion and ability to help public figures who have done wrong, without approving of the wrongdoing, is a reflection of his commitment to the gospel, which admonishes us to love even the sinner.

God has gifted him with a lively sense of humor, a quick wit, a grand smile, and a twinkle in his eye that radiates a spark of divine love, which he has so generously shared over the years. There is no other individual (wife, children, and parents excluded) who has influenced my life, in a positive way, as much as he has.

When Father Bob Lennon reaches the gates of heaven, God will say, "Welcome, good and faithful servant. Enter the kingdom of heaven, for what you did for the least of my brothers, and sisters you did for me." (2014)

Possibilities

In the eighteenth chapter of the book of Genesis, God promises Abraham that his childless wife, Sarah, will conceive and bear a child, from whom a great nation will flow. Sarah laughs at the suggestion that she could become a mother at her age, possessing a barren womb and a reproductive system well beyond childbearing years.

In the natural and normal order of things, she would be justified to laugh at such a suggestion, but she fails, as we all too often do, to take into account that all things are possible with God. With God, it is possible for a rich man to enter the kingdom of heaven. With God, it is possible for a virgin to bear a child. With God, it is possible for a woman of ill repute to become a confidant of Jesus. Sarah's laugh was that of one not open to the possibilities of God's power.

We, like Sarah, have little insight into the realities in which God's power is manifested. God does ask us, in faith, to be open to his power and possibilities regardless of whether or not these possibilities come to fruition in the manner in which we wish. Almost all of us wish for long life and good health. Most people desire good fortune and happiness. But as we know, these things are not granted to all of us. Even the request of the apostles James and John to sit one at the right hand and the other at the left hand of Jesus in heaven was not to be granted. All our wishes, desires, and requests are not necessarily ours to be granted. When we ask for our health or the well-being of our children, we must be open to the possibility of a positive response, but we must also be open to the possibility that these gifts are not ours to receive. These mysteries are truly beyond our comprehension. How and who God chooses and for what reasons will remain a mystery in this life.

God often surprises us with gifts even when our expectations are low, as was the case with Sarah. On the other hand, even when our expectations are high and we are open to God's power, it doesn't always work out the way we expect. Faith gives us an attitude of expectation and possibility without demand because we know all things are possible with God. Faith should also allow us the insight to know that all we hope for, even if what we hope for is good, is not necessarily possible for us. Even Jesus, the Son of God, completely open to God's power and possibilities, hoped and prayed in the Garden of Gethsemane for the bitter chalice to pass, but this was not possible for him.

Sometimes when God chooses not to grant what we ask and pray for, we tend to interpret or place certain meanings on the outcomes. This is acceptable as long as we realize that these interpretations are our personal views, and they do not necessarily reflect God's intentions in these matters. Remember, God's ways are not our ways. These interpretations are our attempts to make sense of things.

Religions often aid us in interpreting events and happenings that are good, but at times, religions can view their interpretations as synonymous with God's intentions. When we honestly think about and analyze this behavior, no matter how well intentioned, we realize it is presumptuous for religion or, for that matter, any person to declare unequivocally what God's intentions are in these matters.

It would seem more honest of us, as individuals and religions in general, to acknowledge that these interpretations are positive, hopeful suggestions to be used when searching for the meaning of God's hand in our lives. To be open to possibilities, to be expectant in the presence of God's power yet wise enough to understand that God's ways are not our ways is to follow in the footsteps of Jesus. (2020)

CHAPTER 9

A Little Different Look

Jesus the Christian Prophet

Some individuals and institutions feel that people who don't work, for whatever reason, or who don't want menial jobs should not receive welfare, Medicare, Medicaid, life-saving medical treatment, or any benefits, "which they did not earn." We need to take a moment to think and reflect on this.

The system is so broken, so corrupt, and so slanted in favor of the rich that true justice is virtually impossible to achieve. Even people of goodwill find it difficult to see clearly the predicament. If we want people to work full-time jobs, we need to pay them a living wage. A living wage is not $15 an hour. How can we expect someone to work a full-time job and not get paid a living wage, not get paid enough to keep body and soul together, pay rent, buy food, pay medical insurance, raise kids, etc.? Try it; you won't like it.

Something is seriously wrong with the economic system. Could it possibly be greed or a lack of will to change things or an inability to empathize with our sisters and brothers? Those at the top often seem only too eager to put the blame on the poor when in fact the institutional systems they endorse keep people from getting ahead. These systems and individuals who create and perpetuate this condition are much like the people and systems of Jesus's day. Those who oppose institutional corruption, much as Jesus did, pay a great price. Some pay the ultimate price.

Jesus was a religious, political, and social prophet at the very least. Because he cared for the sick and the poor, because he cared for the sinner, sought justice, and opposed the systemic corruption found in religion and politics, he was ultimately rejected. We have strayed so far from his message that we have lost sight of the mission he passed on to us. It is one of compassion, mercy, peace, and justice.

Some church communities have decided to concentrate on personal internal issues and concerns of personal salvation to the detriment of the larger commitment to mercy for sinners and justice for the poor. Jesus obviously had a preferential love for the poor and the sinner. Jesus ate with sinners; he walked with them; he cared for them and loved them. Jesus had no agenda; he cared for people without reservation. He said to the woman caught in adultery, "*Go and sin no more*" (John 8:11), but he always forgave.

When Peter asked, "How many times should I forgive, seven times?" Jesus's response was, *"I tell you not seven times but seventy-seven times"* (Matt. 18:21–22). This means always with no condition attached with regard to success or failure. We are all sinners and should be thankful for Jesus's mercy; it includes all of us. However, his mercy will be a reflection of the mercy we show the poor, the sinner, our less fortunate brothers and sisters. *"Amen I say to you, whenever you did this for one of these, the least of my brothers and sisters, you did it for me"* (Matt. 25:40). Remember, we are all sinners.

It is obvious that this largely Christian nation has lost its way. If Jesus is truly "*the way, the truth and the life*" (John 14:6). We "American Christians" need to reorder our lives based on his gospel and not on some rationalized version of that gospel. (2010)

Relationship
War and Peace

What do relationships have to tell us about war and peace? Have we misconstrued the path to peace? Do we in actuality believe war can bring about peace? Ultimately, the only real path regarding war, peace, and relationship is love. This is a vague, nebulous, and unspecified answer. This answer is simplistic without further explanation. An understanding of love can only come when we consider and define the following components: justice, peace, trust, forgiveness, and love.

Justice, as we have stated in the past, is a morally fair and right state of everything in which all people are treated equally. Peace can be defined in at least two ways: as a period when there is no war and as a period of harmony and tranquility. Trust is the belief in the reliability and truthfulness of another. Forgiveness is a conscious, deliberate decision to release feelings of resentment or vengeance toward another who has harmed us, regardless of whether it is actually deserved. Finally, we come to love, which can be defined in many ways. Some see love as an emotional state or a mental state of deep affection. Love is not often described as a will act, but the will is a vital part of real love.

Pope Paul VI said, "*If you want peace work for justice.*" Desmond Tutu summed up the road to peace by saying,

"There is no future without forgiveness." Santosh Kalwar tells us, *"Trust starts with truth and ends with truth."* Pope John XXIII said, *"A peaceful man does more good than a learned one."* The great prophet Martin Luther King Jr. proclaimed, *"Hate cannot drive out hate; only love can do that. Peace cannot be kept by force; it can only be achieved by understanding."* Each of these components is complex in nature. There are multiple ways of defining, understanding, and interpreting these concepts. For our purposes, the definitions given above should be adequate.

It is my contention that without these ingredients, human relationships between individuals or among nations will result in continuing broken personal relations and endless wars. Love is the foundation and bedrock upon which the other components rest. Marriage or personal relationship is analogous to relations among countries. All analogies limp, and personal relationships are not as complex as relations among nations. However, insight into personal relationships can give us, through that experience, some awareness of the method and formula for achieving world peace.

Without the tools of justice, peace, trust, forgiveness, and love, both personal relationships and relations among nations will fail. Anyone who is married or has been a partner in a long-term intimate relationship will recognize that romantic love and real love are quite different. The word *love*, used in long-term intimate relationships, encompasses justice, trust, forgiveness, and peace. Justice, trust, and forgiveness are the means by which we achieve a peaceful and loving relationship. Justice means that there must be some equality between parties, not necessarily on every single issue but in a substantive and consensual way. Trust surely begins with truth and ends with truth. Without trust, a relationship will deteriorate and will eventually end in doubt and suspicion. Forgiveness allows for our humanity; we all fail our partners to a greater or lesser degree, but forgiveness says our love is greater than our offense or failure. It is through these efforts that we arrive at peace within relationships (a state of reasonable harmony and tranquility). The overall condition achieved through this process is called love in personal relationships and peace in international relationships.

At this point, we need to look a little more deeply at love itself. Because we have been so inaccurately and deeply indoctrinated in a false concept of love, we think love to be an unrealistic and Pollyannaish view or means to peace. In many ways, we think war is strong and love is weak. However, if we use personal relationships as a metaphor for war and peace, we find that love is the only answer.

In relationships, violence breeds violence. The same is true in relations between nations. Because we have a history of violence used as a solution to difficult situations, an ineffective one at that, it becomes more and more difficult to break patterns of violence. As in personal relationships, violence causes the participants to become mired in feelings of hatred and mistrust.

In personal relationships, only love can heal these fissures. As any married couple knows, love is not just good feelings and flowers. Relationship is hard work. Love is so romanticized in our society that we fail to see that love is hard-nosed and demanding. However, the happiness and satisfaction that come from that hard work can be truly fulfilling and joyful, but it is not all peaches and cream. The same kind of effort that goes into a relationship must go into peacemaking. Difficult as it may be, it is absolutely required.

The hippies of the '60s had it right: "Make love, not war." Perhaps not 100 percent right. We are not talking about physical love here. We are talking about hard-nosed love, about difficult self-giving love for those with whom we disagree. Jesus and others are exemplars who showed us the cost of love. Relationships are between two flawed people or two or more flawed countries who are striving to form a bond that will sustain and nourish their relationship. Of course, there will be arguments and disagreements, but the hoped-for result is a lasting, caring, complementary relationship that will create and sustain both individuals and nations. Personal relationships can be difficult, but international relationships are even more difficult to navigate and negotiate. We are not always successful, but we should not use failure as an excuse for not trying.

In interpersonal relationships, love presupposes trust, and trust breeds trust. Baby steps work here. Little by little, trust builds upon trust. History, politics, religion, economics, and the like further complicate the matter of international relationships. All this being granted, there are still lessons to be learned in considering personal relationships when considering war and peace.

Martin Luther King Jr. states, *"Power without love is reckless and abusive and love without power is sentimental and anemic. Power at its best is love implementing the demands of justice and justice at its best is love correcting everything that stands against love."* In light of this insight, we see love demands willpower, and it becomes more evident that living in peace or achieving peace requires love, which contains all the above components. The complexity of this process gives additional insight into the reasons why the human race has such difficulty with interpersonal and international relationships.

All this brings me back to the famous and true quote of G. K. Chesterton: *"The Christian ideal has not been tried and found wanting. It has been found difficult and left untried."* Love and all its components are the only answer to truly healthy relationships. Love is the only answer to the question of war and peace, but like Chesterton's Christianity, it has been found difficult and left untried, at least in most cases.

It is not an easy answer. It requires tremendous effort, even for men and women of goodwill. It may be possible that we, in our heart of hearts, don't believe this type of love is possible. I hope this is not the case. We seem to have reckoned war to be a path to peace. Should we not realize by this time in history that war is not the means to peace? What happened to "the ends do not justify the means," or does that only apply when it works to support our position? War is the opposite path to peace, at least to real peace. War often leads not to peace but to domination. We are slow learners; the true path to peace is love.

Wisdom and religion both tell us that self-sacrifice, the hallmark of love, is the way to true life and peace. This counterintuitive wisdom will be resisted, denied, and avoided until some event, positive or negative, opens our eyes to reality, or perhaps we will achieve, over time, a more enlightened attitude and the will to put it into practice. (2020)

Suffering
A Partial Answer

Some Christians and people of religion believe suffering is a gift from God. I have often wondered what that means. How and why they arrived at this belief is a long and complicated process. Others think it is punishment for our sins, and still, others say it is the result of sin. The beliefs regarding suffering are many, and all fall short of a complete explanation of the true meaning of suffering. Does the more you suffer mean the more God loves you? Or does it mean the more God loves you, the more you must suffer? Does suffering have anything to do with sin? Would you give your children the gift of suffering, or do you try to protect them from suffering? Is suffering redemptive? Is suffering the result of evil? Is God trying to tell us something through suffering? It is perhaps one of those realities that will remain forever a mystery.

Suffering, for me, begs the question, if God exists and is all-loving, what do we make of suffering? Curse or blessing or both at one and the same time? Like the cross, some see it as foolishness; others see it as the saving power of God, and for others, suffering is a stumbling block.

To complicate matters, there exist at least two types of suffering: natural and man-made. Natural suffering is the suffering that man has no control over or causal relationship to, something necessarily caused by nature (God?). Some examples are as follows: volcanic eruptions, tornadoes, earthquakes, and hurricanes. These events and their results, suffering would occur even if mankind did not exist. This is not to say that man's activity cannot exacerbate the suffering.

Man-made suffering is just that, suffering that is caused by or the result of man's activity. Man-made suffering comes about through intentional or unintentional acts for which he is wittingly or unwittingly responsible. Murder, war, abuse of nature, and social injustice are just a few examples, all of which bring suffering.

Are there any benefits to suffering? As my father used to say, "It all depends on how you don't look at it." If you don't look at it from a spiritual point of view, it has limited but important benefits. For instance, from suffering can come compassion and empathy and the will to eliminate the causes of suffering. However, if we look at it from a religious point of view (belief in God), it can be so much more. Suffering and evil are bound together but are not synonymous. Just as suffering can be man-made or from nature, so also evil can be man-made or from natural causes. Just as suffering is mysterious, so also is evil. Evil can, and always does, cause great suffering while suffering does not ordinarily cause evil.

If Christianity is correct in its assertion and assumption that the Son of God entered the world to benefit mankind, what is he saying to us? After years of study and examination trying to understand what might be at least a partial explanation for the existence of suffering, I have chosen a paradigm that embraces love, sacrifice, and in effect embraces suffering.

As stated earlier, suffering is possibly a blessing and a curse. We know full well what the curse is: pain of all kinds—physical, psychological, social, spiritual, etc. What about the blessing? I would suggest from a Christian point of view that God came in the form of Jesus as an exemplar—that is, one who shows us the way. Through Jesus's life and death, we see connections. Suffering and sacrifice are necessarily a part of love. Through suffering and sacrifice, Jesus shows us life is about love, which, at its heart, is sacrificial and intimately connected to suffering. The crucifixion is not about sin, redemption, and salvation in the traditional and orthodox sense.

It is rather about Jesus's being an exemplar. He makes himself vulnerable and takes love to the limit. More than likely, we will not have to make the ultimate sacrifice in the name of love. However, in order for us to grasp the dynamic power of love, Jesus embraced the ultimate sacrifice with all its suffering and pain. This should speak to us of the equality and importance of human beings. Suffering is not easy and, for me, has no value for its own sake.

As human beings and especially as parents, we can identify with this type of love. Love and sacrifice are part and parcel of life and nature. This somehow has to be part of God's nature. Richard Rohr, in one of his daily meditations, makes an important point regarding the foremost Christian symbol: "*The cross became the central Christian symbol because the early Christians saw accurately the message of Jesus's love is expressed most fully through sacrifice which always entails suffering.*" The meaning of this symbol, over time, has been lost or denied because power, privilege, and domination are mistakenly believed more desirable and powerful than love, vulnerability, suffering, and sacrifice. The heart of love is sacrifice (or at least the willingness to sacrifice), and the heart of sacrifice is suffering. This is hard to embrace or integrate because we have been conditioned by society and religion to choose power, wealth, and position over love.* (2020)

---

* The paradigm presented is, at a minimum, incomplete with regard to an ultimate solution to the issues of suffering and evil.

Love and Power

In James 2:2–9, a contrast is drawn between love and power.

> *Now suppose a man comes into your synagogue, beautifully dressed and with a gold ring on, and that at the same time a poor man comes in, in shabby clothes, and you take notice of the well-dressed man, and say, "Come this way to the best seat"; then you tell the poor man, "Stand over there" or "You can sit on the floor by my foot rest." Can't you see that you have used two different standards in your mind, and turn yourself into judges, and corrupt judges at that?*
>
> *Listen, my dear brothers: it was those who are poor according to the world that God chose, to be rich in faith and to be heirs to the kingdom which he promised to those who love him. In spite of this, you have no respect for anybody who is poor. Isn't it always the rich who are against you? Isn't it always their doing when you are dragged before the courts? Aren't they the ones who insult the honorable name to which you have*

been dedicated? Well, the right thing to do is to keep the supreme law of Scripture: you must love your neighbor as yourself; but as soon as you make distinctions between classes of people, you are committing sin, and under condemnation for breaking the law.

This reading from James speaks strongly to our present-day realities. He points to the relationship between the powerful and the poor and the lack of real love for our struggling sisters and brothers. Why can't we help those in need rather than just standing by or hindering their ability to just live?

A short true story will illustrate the point. A baggage handler for one of the major airlines, making at least $30 an hour, felt fairly secure in her ability to care for her family during this pandemic—that is, until she lost her job. She has not been able to secure another job even after some forty interviews. She and her family are now food-deprived, homeless, without health insurance, without a car and furniture, and feeling abandoned and hopeless.

There are thousands of individuals and families out there in the same boat. How do you think you would feel without a job, a home, a car, food-deprived, without health care, and no one who gives a damn? Approved supplemental government aid is logjammed, and Congress is taking its sweet time about passing another desperately needed aid package. Where is the outcry of the people of this nation to do something meaningful for those suffering and desperate people? Shame on us! *"As soon as you make distinctions between classes of people, you are committing sin, and under condemnation for breaking the law"* (of love).

This was the thrust of early Christianity: to be loving toward all—the poor and the rich, the weak and the strong—recognizing the dignity and equality of all women and men. However, it didn't take long for this message to be corrupted. Our challenge today is the same as that of the early followers of Jesus: to realize we are all weak and vulnerable, and for this reason, we are all in it together. Those who are fortunate in material assets are obliged to find ways to help the less fortunate. The message of Jesus was and still is love. Love entails sacrifice and suffering, and no one is exempt. It is only when we eliminate these inequities among us that we will achieve the end for which Jesus suffered. (2020)

Direction of Life

If the first stage of life has a solid foundation, then we have a good chance; if not, then life can be a monumental struggle. Some do not get this solid foundation of love, respect, honesty, and good direction. Without it, our foundation and platform from which we move forward will be unstable and shaky. It will require more effort to develop a stable and growth-inducing environment. Richard Rohr calls this "*the first stage of order.*" Even a good foundation has its drawbacks.

For all intents and purposes, a normal foundation is assumed. It feels solid and true. This is a positive good but in some ways can become a protective wall that does not allow us to easily consider alternatives. A relative balance has to be struck. If the negatives outweigh the positives, coming to a balanced and secure way of life is extremely difficult and for some, impossible.

From this platform, Richard Rohr feels one goes on to deal with first things, "*establishing identity, home, relationships, friends, community, security, and building a proper platform for our only life.*" This is the foundation from which we go forward toward, hopefully, a deeper and richer life. If we do not go forward, in many ways, we remain as children and fail to seek the higher meaning of life. We all need what appear to be hard and fast rules in this first stage of life. These give us stability and consistency when we need it most.

However, as time goes by, life becomes paradoxical. The rules that gave us stability at the beginning of life, and could possibly now restrict us, can also afford us the stability to question the validity of those very rules. We allow ourselves to experiment and reach out beyond narrow and static borders to a more dynamic reality. They give us the ability and courage to question, in a constructive way, all that we have held as true without destabilizing our equilibrium.

Much of this essay is a combination of ideas gleaned from Richard Rohr's daily meditations and Karen Armstrong's book *The Great Transformation* along with my own thoughts, experiences, and observations.

Around 900 BCE to 200 BCE, the world started to change in terms of man's understanding of religion, philosophy, war, spirituality, politics, and the concept of God. This has been called the Axial Age or, as Karen Armstrong characterizes it, *the great transformation*. In her book of the same name, she, in great detail, describes what transpired. This period is quite complex, so I am going to focus on two vital life-enhancing principles that developed out of this age. These principles have influenced most of the known religious or spiritual philosophies of India, China, Greece, Persia, Iraq, Iran, Israel, and many others regions. Karen Armstrong explains,

> *The Axial Age pushed forward the frontiers of human consciousness and discovered a transcendent dimension in the core of their being, but they did not necessarily regard this as supernatural and most of them refused to discuss it. Precisely because the experience was ineffable, the only correct attitude was reverent silence. The sages certainly did not seek to impose their own views of this ultimate reality on other people. Quite the contrary: nobody, they believed, should ever take any religious teaching on faith or at second hand. It was essential to question everything and to test any teaching empirically, against your personal experience.*

It was a foundational age upon which Judaism, Christianity, Islam, and even nonmonotheistic spirituality rest.

If we go no further than the foundational times of our lives, we never effectively deal with disorder, change, suffering, God, complex relationships, egotism, sacrifice, evil, and a multitude of issues outside or beyond the foundational truths that seemed so absolute in our youth. Without movement, growth is stunted, and our vision of reality becomes myopic and distorted. Challenges investigated can often lead to growth, while challenges denied or disregarded can lead to anxiety and atrophy.

Long before Jesus arrived, the world was dealing with complex realities, and many of the leaders of the Axial Age (Zoroaster, Confucius, Buddha, Socrates, Aristotle, and a host of others, to say nothing of the Hebrew prophets) were questioning the way of life. This was an age of spiritual revolution, an age of intellectual and religious wisdom. It was an age of wisdom that is sorely needed today—a wisdom devoid of egotism, dogmatism, absolutism, and coercion. Many of the thoughts and ideas of the Axial Age predate Christianity. Whether through constant questioning, meditation, self-discipline, introspection, or a combination of practices, these great religious and philosophical figures came to what we call today the way, enlightenment, or holiness.

Confucius is possibly the first person of historical record to have verbalized the Golden Rule: "Don't do unto others as you would not have them do unto you." Jesus said, *"This is the law and the prophets"* (Matt. 7:12).

Buddha's Golden Rule is a variation on the theme *"A person who loves the self should not harm the self of others."* The Golden Rule has become a major benchmark for almost all who seek the way, enlightenment, or holiness. It is, in my opinion, the first of the two vital life-enhancing principles of the Axial Age.

The second vital life-enhancing principle is paradoxical in nature: *whoever wishes to save his life will lose it, but whoever loses his life for another will find it.* The diminution or diminishment of the ego is, for many of these great thinkers, an absolute necessity in the practice of the Golden Rule. Self-centeredness, which is the product of the ego, is the archenemy of *"do unto others as you would have then do unto you."* The practice of the Golden Rule is as difficult as the rule is simple. Jesus tells us in Matthew 16:25, *"For whoever would save his life, will lose it. But whoever will have lost his life for my sake, shall find it."* Through many different processes, the great leaders of the Axial Age approached these two life-enhancing principles that led them to the way, enlightenment, or holiness. One of the most effective ways to achieve this end is constant questioning of both the status quo and our most strongly held beliefs.

Buddha, Confucius, and Socrates all used this method to come to the way. Almost all spiritual, religious, and philosophical leaders, from the Axial Age onward, have attested to the fact that self-interest or ego blocks the achievement of the way. The more selfless we become, the more fully human we become. Certainly, the Golden Rule is a better solution to the problems of the world than selfishness and egotism. Confucius, Buddha, Socrates, and later, Jesus could be seen as individuals who exemplified what a human being could and should be. Their modus operandi was characterized by respect for the self and others and by practicing the Golden Rule through diverse methods such as mindfulness; constantly questioning the status quo as it relates to individuals and systems; respect for all living things; introspection; and interactions of kindness, compassion, and empathy with all human beings. The thinkers of the Axial Age saw life as dependent on personal responsibility to other individuals.

Unless we attain the ability to "control" the ego, we have not truly reached enlightenment or holiness. This is no easy task. The great thinkers, philosophers, and holy men and women since the great transformation have been seeking this state of being with only limited success. Over the course of these centuries of thought and action, it became obvious that no one person or no one school of thought had or has a corner on all truth or how to achieve the way, enlightenment, or holiness. It also became obvious that for continued growth in our life direction as individuals and a society, we must always search for greater awareness and development of virtues that require us to seek for others what we seek for ourselves (justice, peace, compassion, mercy, respect, empathy, and love).

I have found living the Golden Rule for even one day to be extremely difficult and demanding. To be constantly mindful of the other and how the other would like to be treated takes concentration. One must be totally conscious and aware of his or her interaction with every person and treat every person as he or she would like to be treated. I would say good luck, but it has very little to do with luck. It requires internal change, awaking, conversion, and transformation, just as it did for the great thinkers and doers of the Axial Age. (2020)

Vulnerability

Last night, I was watching on Netflix a very dark series called *Ozark*. Much to my surprise, one episode included a scene in which a corrupt psychologist made an insightful statement about vulnerability: "*It is easy to confuse vulnerability with weakness. Allowing yourself to be vulnerable is a sign of strength.*" Vulnerability can be a quality or state of being exposed to the possibility of being attacked or harmed, either physically or emotionally. The quality of being easily hurt may be seen as weakness, defenselessness, and fragility. There is nothing in this definition that even hints that vulnerability could be a strength.

It seems we are talking about another paradox when we speak of a God who is one and the same time invincible and vulnerable. For believing Christians, God revealed his vulnerability in Jesus. He did not desire the suffering that can come along with vulnerability but rather allowed himself to be vulnerable so that we could see the power and nature of love.

If we look at Martin Luther King Jr.'s movement of nonviolent protest, we see the importance of vulnerability as a necessary component of love. The civil rights protestors could have taken up arms in an attempt to achieve their goals of freedom, equality, and respect. They, however, chose the way of vulnerability, which they knew would entail suffering.

Vulnerability, like suffering, is not an end in itself but a means to achieve the desired end, which is love. Love is the desired end that requires vulnerability, sacrifice, and suffering. Vulnerability is a necessary part of the process of love. This can be a tough message. It is easy to confuse vulnerability with weakness, but allowing oneself to be vulnerable is a true sign of strength. Love is not an easy virtue.

It is rather a tough-as-nails virtue. Naive or romantic love is easy; real love is hard-nosed and difficult.

Today, we are in the midst of what may be the worst week of the coronavirus. Yesterday, New York and New Jersey had a record one-day death toll. This was both good and bad news. It possibly meant that we were approaching the apex, which, in turn, possibly meant the flattening of the curve was not too far off. Let's hope so!

Vulnerability, as an expression of love, is being seen throughout the entire country. The list of brave people who are putting their lives on the line, whether voluntary or because of duty, are the heroes who have made themselves vulnerable to others. Regardless of reservations and fears, in many cases, they have given their lives for others. To lose one's life for others was not the intention, but it was the known and understood possibility. Those who have died and will die in service to others are and will be remembered in a special way by their loved ones. Most of us for whom they died will remember them in a less personal way but, nonetheless, in a special and important way.

Nurses, doctors, hospital workers of all kinds, and other health care workers are and have been putting their lives at risk on a daily basis. Police, EMT personnel, firefighters, postal workers, truck drivers, food store personnel, and anyone who, in any way, participates in transporting people to and from necessary destinations were and are at higher risk and deserve our deepest respect and gratitude. We value and appreciate all those necessary workers who do hundreds or perhaps thousands of jobs that allow millions of us to shelter in place and live in relative safety. They are often little appreciated until a crisis like this reminds us of their everyday value and importance. To all of you, we say thank you for your sacrificial love during these trying times.

Perhaps what we should remember about this time is not political posturing, religious prejudice, social inequalities, and economic disparity, although they are real and can divide us. Rather, we should remember our shared vulnerabilities and the way we overlooked our differences for the common good. We should remember that we did not confuse vulnerability with weakness but saw it as a strength that allowed us to sacrifice and suffer for the love of our brothers and sisters regardless of race, religion, political persuasion, marital status, gender identity, economic status, sexual orientation, or any other accident of the human condition. Virtually no one asked questions of this nature before help was offered. Those who sacrificed for their fellow human beings had no agenda other than the desire to save and protect the lives of all. We were and are all in this together. (2020)

Fear of the Lord

"*Fear of the Lord is the beginning of Wisdom*" (Proverbs 9:11). The meaning of this proverb depends on how one understands or defines fear. Fear in this proverb has little to do with our traditional understanding of the meaning of fear, which can be defined as a feeling of trepidation triggered by the perception of danger, real or imagined. It is a response to a real or potential threat. Fear can be seen as a negative or positive, depending on the situation.

Religion can and does use fear in a negative way to elicit certain responses. For some people of religion, the fear of God's wrath or punishment is a means of keeping people "in line." Fear of hell is a great tool of behavior modification. You better act in this way or that or else. Understanding fear in this way has nothing to do with the attainment of wisdom but has only to do with intimidation and trepidation.

In this proverb, fear of the Lord is seen as something radically different. It has to do with our recognition of, respect for, and gratitude to someone or something we stand in awe of that is infinitely beyond our comprehension. This fear helps us, in a realistic way, to evaluate, understand, and value our relative importance in the universe. It puts our importance in perspective.

Fear of the Lord fosters and engenders humility, a virtue without which we are unable to see clearly or realistically our true relationship to all creation. Poets and philosophers have used waves upon the shores, stars in the sky, and grains of sand upon the seashore as metaphors to illustrate our proper position in the cosmos. We are not the center, but we are an integral and significant part of the whole. Looking at our being and existence through these metaphors should not diminish our significance. They should aid us in the never-ending struggle to see ourselves as we are for what we are. Our first response to "fear of the Lord" should be awe and gratitude that we have been given the awesome gift of existence and life, and the second should be humility. What a blessing it is "to be"! There is no doubt of the dignity and majesty of the universe in which man participates.

A lack of humility distorts our sense of our own importance. Without humility, we fall out of balance with the universe. We become prideful and arrogant. We lose perspective and value the wrong things. We fall out of balance with our sisters and brothers.

Humility is a modest or realistic view of one's own importance. It is a recognition of our dependency, a recognition of the equal importance of our sisters and brothers and the world in which we live. An athlete of great skill and humility recognizes that without the rest of the team, there is no victory. A realization that we are not superior to others but possess unique talents just as they do is true humility. Putting another first is an example of humility in action. Knowing our true place in all our relationships leads to wisdom, which is essentially based on humility.

False humility is the art of portraying oneself as externally humble while internally seeing oneself as superior to one's sisters and brothers. Hubris is the opposite of humility and more. It is a form of excessive pride or arrogance, which puts oneself above others. It is seeing oneself as the center of reality, more valuable than others and acting as such. On the other hand, humility is seeing oneself as a unique individual dependent on other unique individuals in a world of which we are a significant part but not the center, living in gratitude and awe for the privilege of being and life. This is the wisdom that fear of the Lord is about. (2020)

Here I Go Again

I keep coming back to a few key issues that religion tries to explain such as suffering, sacrifice, evil, and love. I do this because I think they are fundamental to the mystery of life.

This essay will be primarily concerned with suffering, sacrifice, and love. These are not new issues for me, but they are still areas of concern. As mysterious as these topics are, evil is by far the most difficult to understand and explain.

If Christianity is correct or valid, it seems to have something to do with suffering, sacrifice, and love. If this were not the case, why would God accept, without protest, Jesus's treatment at our hands? To willingly undergo this suffering and sacrifice seems logically to lead to the idea of vulnerability and love. God shows his concern for us through the power of his vulnerability. He opened himself to suffering and sacrifice as a demonstration of his unlimited and unconditional love for us. This demonstration is a tutorial for life. To suffer for another is somehow redemptive, makes us whole again, and restores balance in the world. It is salvific; it saves us and others from the selfishness of the ego. It is, in some sense, maturing and growth inducing. It is part of the process of growing to be perfect in love as is our heavenly Father. Suffering is redemptive and salvific for both the sufferer and the one for whom one suffered.

As I have said before, true love somehow requires suffering or at least the willingness to suffer for the other. Jesus, again, is our exemplar in the perfection of love. While I was writing this essay, I began to realize that my feelings about suffering were shifting ever so subtly. That suffering for suffering's sake has value still seems like a non sequitur. However, this shift in perception allowed me to see, in a different and more integrated fashion, the relationship of sacrifice, suffering, and love for the benefit and well-being of another. Some would say Christianity was always about suffering, sacrifice, and love. Yes, this is true in theory, but the practical paradigms, over the centuries, have not always reflected that belief. A new living paradigm that reflects Jesus's life and gospel is desperately needed, a paradigm that reflects sacrifice, not selfishness; justice, not injustice; humility, not arrogance; truth, not falsehood; courteousness, not rudeness; vulnerability, not abuse of power; sharing, not hoarding; kindness, not inconsiderateness; nonviolence, not violence; mercy, not judgment; forgiveness, not condemnation; peace, not war; and patience, not impatience. This is what we see in the gospels; this is what we see in Jesus.

If we are honest, we see today far too little of it in our own lives and in our society. Many people hold tightly to the belief that strength is power, vulnerability is weakness, privilege is to be sought after, sacrifice is to be avoided, suffering has no value, love is sentimentality, and doing for others lessens one's strength. Power, position, possessions, wealth, and privilege are the meaning of life and are to be sought after at the cost of love. A God of love, vulnerability, suffering, and sacrifice makes more sense than a God of power and might who is harsh enough to belittle and condemn those he is supposed to love. God tells us through Jesus's life and gospel that the only way to perfection is through love.

This reflection on suffering and love does not resolve many issues around the topic but rather is one more attempt to give additional insight into these mysteries. Life is about striving to achieve the perfection of love. It is not always easy. We all fall short of achieving this ideal, but Jesus makes the way abundantly clear. As long as we recognize and strive for love as our ultimate goal in life, we are on the right path. Love is the way, the truth, and the life. (2020)

Hatred Is the Main Problem

The picture of a white police officer with his knee firmly planted on the neck of a defenseless unarmed, handcuffed black man can be seen as a metaphor for three hundred plus years of white domination, through violence, over the black race. Within the last three months, three killings of black people at the hands of white police officers and angry white men have pushed aside, to some extent, COVID-19 and its devastating effects. I am sure you are familiar with the details of these killings and murders. For that reason, I will not review the gory details. This hatred is rampant in all the United States: North and South, East and West. It is not a regional problem but an American problem. It will take all of us to solve it. The white man has created it and continues to foster it. We must focus on the horror of racism and the devastating effect of this hatred and not be sidetracked by other complicated but less important problems. The riots and demonstrations are not the cause of the problem but rather the result of the problem.

However, unfortunately, the riots, because of their immediate danger, are the main topic of news reports, distracting us from the underlying cause. This allows those who hate to use riots and looting as a diversionary tool to blame the victims.

I was stationed in Newark, New Jersey, in the summer of 1967 when "race riots" broke out all over this country, including Newark. The worst riot took place in Detroit. Forty-three—ten whites and thirty-three blacks—died in Detroit, and twenty-six people died in Newark. There were millions of dollars' worth of damage throughout the country, and thousands of people were injured. The riots of 1967 were among the most violent, deadly, and destructive in our history. A total of 159 riots took place that year. As a result, the Kerner Commission was formed to investigate the causes of these outbreaks. The investigation found that white racism was the underlying cause of the riots. The Kerner Commission's recommendations were ignored amid white backlash against black assertiveness. The same thing is happening today. More than fifty years later, conditions remain much the same.

Police brutality, poverty, and antagonism among the races still exist and thrive. Remove the causes of the problem, hatred and racism, and the violence will not happen. There is a direct relationship of one to the other. Many whites are focusing on the destruction of private property by a small minority of the persecuted black community. Rioting and looting have to be controlled but must not divert our focus from that which causes riots. When hatred rears its ugly head as systemic racism, more than three hundred years of pent-up fury and repressed anger over the despicable treatment of blacks explode. Do we not understand why this explosion of violence happens, or is it we just don't want to know or we just don't care? If our ancestors had been kidnapped and held in bondage and slavery for centuries, raped at will with no recourse, whipped and mutilated, forced into economic despair, lynched for no cause, and more, would we not be filled with pent-up rage? If we answer no to this question, we are either liars or self-deceivers. We should emphasize resolving the enormous injustices and not the reaction of a persecuted people. Stop the hatred and racism, and the violent reactions will stop; there will be nothing to react to.

The evils of hatred and racism are the cause of the violence. The white man and his institutions and systems of racism are the cause. Walk in the black man's shoes for three hundred years; see how it feels. Experience the black man's justice and we just may understand his frustration. No one is condoning the violence; we are just trying to be objective in recognizing causes. We should concentrate on the greater problems of hatred and racism. We should not allow ourselves to be misdirected and sidetracked from dealing with the real cause of the problem: hatred and racism. Riots will continue unless we address the underlying causes.

In 2017, *Kenneth T. Walsh, an American journalist and former president of the White House Correspondents' Association for "US News and World Report," wrote an article on the race riots of 1967 predicting future riots based on the fact that not much has changed over the last fifty years. People have medical conditions that can be cured if the underlying causes for the obvious symptoms are addressed. Treating symptoms, although beneficial, is only a partial solution. Race riots are only a symptom of a larger problem. The issue of hatred is a many-headed monster. Correcting the symptoms is good, but eradicating the cause is certainly preferable—easier said than done.

We know that the opposite of hate is love. Changing hate to love is a slow process, which is internal to a large extent—a matter of the heart, as it were. Changing externals can also contribute to societal changes, which, over time, can alter behavior and the direction in which a society moves. Two great internal changers are family and education; remember, *"you must be carefully taught"* to hate. The same goes for love. *"You must be carefully taught"* to love. To be raised believing that all men are created equal and *"Do unto others as you would have then do unto you"* are the bedrock of love. Love is a truth that once learned is hard to dislodge. External changes can come through laws, customs, and peer pressure that protect and foster absolute equality for *all* people.

Rooting out systemic racism is critical to an external solution to the problem. A city police chief was asked by a reporter what the cause of the murder of George Floyd was, poor vetting of candidates, education of police recruits, or the training of candidates? The chief responded that all three categories were faulty and part of the reason why these murders and killings continue to take place. Systemic racism is not restricted to the police only. Racism is all-pervasive in our society. Banks, politics, housing, education, law enforcement, health care, judiciary, religion, and recreation are all influenced by racism; if you can name it, it has been touched by racism.

African Americans are 2.5 times as likely to be killed by police than white people. A study by Frank Edwards of Rutgers University's School of Criminal Justice found that roughly one in one thousand black boys and men will be killed by police in their lifetime. For white boys and men, the rate is thirty-nine out of one hundred thousand. For more info on statics, go to CityLab.com. Any black person seeking his or her civil or human rights is still seen by many white people as an "uppity nigger." For some, it is easy to see the injustice, hatred, bigotry, and racism of a large minority of white people in this country. An Englishman in 1546, John Haywood, is reported to have said, *"There is none so blind as those who will not see."* In Jeremiah 5:21, it is written, *"Listen O foolish people who have no heart! You have eyes but do not see, and ears but do not hear."* We, for too long in America, have not only shut our eyes and ears but have actively promoted racism. Fundamental and systemic change must come, or we are doomed to repeat history again. Let us make America great by eradicating hatred and racism.*

A Corrupt and Broken System

On a business trip to ski in Vermont, I drove with one of my biggest customers and a friend of his. As we drove along, my customer's friend complained about his tax burden. He was a lawyer and seemed to be pretty well-off. I asked where he lived. He said he lived in Rumson, New Jersey, on the Navesink River—very exclusive! Then I asked what kind of car he owned. He responded, "A Mercedes-Benz." All his kids went to private schools—again, very exclusive! I then asked him how could he possibly complain about his taxes when he was so blessed. To his credit, he had a pretty good sense of humor. He laughed and said, "I see your point."

As the weekend progressed, he questioned me about what I thought his attitude should be in this regard. I responded with a quote from Micah 6:8: "*What does God ask of you? To act justly, love mercy and to walk humbly with your God.*"

---

* Go to USNews.com for the complete article of Kenneth T. Walsh (2020).

This experience came to mind because of the publicity regarding Donald Trump's tax situation. Regardless of how you might feel about Mr. Trump, his tax situation speaks directly to our broken economic system. There is no doubt that many rich people avoid, legally or illegally, paying what would be a fair and just amount of taxes. This is obviously true and evident when compared to what poor and middle-class people have to pay. In this country, the rich are favored. They can live quite comfortably, even when they pay a just tax while the poor and middle class struggle and strain to stay afloat. The economic system in this country is tilted in favor of the rich. Justice and fairness do not seem to be served under this corrupt and broken system.

You might feel that the law allows avoidance of tax obligations, so why not take advantage of the situation. That is just the point; these systems are designed to make it easy for the rich to avoid what most people would see as just taxes. The laws must be changed so they do not favor the wealthy unfairly. These systems make it almost impossible for the poor and middle class to get any relief. When middle-class people say they are against raising taxes, in reality, it means they are against inequitable tax on the poor and middle class. The wealthy can afford to take on their fair share of taxes in order to make the system fairer and more equitable. The system needs to be reformed. The common folk only ask for a system that does not favor the rich and punish the poor and middle class. (2020)

The Devil and Evil

How do we understand the personal nature and the influence of the devil on evil in this world? Is the devil a personal being who roams the earth, seeking souls to devour? The devil is seen by most orthodox religions as personal; however, I believe a creature such as this does not exist. I think of the devil, not as a personal being or force but as a metaphor for man and mankind's inclination or propensity to evil on both a personal or societal basis. Today, more and more people seem skeptical of the existence of a personal devil. Just as our understanding and concept of God are evolving, so also is our understanding of evil and the nature of the devil.

There are internal and external forces, both of which influence us regarding personal and societal evil. It seems that these two forces are so intertwined that it is virtually impossible to separate them one from the other. During the '40s, '50s, and into the '60s, Catholic theology emphasized the personal aspects of sin or evil in relationship to salvation. It is only recently that the emphasis has shifted to some degree. As time marches on, we see this shift toward communal, corporate, and institutional evil being recognized more and more. Could the devil and evil be metaphors for the systemic evil of institutions, organizations, and systems.

We do not get off the hook by blaming the devil or some personal power outside ourselves for being even a partial cause of the evil we do. Unlike Adam, who blamed Eve and the devil for his transgression, we are culpable for our actions. When it comes to societal evil (e.g., slavery, human trafficking, genocide, and the like), it is even more difficult to assign a personal "devil" as the "encourager in chief" of evil. There is no doubt that there is some type of dynamic at play, which has a causal effect on the greater society, but it is highly unlikely it exists apart from us and our institutions. It may have to do with the idea that evil fosters evil just as good fosters good. There is an interconnectedness between individual and societal evil. This is why the Catholic Church rightfully believes Jews alone are not responsible for Jesus's death but all of us who participate in societal and personal evil. As long as we participate in communal evil such as racism, inequality, economic elitism, or any type of systemic evil, we contribute to the advancement of evil.

Although we can never lose sight of the personal aspects of evil, we should take into account the power and influence of communal evil. An example of both types of evil might be helpful. A personal act of violence against another (rape) is just that, but it is more than likely grounded in society's disregard for life among other things. On the other hand, acts of war are perpetrated by societies acting under the influences of power, greed, domination, and a host of other motivating factors. This type of activity goes beyond the personal and has ramifications larger than the personal. This is not to say the personal evil does not have broader ramifications of its own—as you can see, a very complicated situation. We as individuals and as a society should be held responsible for the moral evil in this world. God's involvement will have to be an essay for another day. (2020)

The Front Four

Today is Sunday, November 8, one day after Joe Biden and Kamala Harris were declared, by the projection of all major news outlets, to be the president-elect and vice president-elect of the USA. Of course, there will be thousands of articles and editorials written throughout the world relating to this election and the future. It was and is a big deal. It seems only fitting, as I wrap up this book of essays that, I write an essay on where we are today and what we should be concentrating on in the near future. To go forward, we should take a step back to see how we got here. If we start with Donald Trump's presidency, we might think of him not as *the* problem but rather as a problem.

While discussing this issue with my son Patrick, I was impressed with an astute observation he made regarding Mr. Trump. He observed and noted that Mr. Trump was not the problem, but rather, he was the result of the problems that preexisted in his presidency. Perhaps, the best thing about Donald Trump's presidency was the fact that he made us more aware of the divide. His exacerbation of these divisions did not help solve them but rather increased their intensity. If that is the case, and I believe it is, then the problems are still with us, as has been made evident by the fact that more than seventy million people voted for him to continue as our leader. Some of these issues are more immediate and visible and some seem less imperative and less visible, but they all need attention. Many, if not all, are complex and connected. Most have been with us for a long time, but some are new. It would be beneficial if we could first recognize and agree on the problem areas, for without recognition and agreement, little can be accomplished.

I would like to use a metaphor to illustrate the issue. If you are not a skier, you are probably not familiar with the "Front Four" at Stowe, Vermont. The "Front Four" refers to four ski trails on the face of Mount Mansfield: Goat, Star, National, and Lift Line, regarded by many as four of the most challenging trails in the east if not the entire country. Large bumps, icy cold winds, poor visibility, hardpacked snow and ice, and changing conditions—to say nothing of steepness—are the obstacles that make successfully negotiating and navigating these trails difficult at best and hazardous at worst. This election brought to mind these four trails because of the difficult nature of present-day issues. They remind me of the "Front Four" at Stowe because they offer real and present challenges loaded with hazards and difficulties for this country and the world, both for the immediate future and beyond. In my mind, they are urgent issues that need immediate attention.

First is climate change, which for many does not get top billing. It could, however, dwarf all other issues because the very existence of humanity hangs in the balance if the scientists are right. The other problems would be inconsequential if we are not here, if we don't exist. The second problem COVID-19 is more immediate and more addressable yet complex because it involves life and death, concern for others, planning, action, coordination, economic support, and a viable plan for economic recovery, along with physical, political, and social healing. Poverty is the third issue that needs to be addressed and is a long-term and persistent problem not only in the USA but throughout the world. Without the alleviation of poverty, injustice, and unrest, discontent will be with us. Revolution of one sort or another always lurks just below the surface of poverty. Economics and poverty go hand in hand. Faulty and unjust economic systems along with greed and power are the root cause of poverty. Without fair and just economic systems, society will never be about equal access to life, liberty, and the pursuit of happiness. Last of all, but not least, is racism and its systems, which are a four-hundred-year-old sickness, which will eventually kill this republic if we continue to ignore and refuse to address this American Achilles' heel.

This election has highlighted many issues that need addressing: education, health care, immigration, common-sense gun legislation—the list goes on and on. At the top of my list is first, COVID-19; second, racism, this country's original sin along with genocide; third, poverty, which includes economic justice; and fourth and finally, climate change and environmental justice. These are, in my estimation, the "Front Four" of our national dialogue. They contain terrain, which will be difficult and hazardous to negotiate. There will be conditions, such as, prejudice, hatred, partisanship, greed, lust for power and position, which will rage mightily against our goal—a more perfect union in which all men and women are created equal with the inalienable and undeniable right to life, liberty, and the pursuit of happiness. (Nov. 10, 2020)

Religion and the Afterlife

The more I think about religion and the afterlife, the more I become convinced that the afterlife is really not the point. We are not here to achieve heaven. The point of religion, in my estimation, is how we live our lives in the here and now. I know for some religions, the afterlife is very important—e.g., Christianity and Islam. Afterlife or heaven appears, for many, to be a reward for a life well lived. Is not the good we do for our brothers and sisters reward enough? How does the afterlife affect the purity of motivation and intention?

For some people of religion, the emphasis on heaven and the afterlife overshadow the here and now. This can be a concern because it can disproportionately stress the end and not address adequately the moral imperative of the here and now. There has always been in religion, at least in Christianity and Islam, a tension between an eschatological approach and an incarnational approach. The former puts an emphasis on things relating to death, judgment, and the final destiny of the soul while the latter sees the world charged with grandeur and meaning. It emphasizes the well-being of all in the here and now as opposed to concerns about the afterlife and heaven. As we go forward, a more realistic and balanced approach is needed between these two views. It appears that today, this shift is occurring in favor of the incarnational approach.

I was raised in a church, which perhaps unintentionally stressed our final destination while ignoring, to a large extent, the proper means for getting there. Personal salvation was stressed and that was achieved through adherence to beliefs, dogmas, rules, regulations, and rituals. There seemed to be little outreach to the community at large: politically, socially, spiritually, and ecumenically, except within the confines of our own little world. The communal nature of religion did not extend beyond the members of our own limited group, except maybe to convert or proselytize potentially new members. Large political, social, and economic issues of the time were largely ignored with a concentration on parochial and salvation issues.

There were, of course, reasons for these conditions and circumstances, which have had a lasting effect. The immigrant church was instrumental in fostering this protective atmosphere. In 1840, the Irish Potato Famine triggered the Irish Catholic immigration to this country. The Irish Immigrant Church was very solicitous of its faithful and promoted an inward preservative attitude out of survival concerns. Protestant religions were the predominant religions of the day in the USA and were hostile to Catholics in general. It took over 180 years before the first Catholic president was elected. For this and many other historical reasons, religion in the USA and throughout the world has focused on eschatological concerns. To this day, it has been a long and difficult journey for religion to come to a truly universal view of its mission. We are finally, in this country, realizing that what really matters is not all the orthodox beliefs regarding salvation and end times but rather the ability of religion to assist people in life's journey toward a society and a world that fosters the well-being of all women and men. Religion's purpose is not to justify or condemn but should be to nourish and guide us as we travel negotiating the challenges of honest and value-based living.

In an open letter to Pope Francis, Jose Arregi states, *"The church is not here to define what is regular and what is irregular, but accompany, encourage and support each person as they are, where they are."* If religion doesn't do this or if this is not what religion is all about, then what in the world do we think heaven is about? Should we not be kind to our brothers and sisters regardless of whether heaven exists or not? Today more than ever before, we need to learn the lessons of Martin Luther King Jr., Jesus, Gandhi, and other great spiritual/religious leaders who made the ultimate sacrifice in the here and now to transform this world now and in the future. (Nov. 15, 2020)

Defiance

Part of Donald Trump's appeal is defiance. Defiance against political institutions and systems that frustrate his will and desires regardless of whether these institutions and systems are sound, moral, and beneficial to the citizens of the USA. He has an attitude of defiance toward anything that hinders his wants or desires. A large minority of his supporters identify and laud Mr. Trump's defiance because they feel or believe they have been harmed, taken advantage of, or suffered some type of injustice at the hands of those whom they have seen and still see as a threat to their class status, identity, and economic superiority.

Whether there is a valid basis for those feelings and beliefs is irrelevant. Their beliefs and feelings have more to do with personal perception than with verifiable reality. Mr. Trump is a demagogue with a real talent, intuitive or developed, to recognize, identify, and activate the buttons that motivate people who, for whatever reason, are susceptible to this type of manipulation. This seems to work to his advantage even if it is contrary to his followers' vital interests. He has used this ability to generate defiance in others, which he so often displays himself.

Defiance can be defined as standing up to an opponent or authority, open resistance to any opposing force, open disregard, or contempt. Defiance can be good or bad. It is like obedience, which depends on whom or what one obeys or disobeys. Defiance is good or bad depending on whom or what one is in defiance against. Mr. Trump has aroused defiance, to his advantage, in many dissatisfied people. He has, from their anger, extracted power to achieve his morally suspect ends. Some are unwitting cooperators while others are witting cooperators and active participants.

As we have seen in the past, many people have been educated to see reality through a distorted lens. When their reality is or seems to be threatened, then defiance can come into play, especially when a person in authority not only gives permission but also encourages defiance. If taken to an extreme, defiance can become violent.

Most Trump supporters claim to be devoted Christians, so it might be helpful if we seek Christian principles as a measuring rod for right behavior. We should never let nationalism co-op religion as the source and motivation of our moral obligations and decisions. When national objectives violate or oppose basic Christian ideals and tenants, they should be called out as immoral. When Christian principles take a back seat to politics or national goals, we are traveling down the wrong road. "My country, right or wrong" is never an acceptable way of dealing with national problems; it is neither morally nor rationally correct. Should not all Christians agree on this basic point? Did Jesus not tell us to love even our enemies? *"Love your enemies, do good to those who hate you. And pray for those who persecute and slander you"* (Matt. 5:44).

Love of neighbor must be the measuring rod by which we gauge our success or failure. If this is a foundational belief of Christianity, any activity that harms another is not acceptable no matter what "side" one represents. If we believe this, then the next step is to make a sincere effort to come together in dialogue with some openness to compromise. Defiance on these principles is not a viable option. Behavior that is intended to intimidate or harms people physically, emotionally, or for that matter harms anyone in any way is unacceptable and morally questionable. It is behavior that bars one from the negotiating table, a table that hopefully leads to compromise and solutions. (Nov. 13, 2020)

Compartmentalization

At this point, I am suffering from Trump fatigue; perhaps you are too. Between the election and COVID-19, between racism and economic inequity and the like, life is somewhat emotionally exhausting. Before I go on total crisis overload, I am going to take one last crack at why so many people voted for Mr. Trump. Besides defiance, compartmentalization is another significant element.

During a conversation with my best friend Franklyn, he suggested that compartmentalization was a significant factor in more than seventy million people who voted for Mr. Trump. I could not have agreed more, and because of that, I decided to write this essay. He also suggested that one could, through compartmentalization, support Mr. Trump and still realize he is egotistical and unstable under the guise of "Oh, that's just the way he is." But when it comes to policy, we like what we see: the economy, immigration, law and order, foreign relations, business, stock market, taxes, and environment. This is how many see reality even if the substances of these policies are detrimental and divisive. They are actually on the same page as Mr. Trump.

How does one justify these policies with the beliefs that seem to regulate one's daily life? A partial answer to this question is compartmentalization. It is a process by which one divides reality into categories or separate compartments. Psychologically, it is a subconscious defense mechanism used to avoid cognitive dissonance or the mental discomfort and anxiety caused by a person's having conflicting values, emotions, and beliefs within oneself. I like to call them operational mechanisms. They allow one to work through complex, stressful, and sometimes contradictory feelings and situations while maintaining some semblance of order and stability. To become too dependent on these mechanisms can cloud judgment and distort reality.

Other mechanisms used to shield us from reality that causes conflict can also be seen as partial explanations for contradictory beliefs, feelings, and behaviors: rationalization, denial, repression, projection, and the like. Some everyday examples might be helpful. but we must first realize in many cases, we are talking about good and decent people. How then does compartmentalization justify allowing people to hold and act upon at least two opposing moral views of reality at the same time?

When I was stationed at St. Peter's Orphanage in Newark, New Jersey, I observed a fairly simple custom of individuals and some institutions giving gifts at Christmastime to the children of the orphanage. In and of itself, this was a laudable practice; however, for some, it was a compartmentalization of their need to care for the poor and needy. It allowed them to feel good about the good they, in fact, did, but at the same time, it allowed them to neglect the needs of these children throughout the rest of the year. They felt in some way that they had fulfilled their obligation toward the poor. In fact, they felt absolved of any obligation or connection between paying taxes as a means of supporting the poor in a consistent and profound way.

Businesses give large sums of money to charitable institutions, which is, in fact, a good thing; but they pay their rank-and-file workers either the federal minimum wage ($7.24 per hour) or a new recommended minimum wage ($15 per hour). I would love to see our political leaders live on $15 per hour for a year or two and then give us some feedback on how easy it was.

Both the politicians and business people claim to pay workers a more just and livable wage would hurt the economy. That is no excuse! If the economy can't support a living wage for all, then change the economics of the country through taxes restructuring or change the system. The point is that individuals and corporations or systems can compartmentalize their economic responsibilities so that they feel morally justified with their decisions and behaviors.

Suffice it to say, I am sure you can think of many other situations where compartmentalization gets people and institutions off the hook, at least in their minds. Compartmentalization is a form of myopic vision, which allows good and decent folks to choose what they feel is good for them with only little regard for what is good for their sisters and brothers. Compartmentalization is one of the contributing factors that account for more than seventy million who support Mr. Trump and his agenda. (Nov. 28, 2020)

Paradox

I had just finished writing the essay on paradox when I checked the TV for the latest update on COVID-19 and came upon a news segment that highlighted the book *Why I Am an Atheist Who Believes in God* by Frank Schaeffer. If I were a Fundamentalist Christian, I would see this as divine intervention, a miracle. It is actually a coincidence, not a miracle. A typical "God of the gaps" situation could be applied here.

Frank Schaeffer was an avid Fundamentalist Christian until questions and life experiences challenged the validity of his beliefs. He was cut from the same cloth as Jerry Falwell, Pat Robertson, Billy Graham Jr., Jimmy Swaggart, and a host of others. Disillusionment left him with a paradox: believing and not believing in God at one and the same time. I was never a Fundamentalist Christian but find myself in a similar position. Karl Rahner, a Catholic theologian, touches on the inclination that, for many, faith or belief in God is in a constant state of flux or a paradoxical dilemma.

Who should claim that his or her fantastical religious beliefs are more correct than the next person's fantastical beliefs? No one! Who should impose these beliefs on another? No one! Believe what you like as long as it does not harm another or coerce another into unwanted situations. I have questioned why Buddhism would be truer than Christianity, or why Christianity would be truer than Islam, and so on. Christians often hold beliefs and traditions with tenacity because they were raised in those beliefs and traditions. Would not the same individuals hold with the same tenacity Islamic beliefs and traditions if he or she had been raised in those beliefs and traditions?

I was pleased to see that there was someone else besides myself who saw paradox as part of life, as a reality beyond imagination. To be confronted with paradox regarding such important issues is not the most comfortable position in which to find oneself. It leaves things up in the air. There are no hard and fast rules, no set answers, just lots of questions. But it seems more real than a series of dogmas that are designed to cover all possible situations and eventualities. Hopefully, paradox allows what is mysterious and unknowable to remain mysterious and unknowable without undue anxiety.

In an article I was reading, Frank Schaeffer was quoted as saying, "*They can live by the Bible or live by Jesus. They can't do both.*" Perhaps this was taken out of context or the possibility that Mr. Schaeffer's long exposure to a fundamentalist approach makes it difficult to accept the Bible in terms of simile, analogy, allegory, and metaphor. There is much wisdom in the Bible, and it does not have to be in competition with Jesus's message of forgiveness, mercy, peace, understanding, tolerance, and love. A historical and literal interpretation of the Bible is not the point. In reality, a strictly literal understanding is one of the root causes of religious fundamentalism. The meaning of the text is the crucial point. It is diametrically opposed to a "*fire and brimstone*" approach. The Bible, if understood properly, promotes the above-mentioned virtues.

After all is said and done, I believe paradox is a vital tool, offered by Mr. Schaeffer, for religious honesty and integrity regarding the ongoing discussion of God's existence and the place of religion in our lives. (2020)

CHAPTER 10

Prayer

Prayer on 9/11

A year has passed since September 11, 2001, and much has changed for many people. During the course of the year, prayer has changed for me in important ways. These changes were immediate but grew in intensity culminating on the first anniversary celebrations in New York, Washington, and Pennsylvania.

All prayer recognizes God as the giver and sustainer of life. This truth did not change, only my perception. During the time immediately following 9/11 and especially on the anniversary, this truth became deeper and more apparent than ever before. I understood in a more profound sense the great gift of life, which God shares with us. The awe-inspiring nature of God's creation, especially human life, has become vibrant and alive. My prayer seems to center on the awesome mystery of the transcendent. There has been a shift from praying about wants and needs to concentration on God's generosity expressed in the gift of life. My thanksgiving is no longer focused on the material things but on life, family, and people.

On Wednesday, September 11, 2002, I listened to the names of victims read aloud at ground zero in New York City. In some ways, it reminded me of the Vietnam Memorial in Washington, DC. The stark black marble wall engraved with the names of those who died has an emotional impact and energy that is hard to express unless experienced. I felt this same emotional impact and power during the reading of the victims' names. Although I knew only one victim, in a very casual way, the name reading stripped away the anonymity and surreal nature of 9/11. The reading of the names emphasized the uniqueness and preciousness of every life. With the reading of each name, the relationship between victim and loved one became real and alive. As I listened to the names, representing over eighty countries, it was easy to recognize our common humanity and the universal value of life.

In the wake of evil men's deeds, the goodness and beauty of God are made clear in his life-giving power and love. Often, in desperation and need, God lifts our spirits and fortifies our souls by extending to us his love and compassion. "*In the tender compassion of our God the dawn from on high shall break upon us, to shine on those who dwell in darkness and the shadow of death, and to guide our feet into the way of peace*" (Luke 1:79).

Another change in my prayer occurred when the tenuous and fragile nature of life forced its way into my consciousness. Even when this truth is evident, the tendency is to put it on the back burner. It is hard to believe that control of my life is not in my hands. Granted to some extent I realized this vulnerability, but my sensitivity to my actual helplessness was forced on me with devastating power on that September morning.

We are vulnerable and exposed from the moment of our conception and in every moment thereafter. Scripture tells us that we know not the day or the hour. Who would have imagined, on a day of such brilliance, that so many lives could have been lost in so short a time and in such an unbelievable circumstance?

I still pray for all sorts of things, but my own vulnerability is at the forefront of my consciousness. The recognition of my own helplessness and dependence has become part of my prayer more than ever before. As the realization of my inability to control my own life came into focus, it also became more apparent that the lives of my loved ones were beyond my domain. Of course, this became a concern, but again, the counsel of scripture helped. *"Can any of you live a bit longer by worrying about it?"* (Matt. 6:27). In prayer, I have learned that life is in God's hands. It is not ours to give or take. God tells us that not one hair will fall from our heads without his permission.

Life has been given to each of us for a short time. However long or short it may be, it is a gift to be cherished, protected, appreciated, and respected. God tells us that life is more important than clothes, that people are more important than things, and that we are all his beloved children. He also tells us that we are of great value to him and that we should be of great value to each other.

With a deep sense of my own finiteness and with a renewed and more vivid appreciation for life, I pray that we can live in mutual respect and tolerance. (Sept. 11, 2002)

Glory and Praise to God

As I prayed in my backyard early one beautiful sunny morning, inspired by the hymns of praise found in the Bible, I began to write:

> Glory and praise to God the
> Creator and Sustainer of all life
> Glory and praise to God the
> Source and Ground of all being
> Let all creation bless the Lord for
> he is good and his steadfast love
> and mercy endure forever
>
> Let all creation bless the Lord
> Let the sun and the moon bless the Lord
> Let the stars and the planets
> bless the Lord
> Let the heavens and the
> skies bless the Lord
> Let the universe and all that
> is in it bless the Lord
>
> Glory and praise to God the
> Creator and Sustainer of all life

Glory and praise to God the
Source and Ground of all being
Let all creation bless the Lord for
he is good and his steadfast love
and mercy endure forever

Let the rain and the clouds bless the Lord
Let the winds and the
storms bless the Lord
Let the snow and the ice bless the Lord
Let the hills and the valleys bless the Lord
Let the forests and the
woods bless the Lord
Let the rivers and the
streams bless the Lord
Let the trees and the plants bless the Lord
Let the brooks and the
ponds bless the Lord
Let the lakes and the seas bless the Lord
Let the marshes and the dry
lands bless the Lord
Let the fruits and the
vegetation bless the Lord
Let the oceans and the
mountains bless the Lord

Let the universe and all that
is in it bless the Lord

Glory and praise to God the
Creator and Sustainer of all life
Glory and praise to God the
Source and Ground of all being
Let all creation bless the Lord for
he is good and his steadfast love
and mercy endure forever

Let the animals of the
earth bless the Lord
Let the beasts of the jungle bless the Lord
Let the insects and the creatures
beneath the earth bless the Lord
Let the bugs and the crawling
things bless the Lord
Let the birds of the air and the
creatures of the sky bless the Lord
Let the fish of the sea and the
creatures of the deep bless the Lord
Let the universe and all that
is in it bless the Lord

Glory and praise to God the
Creator and Sustainer of all life
Glory and praise to God the
Source and Ground of all being
Let all creation bless the Lord for
he is good and his steadfast love
and mercy endure forever

Let the inanimate and the
animate bless the Lord
Let all life bless the Lord
Let female and male bless the Lord
Let husbands and wives bless the Lord
Let the young and the old bless the Lord
Let the strong and the
weak bless the Lord
Let the people of the world bless the Lord
Let the nations of the
world bless the Lord
Let all living things in the
universe bless the Lord
Let families and communities
bless the Lord
Let the righteous and the
sinner bless the Lord

Let the inhabitants of the
heavens bless the Lord
Let the just and the unjust bless the Lord
Let all spiritual creatures bless the Lord
Let the people of God bless the Lord
Let the universe and all that
is in it bless the Lord

Glory and praise to God the
Creator and Sustainer of all life.
Glory and praise to God the
Source and Ground of all being
Let all creation bless the Lord for he
is good and his steadfast love and
mercy endure forever. (2014)

Prayer: What Is It?

When I hear the word *prayer*, I automatically think of the Baltimore Catechism's definition, which harks back to my Catholic grammar school days. "Prayer is the raising of one's mind and heart to God or the requesting of good things from God." St. Therese of Lisieux describes prayer as a "surge of the heart, it is a simple look toward heaven, it is a cry of recognition and love embracing both trial and joy." Prayer, for Christians, presupposes belief in God and hope in his goodness. Catholics and all Christian religions feel prayer is an integral part of the spiritual life. The following are my reflections on prayer, which are in no way certain or absolute.

I have been praying all my life, but I am clearly no expert on the subject. I have never been sure just what prayer is or how to do it. Most of the time, I feel like I am talking to myself. Many people feel it is a conversation with God, Jesus, or holy people who have gone before us. In some way, prayer is a conversation with a friend. As Norman Greenbaum's song says, *"When you die and they lay you to rest your gonna go to the place that's the best."*

In the past, and even now, when I pray to Jesus, it feels like a conversation with a friend. When I pray to God, it feels like a conversation with my father. I am sure this is the result of my cultural, religious, and spiritual upbringing. For those who are not so religious or have been raised in a different cultural, religious, and spiritual atmosphere, prayer may take a different form. The process of prayer may be seen as the practice of being in touch with one's own inner being or being in touch with a power or being beyond oneself. Some think that prayer and faith are a process of evolutionary development that fosters, in one way or another, the survival of mankind. If one were brought up in a Buddhist or Islamic culture, one would not ordinarily embrace a Christian spirituality let alone Christian prayer. The fact is that prayer exists and could be a combination of all these processes. The problem is the more one thinks about it, the more complicated it becomes. In prayer, I have always done the talking, for the most part, a kind of one-way conversation.

My expectations early on were that God or Jesus would literally talk back to me. At that time, with prayer and the Bible, I was somewhat of a literalist. Through my reading and study of the Bible, I came to realize that literal interpretations are not the point. The true point is what the text means or what it is trying to say. I think prayer is in the same category—that is, it is similar to or analogous to a conversation but not a literal or traditional conversation. Spiritual writers, theologians, religious institutions, and holy people have weighed in on the subject of prayer: its source, its meaning, its practice, its process, and its purpose. Because prayer is so personal and complex, it is difficult to capture what it is exactly. Prayer is as individual and unique as the person practicing it.

Prayer, like faith and beliefs in God, contains seeds of doubt. Ken Burns, the famous documentarian, in an interview on TV, pointed out that the opposite of belief is not doubt but certainty. If there were only certainty, there would be no faith. Prayer is an act of faith. Belief in God and belief in the efficacy of prayer are acts of faith and hope. Those who believe in prayer do not have scientific certitude but rather what I call spiritual certitude.

There are many types of prayer. We praise God, we petition God, we thank God, we worship God, and we ask God to intercede on our behalf and for the good of others. These different types of prayer seem to tell us more about ourselves than they tell us about God. Does God need our praise or worship? Does God need our thanks and gratitude? Does God need us to ask for his intercession? I think the answer is obvious. Prayer unquestionably is for our benefit. During these days of the coronavirus, many of us have resorted to prayer, even if in the past we didn't pray frequently. Sometimes we pray out of desperation. When things are out of our control, we pray for God to intervene on our behalf. If things work out well, we offer prayers of thanksgiving and gratitude. If they do not turn out well, we offer prayers of resignation and acceptance or perhaps we become disillusioned and stop praying at least for the time being. "After all God knows best; he is in control."

At times like this, it is obvious that we have limited control over much of life. Prayer seems to exist for our benefit and well-being in one way or another. It enables us to cope with the mysteries and unexplainable twists and turns of reality. If God is a God of love and love is creative and sacrificial in nature, then perhaps God gives us prayer as a means to our happiness and sanity. Prayer, thought of in this way, would be a generous outpouring of God's love for us.

Of course, these are unprovable assumptions, not certainties. However, there is in us the drive to express all these needs, wants, feelings, and desires. It seems that we have these needs, wants, feelings, and desires because God possibly created us with them as part of our nature. Possibly there is no God, but we grasp our insecurity and finiteness that lead us to seek something beyond ourselves, which is stable and secure, someone or something that gives our existence meaning and stability. Most of us have made this choice in favor of faith and prayer. Even if there were strong evidence to the contrary regarding the efficacy and veracity of prayer, much like faith, prayer will be with us until the end of time. Prayer is also a recognition and an admission that after all is said and done, for the majority, there is something bigger than us out there; and he, she, or it cares about us. (2020)

Our Father: Matthew 6:5–15

As part of the Sermon on the Mount, Jesus teaches us about prayer and how to pray. He tells us that our prayer should not be ostentatious, and its objective should not be to impress other people. For just as the rich who hoard their possessions have their reward in this life, so too those who pray to impress others will have already been paid in full. Jesus suggests that long hours at prayer and the use of ritual formulas may not be the hallmark of authentic prayer. He asks us to seek the presence of God in the quiet of our own space. In simple prayer, we should recognize that God already knows our needs yet still desires to dialogue with us.

Jesus sets an example for us, as he does so often, in Scripture. He has shown us how to live, how to love, and how to deal with adversity. He now shows us how to pray in this short but meaningful prayer. The Our Father teaches us about our relationship with God, sets priorities, challenges us to live fruitful lives, and deals with fundamental human concerns.

At the beginning of this prayer, we are asked to see God as our Father. We are asked to view God as a person who possesses perfectly all the best characteristics of a human father and more—one who loves, protects, forgives, and respects his beloved children. We in turn should see ourselves as children who love, respect, and cherish our Father.

In the same breath that we call God our Father, we speak of him as distant from us. We call him holy and see him as a person who resides in a place removed from this earth. This person, at one and the same time, is Father with all the closeness and intimacy that encompasses yet is a being beyond the grasp of the human mind and heart. He is Creator and sustainer of all that is, of all that was, and of all that is to be. For the Israelites, holy referred to the one who was totally other, one who was outside their realm of comprehension. We learn right from the start that although God wishes us to conceive of him in ways we can comprehend, he also wants us to realize that we can never really grasp or fathom the depths of the mystery of God.

In this prayer, Jesus challenges us to bring God's will and God's kingdom to fulfillment on earth. This is no pie in the sky religion; it is a religion of relationships that demands attention to our obligations toward our brothers and sisters. Jesus gives us the tools to accomplish this in the Sermon on the Mount.

As we pray, God helps us to verbalize and visualize what our needs are and where they stand in relation to him. God, through Jesus, tells us the things we need as we pray,

"Give us this day our daily bread." These are the things that sustain our physical and spiritual life: food and drink, family and friends, love and respect, and compassion and forgiveness. These are simple things that nourish us as persons in our relationships with God and each other. This is what our daily bread is all about.

Jesus makes it very clear that forgiveness for our wrongdoing is tied to our own spirit of forgiveness toward other people. On this occasion and on many others, Jesus stresses that God's forgiveness of us will be in direct proportion to our forgiveness of others:

> *Do not judge others, and God will not judge you; do not condemn others, and God will not condemn you; forgive other and God will forgive you. Give to others and God will give to you. A good measure, presses down, shaken together, running over, will be put into your lap; for the measure you use for others is the one that God will use for you.* (Luke 6:37–38)

It is important to realize that although forgiveness is essential, it is a process. Forgiveness on a human level is not instantaneous; but it is a course or journey that, once started, has a potency that cannot be underestimated. Forgiveness has the power to redeem and save not only the person being forgiven but also for the person forgiving. Forgiveness is at the heart of the gospel message. It is not magic; it is in fact like love, an act of the will, which perhaps cannot eradicate feelings of anger, hurt, and revenge but can start us on a path of healing. What this means is that we are willing to try to relinquish our right to these feelings. Jesus here again is our exemplar. *"Father forgive them for they know not what they do." (*Luke 23:34)

Finally, we ask our Father to help us resist temptation and keep us safe from evil. Jesus knows the world can lead us away from God and our true selves. Even those things that are good and wholesome, if substituted for God and others can, at best, distract and tempt us away from God and others and at worst can lead us to that evil, which we seek to be delivered from.

The Our Father should not be a recitation of meaningless words but rather a reflection on our relationship with our sisters and brothers and God our Father. (2007)

CHAPTER 11

Racism

Ahmaud Arbery

I no sooner finished the essay "An Opportunity Missed?" when the horrifying news of the killing of a young unarmed black man by two white men was all over the media. Ahmaud Arbery, a twenty-five-year-old black man, was hunted down like a dog and shot to death by a father and son, Gregory and Travis McMichael. The entire incident was captured on a cell phone video and has been on TV for the last few days. By this time, I am sure you know all the details about the killing of Ahmaud Arbery.

Two days ago, in an essay, I suggested that we had an opportunity to recognize who the most vulnerable among us are and who the most essential among us are. It turns out that people of color and the poor are both the most vulnerable and the most essential among us. They are more at risk because they are doing essential work, which translates into being on the front line, supplying us with food and the ability to social distance, thus keeping us physically alive and protected from this dreaded virus. Hopefully, we will see them as they are—of great value and worth—and translate that into proper respect and more just compensation in the future. We are all in this together, and we are all of equal value.

Terrible as this incident is, the fact that it only came to national attention on May 6 bespeaks something sinister was afoot. The actual incident took place on February 23, 2020. It came to national attention over two months after it occurred. Even more startling is the fact that no one was arrested even though authorities had the video evidence in hand. It suggests that if there had been no video, the incident would have gone without notice. It is now being looked into only because of pressure from black citizens.

It turns out that Mr. McMichael is a retired police officer and a former investigator for the Georgia Bureau of Investigation. Finally, an arrest was made in the last few days. Mr. McMichael and his son were charged with aggravated assault and murder. Hopefully, this is the beginning of an honest pursuit of justice.

Disturbing and horrific as this killing is, more troubling is the realization that behind this tragedy exists an attitude that fosters, approves, and allows this hatred to continue to thrive in our land. The growing uptick in racial violence and prejudicial attitudes is extremely troubling. Systemic racism is rampant in this country, and denying it is just an excuse for its continued existence. The carnage goes on and on.

- Travon Martin—murdered, Florida, February 26, 2012
- Emmett Till—murdered, Mississippi, August 28, 1955
- Michael Schwerner, Andrew Goodman, James Chaney—murdered, Mississippi, June 21, 1964
- Martin Luther King Jr.—murdered, Tennessee, April 4, 1968
- James Byrd—murdered, Texas, June 7, 1998
- Medgar Evers—murdered, Mississippi, June 12, 1963
- Michael Brown—murdered, Missouri, August 20, 2014
- Eric Garner—murdered, New York, July 17, 2014
- Ahmaud Arbery—murdered, Georgia, February 23, 2020
- Addie Mae Collins, Cynthia Wesley, Carole Robertson, Carol Denise McNair—murdered,

Alabama, September 15, 1963 (four teenage black girls murdered in a church bombing)
- Sharonda Coleman-Singleton, Rev. Clementa Pickney, Cynthia Hurd, Tywanza Sanders, Myra Thompson, Ethel Lee Lance, Rev. Daniel Simmons, Rev. Depayne Middleton, Susie Jackson—murdered, South Carolina, June 17, 2015 (nine black men and women murdered in a church in Charleston)

I have included names and dates to emphasize that these people were human beings like you and me. This list is long and disturbing but only the tip of the iceberg. These murders, assassinations, and executions are just an extension of the lynching and mutilations common place during slavery, reconstruction, and redemption. The hatred, bigotry, and degradation have been carefully and systematically handed down from family to family and from community to community. These attitudes are found throughout this nation. They initiate with family and community.

The song from the play *South Pacific* says it all when it comes to hate: "You've got to be carefully taught!" The south is more blatant and obvious about it, but the rest of the country is not without blame and responsibility. Fredrick Douglass commented, "*Opposing slavery and hat-*

ing victims has, become a very common form of abolitionism." These words of Fredrick Douglass could perhaps be updated to "opposing racism and hating the victims has become a very common form of civil rights." Martin Luther King Jr., at a demonstration in Chicago, said that even in Alabama and Mississippi, he had not encountered mobs as hostile to blacks' civil rights as those in Chicago. This latest killing of Ahmaud Arbery is just another manifestation of the deep-seated and pernicious hatred that lies barely beneath the surface and rears its ugly head as a reminder to people of color and to all of us that racism and white supremacy are alive and well in the USA both in the form of active violence and in subtle and not-so-subtle attitudes of discrimination.

Take for example the voters' rights issue. Under the not-so-convincing guise of concern for the integrity, accuracy, and legality of the vote, obstacles are put in place to prevent citizens of color from exercising their right to access the voting booth. It is very much in the tradition of the Jim Crow laws that were installed to keep black citizens from casting their vote. It was and is an effort to undermine the power of people of color. Jim Crow was more obvious, but the intent is the same. People who endeavor to restrict the black vote, for the main part claim they are not racists but are protectors of the sanctity and integrity of the electoral system. This is just an out-and-out lie. It is an attempt to control legislation that might bring people of color into greater prominence, equality, freedom, and power—the very things white supremacists and racists are losing control over.

The ascendance of people of color, as embodied in President Obama, is a cause for great concern among bigots and racists all over this country. The slightly repressed hatred, anger, and fear regarding race have again been rekindled and loosed by the present political atmosphere. In light of this latest murder of a defenseless black man, there is a need to redouble our efforts to do away with racism, bigotry, and white supremacy. After more than 150 years since the Civil War, we are still dealing with these demons. Racism is a potentially catastrophic flaw jeopardizing the future of this nation. Where we are today with regard to progress against racism is, at best, bittersweet. While great progress has been made on the road to freedom and equality, we still have miles and miles to travel. (2020)

You've Got to Be Carefully Taught

You've got to be taught to hate
and fear. You've got to be taught
from year to year.
It's got to be drummed
in your dear little ear
You've got to be carefully taught.
You've got to be taught to be afraid
of people whose eyes are oddly made.
And people whose skin is
a different shade.
You've got to be carefully taught.
You've got to be taught before it's too late.
Before you are six or seven or eight.
To hate all the people your relatives, hate.
You've got to be carefully taught.

These lyrics from Oscar Hammerstein and Richard Rodger's play *South Pacific* accurately identify the most significant means of transmitting love or hate from one generation to another. Families, communities, and nations have come to realize the power and importance of teaching for better or worse. St. Ignatius of Loyola is reputed to have said, "*Give us a child till he is seven and we will have him for life.*" It is through the basic teaching unit, the family, that racism and bigotry will grow and flourish or will be stamped out.

This conflict between right and wrong has been with the human race from the beginning. In our country, there has been no greater or more enduring problem than racism, with the possible exception of poverty. As a nation, we are faced with the task of reeducation and truth-seeking with regard to this issue. It is difficult to uproot pernicious attitudes and feelings that have been passed on from generation to generation for over three hundred years. These attitudes and feelings are so deeply engrained that even with great effort, they will be difficult to expunge. Racism in this country has been fine-tuned for over three hundred years and will take generations or even centuries to overcome. Even this estimation may be too optimistic.

American racism is just a variation on a theme of hatred and domination. When we view history, we see situations that in some ways are analogous to ours. There is an abundance of learned hatred and racism as seen in conflicts between Jews and Arabs, Irish and English, Turks and Armenians, Christians and Muslims, blacks and whites. We must strive to eradicate the feelings of mistrust and hatred that poison the minds and hearts of our children. The existence of hatred and violence is perpetuated through carefully teaching our children to see others as enemies or the cause of our problems. What is taught does not necessarily reflect the truth and reality of the past or present. The antidote to hatred and racism is love and tolerance taught in our families and expressed in our society. This is a long and difficult process that requires the "teachers" to be honest and truthful. This honesty and truthfulness cannot be taught or passed on to generations to come with hate in our hearts.

My wife and I are the proud parents of three boys who are appalled by the racial violence that emanates from hatred. We tried to teach our children tolerance and truthfulness to the best of our ability. The equality of all people is held in high regard regardless of differences such as color, sex, wealth, education, and the like. Hopefully, the quest for truth will, over time, trump misinformation and lies.

Fortunately, the overriding message in my childhood family was not one of hate and bigotry; it was actually one of love and tolerance. However, even in the best of family circumstances faulty information gets passed on. Although there was no overt teaching of racism in my childhood home, there was an underlying attitude that clearly saw people of color as inferior. It was not until my early twenties that I begin to realize I was racist. It was not intellectual racism but emotional racism.

Growing up during the era of civil rights (1950s and 1960s), I became more and more aware of the evil of racism and its pernicious results. I began to feel uncomfortable regarding the unintended racism of my youth. Little by little, I began to unlearn what my parents, relatives, and community intentionally or unintentionally taught me to believe. It was not done in a vindictive way, but it was nonetheless a negative influence. Thanks to heroes and prophets like Fredrick Douglass, W. E. B. Du Bois, Harriet Tubman, Martin Luther King Jr, Malcolm X, and Muhammad Ali, my racist attitudes and their attendant evils have been positively altered.

The process of learning the truth can be long and difficult, but it should always start in the home. The truth-seeking and learning process should also be supported in the community through law, customs, politics, religion, and national education.

Even with a healthy and strong education, the resistance to truth is deep-seated and powerful, as demonstrated by the latest but not unusual display of racism: the murder of Ahmaud Arbery. (2020)

Angry and Selfish

This is a difficult essay to write because of the volatility of the subject. My intention is not to offend, even though I know the topic will be offensive to just about everyone. The following is an attempt to put on paper my personal observations regarding conditions in this not-so-perfect union we call home. You may reject or accept these observations as true and accurate, or you may find them to be only partially true and accurate or not true and accurate at all; the judgment is yours. I make these observations with no malice but with great concern for the well-being of individuals and our society as a whole.

The basic premise I am presenting is that our country, since the time of its inception, for whatever reasons, was founded on inequality and operated with inequality for hundreds of years. The Emancipation Proclamation, at least in theory, freed the black man from the bondage of slavery but left total equality for later generations to achieve. We are still enveloped in that process.

As a result of the Civil War and the Emancipation Proclamation, great resentment for the federal government and people of color flourished. These drastic changes resulted in large numbers of angry people, people who did not and do not want to be told what to do or how to feel.

This is understandable, but instead of seeing people of color as victims, many people consider themselves to be the ones victimized.

Emancipation angered many. Large numbers of people despise the government for what they feel was and is an attempt through federal legislation to enforce and protect the civil rights of black people. After President Johnson achieved massive civil rights legislation, the South forsook the Democratic Party and became solidly Republican. If there was ever any question of where the South stood on civil rights, this left no doubts.

Because of these changes, many people feel emasculated, angry, and belittled. The anger and hatred have come to include, through the promotion of bigoted politicians, anyone who is or looks different or foreign—nonwhites, in other words. Many people feel the political system has treated them as if they were second-class citizens. The uneducated and the poor, much like people of color, feel they have been ignored and neglected, and indeed, they have been. People are angry because they feel disenfranchised. Citizens are looking for someone to take up their cause.

All this and more leave the country open to the demagoguery of opportunistic politicians. We see angry and hateful people participating in the uptick of violent and gun-related crimes. The anger is so deep against our fellow citizens that many choose to support candidates who reflect their anger but do not represent their best interest; these candidates serve their own political agenda. A great number of people reside in the lower socioeconomic strata of society, which only exacerbates the problem. Angry people on all sides are harmful to the common good.

Alongside the angry, we have the selfish who, for the most part, do not reside in the lower socioeconomic strata. These people are the money grabbers, those who have but want even more and are willing, in many cases, to sacrifice fellow citizens on the altar of greed. They are interested in the financial health of the country and lining their own pockets with little regard for the angry or for people of color. They are willing to garner enormous wealth and power at the expense of the common folk. Those who have the power to promote a more equitable society, in many cases, seem to have more interest in amassing greater wealth. These people are also angry when they think anyone criticizes their right to possess an inordinate and disproportionate amount of the wealth of this country.

Corporations, like people, can disregard the rights of consumers in the quest for profits. A few examples will make the point: cigarette manufacturers knew full well that tobacco was addictive and did nothing to protect the health of their customers. Again, knowing full well that cigarette caused cancer, they added addictive chemicals to keep people hooked. Chemical and pharmaceutical companies continued to sell products they knew caused cancer. Lawn care products and talcum powder are among the many cancer-causing products that manufacturers knew to be deadly. Their concern was not for the consumer but rather for the almighty buck. This greed and selfishness continue to be rampant today.

Where does all this anger and selfishness come from? Some of it is driven by pure unadulterated racism and xenophobia—the hatred of people of color, Jews, Asians, foreigners, and in general people who are not like us. Greed is an intense desire for wealth, and selfishness is a personal expression of greed. It is a lack of consideration for others when it comes to money and wealth.

In an interview before Donald Trump became president, he was asked how much money was enough. His answer was 100 percent correct, at least for many rich people. His answer was short and sweet: *"Just a little bit more."*

This is the problem for the selfish. There is no satisfying the need for more. It is reminiscent of the Lay's potato chip commercial. *"Bet you can't eat just one."* Bet you can't be satisfied with $1 million when you can have $2 million. Bet you can't be satisfied with $1 billion when you can have two billion. Those who are in this economic stratosphere seem blind to their selfishness. You don't have to give up what you have, but at the same time, working for others to have more is a step toward a more equitable society. The problem is that we are all selfish and angry to some extent. The solution is that only we can make a difference by ameliorating and controlling our own anger and selfishness. If we continue in unabated anger and selfishness, our democracy will slowly but surely deteriorate. If the shoe fits, wear it. (2020)

SNAFU
Breonna Taylor

The killing of Breonna Taylor, if not murder, and the subsequent charging of Kenneth Walker with assault and attempted murder is at minimum a terrible SNAFU, a life-obliterating event with grave racial overtones. At worst, it is the out-and-out murder of an innocent black woman and a continuation of tacit systemic racist policing. From the very start, it seems that due diligence was not exercised. It appears that the police were looking for a suspect in a drug investigation, Jamarcus Glover, who was in police custody before the raid on Breonna Taylor's residence took place.

Much is not clear about this case, and one wonders if this investigation, just announced by state and federal governments, would have been undertaken at all had not this incident gone viral. From the outset, the circumstances of this killing begged for an impartial, thorough, and independent investigation. Remember, this killing took place on March 13, 2020, but it is only recently that state and federal investigations have been initiated.

In the final analysis, this may not have been premeditated murder. It may have been a SNAFU, but in the end, one more black person has died at the hands of white police officers. How do you think the white population would react if the numbers were reversed, if the same number of white people were killed or murdered by black police officers?

I have no ax to grind. My son is a police officer. What I am promoting is equal justice for all citizens regardless of color, race, religion, country of origin, and education, etc. This is one more case in which white lives matter more than black lives. How many more people of color have to be killed by the police before we take serious systemic reform of law enforcement procedures? In fact, the entire justice system is weighted against people of color. Reform is needed in the fowling areas: legislative practices, enforcement procedures, judicial practices, codes and sentencing guidelines, and an increased effort to emphasize restorative justice over punitive justice.

The racism I spoke about in prior essays is rampant throughout the federal, state, and local prison systems of this country. Shockingly, we have the highest rate of incarceration per capita in the entire world, 716 per 100,000 people, according to the International Centre for Prison Studies. African Americans are incarcerated in state prisons at five times the rate of whites—a five-to-one ratio. Education that starts at birth and speaks to the values of equality, justice, mercy, and love is ultimately the best and perhaps the only way to eradicate racism and promote peace and harmony among human beings. (2020)

An Ugly Fact

Today is May 18, 2020, and we are still embroiled in the COVID-19 pandemic. The pandemic is a major medical event of devastating proportions. It has also become a major economic event, which is having serious economic consequences for the most vulnerable among us. Beyond the medical and economic ramifications is the politicization of these events that complicates any cooperation regarding the paths to "solutions" for the problems facing the nation.

You perhaps saw on TV the demonstration on the steps of the Michigan Capitol Building. The supposed purpose of the demonstration was to implore the governor to reopen the state to promote economic relief for all those suffering monetary hardships. This was the stated purpose and is a true concern for all of us. However, the overarching concern of the demonstration, in actuality, supported a darker and more sinister agenda.

It is my firm belief that both health and economics are, and should be, important issues to both the left and the right. Who wants to die? Who wants to go hungry? Who wants their children, parents, or grandparents to die? Who wants to lose their economic stability? The simple answer to these questions is no one! Then why the political conflict? Is it just that people can't agree on the best way to approach these problems? Although that's part of it, the answer is no. It is more deeply rooted than that.

There is, in this country, a great divide regarding the value of human beings and how we view civil and human rights. We all value our rights, but some of us value our rights more than we value the rights of others. The demonstrators on the steps of the Michigan Capitol said a great deal about this country and what they believe it stands for. The health and economic problems are not at the center of this issue. In the short term, they are just the external representation or manifestation of something thinly veiled which, in the long term, is more apt than COVID-19 to take this country down.

What did you see on these steps? You saw angry people. You saw Confederate flags and guns, the kind that kill at rapid rates. You saw swastikas and hateful placards. You saw a message, loud and clear. It was one of hate and racial superiority. It was one of approbation of human bondage and of human annihilation. It was one of hate toward fellow human beings. The message revealed an ugly fact. It is despicable, but it is a message that reflects the attitudes of a fairly large minority of our society.

The Confederate flag and the swastika are brazen symbols of human bondage and genocide. Parts of this country wish to return to the darkest and most depraved times of our history under the mantra "Make America Great Again." Slavery, bigotry, and white supremacy are sadly deeply embedded in our history and are yet to be uprooted from our society. We have been making slow progress toward this goal, and we must continue on this journey; it is a moral imperative. (2020)

Bloody Sunday
George Floyd

On Sunday, May 7, 1965, fifty-five years ago, on a peaceful civil rights march from Selma to Montgomery, the nation watched on TV a horror beyond belief. The visual effect was profoundly disturbing. People saw with their own eyes the police, with utter disrespect for life and limb, inflict brutal physical punishment on innocent citizens. The TV pictures reflected back to a nation the evil that many of us either ignored or denied. To some extent, to ignore or deny is actually to participate. This event on the Edmund Pettus Bridge became the catalyst of the civil rights movement for many years to come. White America, at least those of open mind and goodwill, were horrified and saw the unacceptability and immorality of treating human beings in this fashion.

The cold-blooded murder of George Floyd feels like another Edmund Pettus Bridge moment. Through the medium of a cell phone camera, we saw another horrifying and almost unbelievably cruel and inhumane treatment of a black citizen by a police officer. The visual of this murder will leave an indelible mark on this nation. This act of murder, perpetrated in such a nonchalant fashion, shook us to the core of our being. It was hard for us, the white population, to believe that a police officer could act in this subhuman way.

In another incident in Buffalo, New York, we saw this same disregard for human life. An unarmed seventy-five-year-old man, Martin Gugino, was shoved to the ground by two police officers while surrounded by at least thirty policemen in riot gear. He posed no threat to any of the officers, and yet they chose to brush him aside as if his life didn't matter. This again could be taken as a metaphor for the way white folks have brushed aside black lives as if they didn't matter. The fact is they didn't and, in many cases, still don't matter to many white people. Officials of the Buffalo Police department released a statement that Mr. Gugino tripped and fell. Little did the police know that at least two individuals had recorded, on iPhone video, the whole incident. It was quite clear from the video that Mr. Gugino was pushed for no good reason. It was shocking to see this gentleman fall and strike his head with such force that blood immediately gushed from his head around his ear. These moments captured on civilian iPhone videos seem to be the watchdog of the future. Again, these videos reflect back on the nation the injustice and racism still alive and active in our society.

As in the case of Bloody Sunday, the visuals were profoundly disturbing. This incident also revealed the systemic nature of violence and racism in law enforcement. As shocking as the video was, the reaction of fifty-seven police officers to the charge of assault leveled against the two officers was astounding. All fifty-seven officers reportedly resigned from that special unit to show solidarity and protest the charge of assault. What might the Buffalo Police Department do to rectify the situation: fire all of the officers because it is not obvious to them that this type of behavior is unacceptable? For this reason, they should not be entrusted with the safety of the community. At a minimum, should all these officers be suspended, have psychological evaluations, and be required to participate in sensitivity training? I am sure there are many options that will be considered by the Buffalo Police Department, but perhaps not.

With the advent of cell phone videos comes an important tool for civilians to help keep law enforcement on the straight and narrow. Research has provided strong evidence that when individuals are being watched, they become self-conscious of their actions and often will alter their conduct.* Aside from informing the public, cell phone videos can be a strong deterrent to police violence. They will not root out systemic racism in law enforcement or root out hatred in our society, but they will hopefully make law enforcement think twice before applying force and violence.

The work ahead is hard. The questions are many. The issues are complex. The solutions are difficult. But to continue on the present path will be catastrophic. We will not come up with all the answers quickly or easily, but we must show strong resolve regarding solutions. If we maintain the present system, we will continue on a downward spiral. As one reporter stated, *"We must change the culture and systems to reflect the values of justice and equality for all."* This cannot and will not happen unless white people really listen to their black and brown brothers and sisters (bbc.com, "How Does Being Watched Alter Behavior"). (2020)

Peace on the Left, Justice on the Right

"If you want peace, work for justice." This simple yet profound declaration was part of a presentation by Paul VI on a Peace Day celebration in 1972. Although I am not in lockstep with Paul VI on all issues, I could not agree more with what he said. His basic message, given in 1972, was and still is relevant and important. He states in strong terms:

Every person therefore has an inherent dignity that no individual, no government, no social or economic system may compromise or deny. Justice therefore requires that we honor, respect and protect the dignity of all human beings. To respect, honor and protect the dignity of all human beings requires that we work to eliminate all those things that threaten the dignity of human persons. This means that we work to end capital punishment…this means we work to ensure that all persons have access to what is necessary to live in dignity-affordable housing that is in good condition, access to health care, sufficient food, secure communities, opportunity for rest, and opportunity for secure retirement. When the prerequisites of justice are absent in a society, there can be no peace as persons struggle to secure what should be theirs by right.

This is the work ahead of us. This is what BLM is about. This justice is for blacks, browns, whites, and every color of mankind under the sun.

However, right now and over the past three hundred plus years in this country, it is the black race who has literally been under the gun. A just society must demand these rights for all its citizens but especially for the disenfranchised. These rights we speak of today—housing, education, health care, just and living wages, food security, just legal and judicial systems, equal opportunity, and the like—are part of the process and the growing awareness of citizens to evolving inalienable rights. These are the very rights that will allow us to form a more perfect union. Without the fulfillment of these rights, true peace will remain elusive. These are the rights all women and men desire and deserve. The achievement of these rights for all people is the actual bending of the arc of the universe toward justice and peace.

Religion asks, Why are we here? What is our purpose? Well, this is it. This is the answer: to achieve justice and peace for all. To do otherwise is to deny the dignity and equality of all humanity. Regardless of whether one believes in God or Allah or some power beyond self or just believes in the dignity of mankind, we can live in peace only if we practice justice, equality, tolerance, and freedom.

All the other beliefs that keep women and men in bondage are empty and false and a deception. Keep in mind, there can be no peace without justice for all.

Where and when do we start? The iron is hot; we should strike now! A good place to start might be the justice and law enforcement systems. Notice I did not use the awkward, easily co-opted, and misunderstood term *defunding police*. Allocating funds in different ways is not "defunding police." It is perhaps a better way of using funds to address, in a more humane way, the solutions to local community issues. Reforming and restructuring, not defunding, is a better way to describe the process and is as good a place to start as any.

Justice is applied unevenly toward black and brown people who almost always end up on the short end of the stick. Perhaps we should start the process by listening to the victims of this racism, the people of black and brown communities, rather than the white "leaders" offering solutions without understanding the complex problems of these communities. Only when we begin to dialogue on a national and local level will we begin to better understand what is meant by "defunding police" or reforming and restructuring the justice system. (2020)

Rayshard Brooks
Why?

Hard as it may be to believe, another fatal shooting (looking a lot like murder) has been perpetrated by two white police officers in Atlanta, Georgia. We saw an unarmed black man, Rayshard Brooks, shot in the back twice by white police officers. The incident seems as if it could have been handled in a multitude of ways with a much better outcome. All the details will be investigated eventually, and a determination of charges will be made.

I have been trying to write an essay concerning the killing of Mr. Brooks but have had some problem identifying why this killing/murder seems so important to me and the cause of racial justice; finally, it came to me. The taking of any life is a travesty and a misunderstanding of the true value of life itself, but there is another important truth to be learned here beyond the obvious. It somehow speaks to the idea of systemic racism even more strongly than the murder of George Floyd. The George Floyd murder was significant and earth-shattering because of the visuals and the sustained nine minutes and twenty-nine seconds it took to murder Mr. Floyd. The evilness of this act was obvious and unencumbered by circumstances. It was a straight-up murder, no doubt about it. The nation was shocked into a profound realization of the reality of racial hatred and systemic police brutality toward blacks. It was an Edmund Pettus Bridge moment and has sparked the coming of a new era in racial justice as did Bloody Sunday in 1963.

One might think with all the upheaval caused by the murder of George Floyd that police and police departments throughout the country would be on hyperalert to deal, in a cautious and careful manner, with any racial situations. Two officers knew full well what the consequences for mishandling racial conflict, especially in this racially charged atmosphere, could mean, yet they did the unthinkable. They shot and killed an unarmed black man, Rayshard Brooks.

Ahmaud Arbery was hunted down like a dog, Breonna Taylor was shot eight times in the middle of the night, and George Floyd was suffocated to death in plain sight. Charges against all involved should have been warning enough to law enforcement that life-altering consequences could result from these racial incidents, such as loss of career, lengthy prison terms, emotional upheaval, and loss of family contact. The price could be very high.

With all this being known, why would these officers allow themselves to be so out of control as to shoot an unarmed black man in the back while he was running away from them? At that moment, he posed no threat to life or limb. They had to know this was a bad thing to do with potentially disastrous consequences. Why then would they do such a thing? Was it an instantaneous reaction, or was it something more significant?

Did it have to do with conditioning? I strongly think conditioning is a major factor not only in this case but in many other similar cases. It is critical for us to understand the importance of this killing because it gives us an insight into the power of negative conditioning and the possibilities of positive conditioning. Conditioning starts in the home with hatred for blacks. Conditioning by the greater society gives, at best, tacit approval of racial and prejudicial conduct toward blacks and people of color and at its worst gives permission to abuse power in racial situations. In Mr. Brooks's case, conditioning seems to be a significant factor that was fostered or at least condoned by systemic racism.

Some examples of this type of behavior go back more than twenty years as in the case of Amadou Diallo. Mr. Diallo was a twenty-three-year-old unarmed black man in New York City who was shot forty-one times by four New York police officers. These officers were charged with second-degree murder and reckless endangerment, and all were found not guilty.

Many years later, in 2014, in the case of an unarmed black man, Eric Garner, an illegal choke hold was the cause of death by a police officer in New York City with no criminal consequences. Over the last twenty years, there have been many similar cases with the same types of outcomes testifying to the fact that not much has changed. If these two Atlanta, Georgia, police officers acted as they did because they believed the system would protect them, it is not much of a leap to conclude that conditioning over the years has contributed to systemic racism in law enforcement.

The fact of this type of killing/murder at this time in 2020 shows that the system has not moved forward on the issue of racism and still seeks to protect and shelter its own rather than serve communities of color. Had an unarmed white man been shot forty-one times by black officers, which would be highly unlikely in the first place, or if an unarmed white man was shot in the back twice by black officers in Atlanta, or if a black officer murdered a white man by applying deadly pressure with his knee for eight minutes and forty-six seconds, there would be a drastically different response. The conditioning of officers and police departments regarding white men is totally different both on a conscious and subconscious level. Perhaps systemic racism is so strongly ingrained that no amount of self-interest or self-protective mechanisms can control feelings and emotions that display unchecked disrespect for black people, especially black men and boys.

Condemnatory sentiment shows that 80 percent of US citizens now believe there is systemic racism and injustice in law enforcement. Considering these numbers, police still seem to be incapable of containing rage against black men. The killing/murder of Rayshard Brooks, even with all the strong feelings and the possible long-term and catastrophic consequences, could not overcome the embedded belief that the system will somehow protect and defend police for their misdeeds as long as they are against black people.

The point, for me, is that the killing/murder of Rayshard Brooks is vitally important because it tells us how difficult it will be to eradicate years of negative conditioning with regard to systemic racism in law enforcement. The good news is that with the change in attitude, positive conditioning, institutional changes, and transparency at the top, we have a fighting chance to turn things around. It won't be easy, but it is a moral imperative. (2020)

Stupid as in Angry and Selfish

A month or so ago, I wrote an essay called "Angry and Stupid." It was a scathing rebuke of the anger of many toward blacks and nonwhites. It was an indictment of the richest among us who feel totally entitled to amass personal and corporate fortunes while large numbers of our population are going without the necessities of life. I was going to call the essay "Angry, Selfish, and Stupid." However, when I had finished with angry and selfish, I thought stupid might be over the top. After a month or so of dealing with "stupid" regarding the COVID-19, I realized that I had made a mistake.

First of all, I should explain what I mean by the word *stupid*. Some of the supposedly smartest and best-educated people I know are stupid. On the other hand, some of the least educated and supposedly stupid people I know are quite smart. This seems to be an oxymoron situation. You be the judge.

If a supposedly smart and well-educated person says we have more infections because we are testing more, does that make sense to you? Many "smart" people have said this, including you-know-who. Does more testing increase or lessen infections, or does testing have any causal relationship to increasing or decreasing the infections? You smart, well-educated people, be careful; that's a tough question to answer.

The common, uneducated folk with no ax to grind realize testing just tells us how serious the problem is in reality. There is no causal relationship between more testing and the increased number of cases, except that cases beget cases. Testing is a method of evaluating the number of infections and extent of the problem and then doing something positive to correct the situation. The numbers help us outline a strategy. It is only what we do with the testing information that will lessen or increase the spread. Counting the number of cases will not increase or diminish the cases of the virus in and of itself. The smart, educated people—I hesitate to include our stupid leader—are either truly stupid or have an agenda that makes them incapable of seeing things reasonably and rationally and dealing with them through a scientific process.

Unfortunately, in this case, "stupid" is colored by various other motivations. Because of pressure from the top, people will choose things that are blatantly stupid for political, religious, economic, and other reasons, including anger and selfishness. Their judgments are clouded by what they see as self-interest.

To say we are doing well in the fight against COVID-19 is clearly not the case. It is a stupid remark. The USA has more deaths (135,000 and rising) than any other country in the world. Death projections go as high as three hundred thousand or more. We also have the highest number of cases in the world, according to present testing. We now appear to be on an upward trajectory in many states, especially in Florida and Texas. Florida had the highest number of cases in a single day, over fifteen thousand. Under pressure from the White House, over thirty states reopened for business (some in a limited way) without achieving the federal health guidelines of the White House. The messaging from the White House is confusing and many times contradictory.

After some thought, angry, selfish, and stupid seem to go together. As a result of our anger and selfishness, we allow ourselves to make stupid decisions that come back to bite us in the proverbial behind. Only now some of us see that decisions based on dubious knowledge and information may have been the product of "stupid." (2020)

Monuments

Caste, a book by Isabel Wilkerson, and *Learning from the Germans* by Susan Neiman can give us insight into the meaning and significance of monuments. Considering the age we live in, these are two books you might want to put on your must-read list. The Civil War and World War II are two wars that had at their basis the subjugation or annihilation of classes of people who were seen as a threat to white superiority or Aryan supremacy. The ruling class in power was willing to go to any lengths of brutality to maintain and sustain their position of dominance.

These two lost causes, black slavery and the Final Solution, are seen by most people as totally reprehensible and brutal. They represent a complete and total lack of understanding for the rights and dignity of all people and the willingness to use any means to achieve domination and control. Slavery and the Final Solution were absolutely and completely immoral. This fact should be self-evident, but it is clearly not for large groups of people even today. The reasons for this are many and complex, but these two books give great insight into this state of mind.

Monuments and the dismantling of Civil War monuments have become an issue in the USA. They could be seen as a metaphor for the struggle to continue the spirit of slavery and the will not to change the hearts and minds of those who cling to the mistaken ideals of the Lost Cause. "Make America Great Again" is a desire, if not to bring back slavery, to continue the domination of black people in any way by white people who feel they are the victims and not the blacks. MAGA hats and monuments represent a desire to return to days when black people shut up and did as they were told.

The same can be said of some Germans. Instead of seeing reality as it is, some Germans feel they are the victims and not the Jews. The Germans, to a lesser degree than the Americans, feel resentment and hostility toward the real victims of the Final Solution, the Jews. This can be seen in the attitudes of Germans and Americans regarding monuments to "war heroes" and members of these lost and immoral causes. I think we can learn from the Germans regarding attitudes about monuments. The Germans have no statues or monuments to Hitler, Goebbels, Himmler, or any war leaders. Instead, they have "stumbling stones" in the pavement to remind themselves of the atrocities of the Final Solution. The message here is that the Germans, for the most part, recognize the evil of the Holocaust and are sorry. Germans are attempting to rehabilitate, reconcile, and make reparation for the wrongdoing of the Third Reich.

In contrast, there is a very large minority of people in the USA who desire to keep monuments to evil men who went to war to keep human beings in subjugation and terror. Many Americans see monuments as a sign of the correctness of slavery and all its attending beliefs. To maintain the monuments is to maintain the attitudes of the slave era. It is to continue to exert superiority over black people and a wish not to recognize their lost cause. There is no recognition or remorse for the evil perpetrated upon fellow human beings, no "stumbling stones" in the USA!

From these two books, two main themes seem to me to continue to be dominant even today. The idea that people will vote for a candidate who does not represent their best interest is to misunderstand what drives their attitude. In the case of slavery, white people wish to keep and prevent black people from rising above their white master through constant and enduring economic and social domination. For the Nazis, it was to establish and maintain the superiority of the Aryan race through extermination used against the imagined threat of the Jewish people and non-Aryans. They see their best interest, consciously or subconsciously, as not economic prosperity, or health concerns, and the like but as not wanting to be lower in status than the black persons who are, in their estimation, the dregs of civilization.

White people, especially in the South, both rich and poor alike, could not stomach the idea that a black person could ever be equal or superior to a white person. For this reason, whiteness was considered by whites as intrinsically better than blackness. Even the poorest of the poor could take solace in this concept, which is still prevalent today. Whiteness represents the essence of this superiority. "No matter how low we go or how high blacks go, you can never take this whiteness away from us" is the sustaining attitude. For many, it is possible to live without many things and yet still feel they will always remain superior because of their color. So it becomes essential to hold down black people to maintain the status quo.

This country is in crisis because many whites see in the near future that the white race will no longer be the majority, and this is frightening, so they will vote for the person who will maintain white power and control. Fear that they will become the lowest caste in our society outweighs all other considerations. Things are changing, and white supremacists think by becoming more aggressive in their opposition, they will somehow turn the tide in their favor. They are wrong; we won't let them. (2020)

Jacob Blake

Racial hatred and disregard for black lives reared their ugly heads once again. Over the last six months, there have been five killings of black people—Breonna Taylor, Ahmaud Arbery, George Floyd, Rayshard Brooks, and now Jacob Blake. Three of the five have been murdered or killed by white police officers, all under questionable circumstances. Over the last one hundred years, murders and killings of black people have gone almost unnoticed and virtually unpunished by white society. All of these recent killings, with one exception, have, to a lesser or greater degree, been recorded in video form, but even that kind of evidence is strongly resisted by a large minority of white citizens. If we deny, without reason, what is seen on video camera, how much more easily will we hide and deny the unseen truth for the protection of racist individuals and a system rife with racism?

It is hard or almost impossible to believe that these are not racially motivated incidents. In Mr. Blake's case, it is difficult to see how a man with his back to an officer can be an imminent threat—that is, an immediate serious risk of death to anyone but especially to a trained police officer with a gun in his hand. The officer's seven shots were all into Jacob Blake's back. It is unreasonable to believe that seven shots were necessary. We know from past experience that very little justice has been done in many of these cases over the years. How can we deny racial hatred when we see over and over again white police officers shoot and kill unarmed black people?

Why is this? The reasons are multitudinous and complex. Hatred and systemic racism are not just seen throughout law enforcement and the justice system but are seen throughout the fabric of our society. Racism is embedded in every aspect of life in this country—health care, housing, sports, education, economics, socialization, and politics. As I have said before, if you can name it, it has been influenced by racism.

The problem is three hundred to four hundred years old, and like it or not, the white man is responsible. We have lived with it for so long that many of us fail to recognize or admit that it exists. Some even blame black folks for the horrors of racism, which are mostly perpetrated against black folks. This type of thinking harkens back to the idea that black people were the cause of the Civil War. White folks fail to see the pernicious effects of hatred and racism on both blacks and whites.

This shooting of Jacob Blake, an unarmed twenty-nine-year-old black man, by a white police officer seems to be another example of the monumental disregard for the life and limb of a black person. Our society and political system use time and procrastination as weapons to effectively undermine the political will of the country to do something meaningful about racial inequity. What do you think the response would be if a black police officer shot an unarmed white man seven times in the back in questionable circumstances?

Several months have passed since the shooting of Rayshard Brooks, which I warned was a signal of how difficult it would be to slow down the violence against blacks and to change attitudes and laws. If the murder of George

Floyd and the other recent racial incidents were not a warning and a call to restraint in these racially charged moments, what would be? As it turns out, nothing short of strict laws and severe punishment may be the only option at this time. I can't help but think that lawmakers who drag their feet when it comes to making laws that are for the protection of all—but especially blacks, who are most vulnerable—are not motivated by bigotry and racism. It reminds me of the inability of many lawmakers who, for financial gain, refused to enact common-sense gun laws.

I am still hopeful that a large majority of people in this country have become more sensitive and aware of the need to press forward with regard to the civil and human rights of black people and all people of color. Remember what this country should be all about: the right of all men and women to life, liberty, and the pursuit of happiness, but before this becomes a reality, there must be justice. (2020)

What Do You Have to Lose?

This was a question Donald Trump asked an audience of black voters at a rally on August 19, 2016, in Dimondale, Michigan. It turns out the answer to that question was and still is "just about everything." How about for starters, your life! Systemic racism has reared its ugly head in an increasing rash of shootings and killings of black men by white police officers, all occurring on Donald Trump's watch. Again, black lives are in greater jeopardy than white lives, and Mr. Trump has shown no special interest in solving that issue.

As first responders and "necessary workers," people of color die at a higher rate than white people and are paid wages that in no way reflect their necessity and importance. The reality is that black people are just more expendable than white people of privilege, at least in the eyes of many whites.

What about lies and deceptions about blacks and their intentions? It is blacks that are being killed and targeted, not whites, as this administration would have us believe. Mr. Trump is the demagogue in chief, a master of using fear for ascertaining political power and intimidation.

We have an economy that is plummeting to the bottom for middle- and lower-income groups. This doesn't seem to bother Mr. Trump and his base as long as it works for them. Even for some poor people, support for Mr. Trump is the way to go. As long as white liberals, blacks, people of color, and foreigners are seen as second-class citizens and the enemy, they will continue to support this administration. Little do they understand that they are useful fodder and nothing more for his political ends. They fail to see how they are being used to maintain and sustain his political power.

Is the failure of the economy this administration's fault? Perhaps, perhaps not. But neither can they take credit for the good economy prior to COVID-19. It is almost impossible to assign a presidency praise or blame regarding economic conditions either during an administration or just after an administration leaves office. That being said, it seems fair not to attach all the blame for this economy to the present administration. There are so many complex factors contributing to the success or failure of an economy that only history will tell the tale; this can often take years. When it comes to the economy all politicians, regardless of party, take credit when things go well and try to blame the other guy when things go badly. My thought here is to neither credit the Obama Administration for success or blame the Trump Administration for failure. Judging the responsibility of success or failure of an economy is usually a long-term process.

Black people must judge for themselves what they have to lose regarding law and order. The issue of law and order is being manipulated fairly effectively by the present administration. Trump characterizes a Biden presidency as one of lawlessness while he presides over a country that he is incapable of healing and uniting but rather sees division and brute force as the remedy. You know who will receive the brunt of that strategy.

The fact is that we have been on a downhill spiral since Mr. Trump took office, and there is no meaningful strategy in place or being developed to correct the race situation, to say nothing of COVID-19. The response to demonstrations is to crush them with force and to characterize them as an attempt by blacks to bring about anarchy. This use of fear preys upon the folks who, perhaps through no fault of their own, have feared blacks because of faulty education, misunderstood or neglected history, negative propaganda, and outright lies about people of color.

Right now, things are not good between many black people and white people, and this is largely the administration's fault. Instead of seeing the demonstrations as a cry for help, justice, and mercy, they are viewed as a tool to divide and conquer by encouraging the base to unleash pent-up fear and anger that has existed since before the Civil War. There is no doubt that one of the weapons of this administration is fearmongering based on a lie that black people are looking to hurt and kill white people, but as the facts reveal, it has always been the white man hurting and killing the black man.

So all in all, I would answer Mr. Trump's question, "What do you have to lose?" by saying if things continue to stay as they are or to escalate, we may lose our country. Our fate will be similar to the sick man who would like to get better but does nothing to improve his health and, in fact, continues behavior detrimental to his well-being; it eventually brings death to both body and soul. (2020)

Shut Up and Dribble

That says it all, unfortunately. Laura Ingraham, a Fox News commentator, famously said to LeBron James in February 2018 while discussing racism in this country, "Shut up and dribble." This was and is a self-revealing statement. If there was any doubt about Laura's closed-mindedness, self-righteousness, and downright nastiness, this statement dispelled any scintilla of doubt. In these four words, she laid bare her disregard for the thoughts, feelings, and opinions of anyone who might disagree with her.

We can all be closed-minded at times, but Laura Ingraham is consistently closed to facts and opinions other than her own. She capsulized in a few words not only her own ignorance and closed-mindedness but that of all who refuse to even consider another's thoughts, feelings, and opinions. By statements like this, she seeks to relegate her opponents to nonentities. This is the modus operandi also used by Mr. Trump. By belittling opponents, by dismissing other's viewpoints, he tries to negate anything of value said by an opponent.

Money, power, and personal privilege seem to be the drivers of this type of behavior, but that is another topic for another essay. Truth, honesty, and concern have very little place in this philosophy.

It is clear that Miss Ingraham cares little about what you think and feel. She has no problem using her platform to express her feelings and opinions but would like to disallow professional athletes and others she disagrees with from using their platform to express their feelings and opinions. However, Miss Ingraham is not beyond being hypocritical. She was critical of Mr. James voicing his opinion because he is, in her estimation, a know-nothing athlete while Drew Breese is given a pass. She said, "*He's allowed to have his view about what kneeling and what the flag mean to him.*" From these two incidents, it seems obvious that what's good for the goose is not always good for the gander, at least in Laura Ingraham's world. She seems to have that mind of which Dean Spanley speaks: "*Only a closed mind is certain.*" And she seems to be very certain. (2020)

Qualified Immunity

"Qualified Immunity is a legal doctrine in US Federal Law that shields government officials from being sued for discretionary actions performed within their official capacity, unless their actions violate *'clearly established' federal law or constitutional rights*" (Wikipedia 2019). Today, it can be seen as an effort by authorities to protect police officers from unjust prosecution and unjust lawsuits stemming from a legal and justified means to properly exercise his or her duty as an officer of the law. It is designed to protect officials from unreasonable lawsuits and prosecutions when in fact they respond in a reasonable, competent, and lawful manner. It is also designed to protect a citizen from incompetence or a knowing and willful violation of the law by an official against a citizen. If applied evenly and justly, it should protect both parties.

Unfortunately, today and in the past, qualified immunity is and has been used by some as cover and protection not for legal and just activity but as a license to act in a blatantly racist, illegal, and unjust manner. We are also at the point now where it is being used to slow down the efficient, timely, and proper execution of justice. Much of this is done in the hope that lack of urgency and untimely resolution will dull the public's desire for swift and honest justice. Faulty qualified immunity has become a desired barrier for some angry and prejudiced people to delay justice for black folks.

Using devious methods to paint people of color and white protestors as rioters has become commonplace. The fact of the matter is that extremists of the right and left are fomenting violent activities, and this activity happens almost exclusively at night under the cover of darkness. Darkness perpetrated in darkness. It seems that the thrust of this activity is threefold. First, to pin the riots on BLM people and their supporters; the fact is they are the legal protestors and not the illegal rioters. Second, black people are the cause and the blame for the riots; this is much like slaveholders blaming black slaves for the Civil War. And third, that white folks respect law and order while black folks are lawless and desire anarchy when in reality, black folks want only justice and to be treated with the same respect as white folks.

When is the last time you saw a police officer of any race shoot a white person in the back or put a knee to the neck of a white citizen? Do you think a black man carrying an AR-15 or some type of assault rifle in a "riot" zone would not have been shot down by police or at the very least stopped and questioned regarding his motives and intentions? In Kenosha, Wisconsin, a white man carrying an AR-15 was offered water and allowed to go home after killing two people and wounding a third without a question of his activity. Tell me there isn't a double standard being applied here in favor of white people.

Vigilantism isn't being promoted by the right? It seems permissible for white vigilantes to shoot black people if they think the law is being broken. Law enforcement undertaken without legal authority by self-appointed individuals or groups of people is illegal. However, it is now being portrayed by the right as a good activity and worthy of praise. I guess it would then be okay for black vigilantes to shoot white people whom they feel are breaking the law. Irrational logic? You tell me. (2020)

Walter Wallace Jr.

The list keeps growing. Another black man is dead at the hands of white police officers. The Walter Wallace shooting, whatever the legal or criminal ramifications, is another reason or motivating factor to act now in a positive and meaningful way toward the correction of a faulty system. I have mentioned before that between the presidential election and COVID-19, all the oxygen has been sucked out of the air with regard to any immediate and meaningful progress toward solving the problems of systemic racism.

Mr. Wallace's death could have been avoided if adequate and proper procedures were in place as part of the training of police officers; perhaps they were, but obviously not effectively absorbed. Clearly, I am not an expert in police procedures, but I think a better solution to this type of problem could be put in place through the efforts of qualified instructors. This will only happen if encouraged by the system and its leaders. The lack of care and concern for the lives of black and brown people is at the heart of the problem.

The unfortunate slogan "defund the police" has at its core negative connotations that are and have been being exploited by racist individuals. Defunding the police is not the solution; rather, redirecting and increasing funding to support training and sensitivity programs regarding the needs of black and brown communities is a more thoughtful and productive approach to a complex problem. It is unfair to our police officers, who are mostly decent caring people, to be put into situations for which they are unprepared. Additional funding and innovative thinking and planning should lead the way to reform our institutions of justice. Honestly listening and responding to citizens of black and brown communities will be absolutely necessary and critical for effective planning and implementation of these programs. Until we address the essence of the matter—racism in both its systemic and personal forms—in a just and thoughtful manner, we will continue to experience these horrendous situations that end up with the killing or murder of black and brown citizens.

The Walter Wallace Jr. killing, just as many others, could have been resolved differently if our society had put in place plans and methods to deal with racism at large. Unfortunately, the nation has resisted mightily most corrective measures over the centuries. To make changes demands a desire and will to move forward with plans and programs that address these difficult situations efficiently and successfully. We cannot continue to fly by the seat of our pants. This is a big lift because it means not only addressing systemic racism in the justice system but addressing systemic racism in just about every institution in the USA.

With the presidential election only two days away, we have a big choice with big ramifications for our future. It is my belief that Mr. Trump will not only not address the racial divide but, in fact, will continue to ignore this grave state of affairs. It would not be a surprise, if elected, that he would continue to fan the flames of division and discord. It is our responsibility to put constant pressure on either Mr.

Trump or Mr. Biden, depending on who wins on Tuesday, to address this crisis. Regardless of the COVID-19 pandemic, we must not let the renewed civil rights flame, rekindled by the murder of George Floyd, flicker and die out. Remember all lives matter, but black lives are under siege, and for this reason, we must continue to fight for the lives of our black and brown brothers and sisters. (2020)

Anjanette Young

On February 21, 2019, Anjanette Young's home was raided by a minimum of six Chicago police officers. She had just stepped out of the shower and was about to get dressed when these officers smashed the front door and handcuffed her. She was naked! She feared for her life. For at least thirty to forty minutes, she remained naked and handcuffed, protesting that a mistake had been made and that the police were in the wrong house. Her protests were expressed a minimum of forty times and only responded to with insensitive rebukes by the police. Would this operation go down in this fashion? It is my strong belief that it goes down this way more often than not. There is a long history of police abuse of people of color. It stems from a dehumanization process long practiced regarding the poor and people of color.

The poor, the immigrant, the criminal, the people whose skin is a different color or whose eyes are shaped differently are not only seen as the other but are in many cases seen as the enemy. Those individuals who are at the top and the faulty systems themselves communicate and promote, overtly or surreptitiously, this dehumanization, which leads to attitudes of contemptuousness and disrespect at the least and mistreatment and hatred at the worst. This dehumanization process has become so embedded in the fabric of our society that we are only subliminally aware of it, if at all.

The case of Anjanette Young is a horrific demonstration of the results of this dehumanization process. This incident spotlights a host of characteristics that point to this process and to systemic racism. There were legal, social, moral, and ethical aberrations brought to our attention in this case.

There was a total lack of due diligence regarding procedural details. The fact that the subject of the investigation was wearing an electronic monitoring device for location purposes and that a different address was the target of this warrant indicates little concern regarding the outcome of this operation. This was the same type of lack of attention to detail that ended in the death of Breonna Taylor.

Miss Young, fortunately, was not killed, but she is scarred for life. Not only was it morally and socially unethical to allow Miss Young to remain naked in the presence of a task force of all-male police officers but it also violated every code of human decency and respect. Her pleas for a modicum of consideration were ignored until one officer finally covered her naked body.

When we see the nakedness of Jewish Holocaust victims, we shudder. We should shudder with outrage in the same way at the humiliation and dehumanization Miss Young endured. She was relegated to the status of subhuman and nonperson, stripped of all rights and respect. How would you feel and react if this were your mother, your wife, your daughter, your sister?

After the incident, it became obvious that a cover-up would have occurred, if at all possible. This, of course, begs the question, "How many incidents were covered up just because it was possible to do so?" Police tried to withhold the camcorder video and denied Miss Young access to the video until a judge forced its release. Officials also went to court to try to block the airing of the video on a CBS news special. Had these legal maneuvers worked, this atrocity would never have reached the light of day.

While this dehumanization process continues, the justice system stresses punitive measures as the solution to these problems. I don't know why this would be since they have not worked thus far. A restorative approach could be a possible positive attempt at rethinking the system. It seems that these flawed solutions just add to and continue dehumanizing real people.

If society has something to do with the success of many, can the converse be said? Does society contribute to the failure of many? Anjanette Young's experience has all the earmarks of a system that is in such need of reform that it is almost inconceivable that anyone could deny the need for change from top to bottom. Perhaps even that is not enough. Perhaps a new conception of race, law, and justice is in order. The process of dehumanization is deep, old, and intransigent and will demand energy, time, and imagination to dislodge and dismember. (2020)

CHAPTER 12

Questions

Asking Questions

Seek and you shall find. Knock and it will be opened to you.

—Luke 11:10

"Seek and you shall find" is about asking questions about many things but especially about truth, the meaning of life, and what life demands of us. Is there more than one truth, or is there one truth with different manifestations at different times and in different locations? Is it simplistic and arrogant for any one person, one group, one society, one church, or one political system to think or feel that it alone has the truth in this time and place, let alone forever?

When individuals, groups, organizations, and institutions act in this way, bad things can and usually do happen.

Motivations for these types of attitudes have to be called into question and examined carefully. We all know behaviors are influenced by both positive and negative factors and at times, a mix of these factors: love-hate, altruism-selfishness, greed-generosity, etc. The more questions we ask, the more complicated it gets. This can become confusing, but being puzzled, confused, or scared is no reason or excuse for not asking questions.

Another question is, how can we be sure of the truth of the answers we ascertain? In many cases, we can't be. You might be thinking, *Then why ask?* If we don't continue to ask, we can fail to take up the challenges of value-based living and will perhaps start to accept blindly, without a critical eye, the opinions and conclusions of others.

Is there an infallible guide for judging the truth of the answers we achieve? Perhaps not, but for each of us, conscience is the ultimate guide. What does that mean? I think it means we must do everything in our power to gather, study, and interpret all facets related to an issue. Even more importantly, we should establish for ourselves some guidelines or some principles by which to live. Some examples: do no harm; seek the freedom and welfare of all concerned, including oneself; be empathetic; be critical in your judgments; recognize there are many sides to an issue; be open; always ask questions. Perhaps Christian virtues and values could be a guide. These are only options; these are your decisions and yours alone to make. No one can dictate to you or anyone else what principles will guide one's life. The answer to the question must come from inside of you. Let your conscience be your guide.

In the end, the proof is in the pudding. If how you believe, act, and live leads all you've come in contact with to a better life, then you are on the right track, whichever track that might be. (2019)

A Mystery

Does God intervene in our lives? And if so, how does he accomplish this? How is he present in our lives? Is he personally, actively involved, or does God set all creation in motion and then step back and let things take their course? Is God actively involved in every minor detail of our existence, or does the truth of God's involvement fall somewhere in between? Is God responsible for evil as well as good? When things go well for us, do we thank God and give him credit? How about when evil befalls good people, who gets the blame? Did God dictate each and every word of Scripture? Is Scripture literally the Word of God, or are the human authors simply spiritual people grappling with the nature of man's relationship with his Creator? Should we take Scripture literally, or is its meaning the real point? Religion grapples with these questions all the time. Over the centuries, individuals and religions have constructed elaborate explanations in an attempt to plumb these mysteries. It seems a bit simplistic to give God the credit for all that is good and blame the *devil* and man for all that is wrong. All explanations seem to leave us with more questions than answers.

Many explanations regarding Scripture as the Word of God are like our suppositions about God's involvement in our lives. Some religions would have us believe that they alone have the answers. The fact of the matter is that we really don't know how God acts and influences our lives on a day-to-day basis or if he even does. These are all beliefs, not facts about which our certitude is spiritual but not provable. Christians believe Scripture is the Word of God written by men and inspired by God, but exactly how this is accomplished or whether Scripture is actually the Word of God is truly beyond us. Although this is a mystery, Scripture scholars and ordinary men and women of faith need to try to explain the process of both God's involvement in our lives and God's part in the authorship of scripture.

There are theories of inspiration that present simplistic explanations, somehow preventing the human authors from making errors. This could hardly be the case since it is obvious from factual errors, the inconsistencies in the chronology of events, and the anthropomorphic nature of God's activity that absolute literal truth is not the point or purpose of Scripture. Just as no one knows exactly how God involves himself in our lives, no one knows precisely how God influenced the writing of the Bible. What we can safely say is that we need to search for the meaning of both the Bible and human existence.

It is always helpful and healthy to explore different points of view regarding faith and our relationship with God. Asking questions and being open to new possibilities are always spiritually beneficial. Question everything!

Is it possible that God is totally involved with our lives and at the same time regulates creation through fixed laws in an orderly way? Did God influence Scripture and still allow the author to be free and self-expressive? Is our very birth, our very existence partially random? Did God choose this egg and this sperm, or did he allow nature and the natural process to take their course or both? When Jesus, in Scripture, asks us to pluck out our eye if it is the cause of sin, isn't he really asking us to earnestly avoid sin? In nature, does God choose one lion to live over another, or does he allow the natural law of survival of the fittest to govern these events? Did God allow Scripture to have errors and yet still communicate his truth? Does God choose the death of a particular individual at a particular time? Can God's plan, because of the mystery of freedom, allow for both good and evil? Do any of these scenarios even begin to explore the nature of God's involvement in Scripture and our lives?

God's participation in our lives and in Scripture is not so clear-cut. It is not a question of black and white even if we desperately want it to be. It is mysterious. (2008)

Religion
Not So Simple

Religion is a complex system by which man relates to the transcendent. It encompasses worship, sacred writings, moral precepts, and dogmatic beliefs within a community of like-minded people. Despite the fact that most religions purport to possess the truth about ultimate realities, it seems that all religions, although they contain truth, fall short of their claim. The truth they claim to possess in many cases pales when compared to reality. The beliefs we hold are only a partial, incomplete, and unclear view of the great mysteries into which religion delves. Complexity is in the very nature of religion. Even if God, Allah, or some transcendent being has revealed himself/herself/itself to us—either through creation, a prophet, a book, or an individual—it does not mean a church possesses all the truth there is to know about the transcendent. It does not even mean we have a clear and complete knowledge about creation or any other supposed revelation regarding the transcendent. God is constantly being revealed to us through the course of history.

When man tries to systematize or institutionalize religion or God, he begins to define, confine, and restrict the transcendent. Man should always remain aware that his efforts in this matter will always fall short of the mark. In his efforts to understand God, man attempts to limit the limitless, to define the indefinable, to express the inexpressible. In and of itself, there is nothing wrong with trying to come to a better understanding of God. We are finite beings trying to understand and relate to the infinite. Categories and definitions, tenants, and dogmas serve us well but of their very nature are limited, faulty, and prone to error and malformation. These theological constructs and categories try to explain and make understandable certain aspects of the God-man, man-God, and man-man relationships.

As Christians, we have, over the centuries, examined and defined our relationship to God in many different categories (e.g., sacraments, liturgy, Scripture, moral precepts, and church dogmas). We cannot and should not lock God into categories that are immutable and unchangeable; aside from being wrong, it opens us to possible absurd and catastrophic error.

For Christians, next to God and Jesus, the most fundamental category is the Bible. It is a book that Christians accept as foundational to their faith. However, even among Christians, there is much confusion, misunderstanding, and difference of opinion regarding the Bible. Some Christians take a literal and fundamentalist approach to Scripture. Other Christians believe a great deal of the Scripture should be taken literally with some exceptions (e.g., "*If your right eye causes you to sin gouge it out and throw it away*" [Matt. 5:29]). Still, other Christians understand the Bible to be a book that puts us in touch with the sacred through symbols, myths, metaphors, parables, stories, and other literary forms. All of these approaches help lead Christians to their foundational beliefs about God and our existence. Any approach that allows us to encounter the truth of the Bible by extracting its meaning and sense is an approach worthy of consideration.

Over and over again, we see questions that suggest inconsistencies in Scripture that might cause us to be skeptical if we take a literal approach. For example, is the Eucharist the body and blood of Christ? Did God create the world in six days? Does God position himself on one side or the other in a war? Does the sun revolve around the earth? Do we really get whatever we pray for? Can faith move mountains? How do we explain violence perpetrated by the Israelites on their neighbors in the name of God? These suggested inconsistencies are hard to explain unless we temper our religious beliefs with honesty and humility about our ability to know and understand the ways of the transcendent. If we have such divergence of opinion about a foundational book, how can we be so dogmatic about other religious questions?

Religion by its very nature not only involves the relationship between God and man but also includes the relationship between man and man and man and nature. People of religious belief are faithful to God's Word only insofar as they actually and truly reflect God's love, mercy, and justice in the real world. If dogma, belief, and ritual harm people or degrade individuals or classes of people, we can be quite sure that we are out of touch with the truth. If a church or religion practices repression instead of freedom, closedness instead of openness, suppression of intellectual pursuits instead of promotion of intellectual curiosity, then we should be suspicious of the truth they proclaim to teach. Where is their faith in the power of the truth?

Some dogmas that accrue to religion today are suspect and have little to do with the essentials of religion. What we believe, for the most part gains its credibility and relevancy only in relation to how we act. John tells us in the simplest of terms, "*If someone says he loves God but hates his brother he is a liar. For he cannot love God, whom he has not seen, if he does not love his brother, whom he has seen*" (1 John 4:20–22). (2010)

Natural Law Theory and Religion

Pope Benedict XVI recently referenced the natural law, to support his opinion, in a lengthy article dealing with the sexual abuse scandal in the Catholic Church. Natural law theory was a back burner issue for most people and perhaps still is for many. The Catholic Church has treated natural law theory as a guide that leads to truths that never change. It is basically seen as a standard for determining right from wrong, and that which flows from it are immutable truths.

The Catholic Church never uses the word *theory* when referring to the natural law. It is a foregone conclusion that it is simply fact when in reality, it is still a theory. The laws of nature are seen and interpreted in different ways by different people. It is not a hard and fast fact but rather a particular way of looking at how we determine right from wrong or how we believe God communicates what are the right and wrong actions.

There is confusion about what is natural and what is moral. Mixing nature and morality can be somewhat confusing. Nature is not necessarily moral, and morality is not necessarily natural. An article in *US Catholic* said of natural law, "*Put simply, natural law argues that nature reveals the difference between good and evil.*" But who gets to decide what is natural?

For St. Thomas Aquinas, the most fundamental principle of the natural law was good is to be done, and evil is to be avoided. The question "*What is the natural law?*" is never defined in the catechism of the Catholic Church; it is only described (see the *Catechism of the Roman Catholic Church* pages 526–529). Natural law is supposedly written in the hearts of men and women and is immutable and permanent. This is of course another supposition. It enables men and women to discern, by reason, the good and evil, the truth and the lie. It seems natural law is left vague enough for diversity of opinion.

Some religions believe we can see God's will for human activity in nature. Christianity seems to believe the natural law is immutable and unchangeable, that some things are always wrong and can never be right. This may be so, but determining which are always wrong and which are always right may be more difficult than first believed. Natural law is used to discern truths that are absolute and objective in all circumstances. The natural law is often used to denounce "unnatural acts," which are labeled immoral. More often than not, the natural law is used with regard to sexual activity and reproductive rights. Pope Paul VI used the natural law argument in his condemnation of birth control in his encyclical *Humana Vitae*. There is no question that activities thought to be wrong years ago are perfectly legitimate and moral today (e.g., interracial marriage).

The opposite is also true. Activities thought to be moral and correct years ago are now seen as immoral and wrong today (e.g., slavery). It is a convoluted thought process that tries to use logic and logical progressions to justify positions, but somehow, reality does not cooperate because it is not always logical.

Scripture was also used erroneously to support the conclusions of natural law. In the above examples, these activities were always wrong or right. It is just that men and women using natural law and Scripture have interpreted them differently and incorrectly. Is there some type of immutable right and wrong, or is it just our inability to judge right and wrong in an infallible way? We would all agree that killing is wrong, yet we have for many years called self-defense moral. We call war immoral, and yet we justify it through intellectual and moral gymnastics. Some still argue about the rightness or wrongness of state execution. Right to life is seen as absolute; its proponents proclaim the goodness of life while at the same time condemn in vitro fertilization based on the fact that it is not a natural process and, therefore, is immoral. Why can't institutions who hold life to be sacred see the life-giving reality of in vitro fertilization? Activities contradicting natural processes are going on all the time and are seen by almost all people as moral (e.g., blood transfusions and medical transplants). None of these things are found in the natural order but are clearly accepted by most Christian churches as moral. There is much room for discussion here.

The natural law theory seems to be applied by Christians in an obsessive way to areas of sexuality and reproductive rights. At one time, when it came to "sexual sins," there was no such thing as poverty of matter. Anything having to do with physical sex outside of marriage was seen as worthy of everlasting punishment. This today is seen by most people as absurd.

As the world has become technically and scientifically more sophisticated, natural law and morality can no longer be based on literally and narrowly interpreted Scripture and a moral code that does not hold up under scrutiny. Moral questions are more complex and nuanced. Natural law positions tend, consciously or subconsciously, to be considered absolute. Natural law theory is a construct devised to determine right from wrong and to support and reinforce a moral code developed over the centuries by Christian institutions.

The natural law theory was first developed by the Greeks who concluded that through the observation of nature and the use of reason, one could live in conformity with nature. Christians adopted the natural law theory from the ancients and came to believe that through observation of nature, one could deduce aspects of God's will to which women and men must adhere. Even the premise that God is revealing through nature what is right and wrong is a questionable supposition. There are many examples in nature of behavior that Christians would not care to emulate. Christians reject homosexuality, yet homosexuality is well documented in nature among animal species (e.g., chimpanzees). Survival of the fittest, one of the first laws of nature, is not seen as moral behavior for human beings. Fitness should not be a prerequisite for survival.

In many ways, Christianity has made natural law theory static and inflexible when in reality, it is flexible and dynamic. In some ways, it is an attempt to simplify and universalize the process of making moral judgments. Instead, it makes moral judgments simplistic and void of intellectual and rational scrutiny. This, in large part, is due to the irrational fear of relativism, which for some would complicate the process of moral decision-making. It would mean, for some institutions, a loss of control in dictating behavior to its members. It betrays a lack of trust, which implies that we cannot use our minds and wills to analyze and implement correct moral judgments. We would have to use our intellects to think and reason in order to come to judgments about our behavior and choices based on the cumulative knowledge and wisdom available at the time. It would mean that individuals could make judgments and decisions that don't agree with ancient institutions.

At one time the Bible was understood literally and, by some, still is and thus is seen as a literal and reliable source for understanding nature and reality. This is no longer the case. The complexity of the world and the discoveries of science have made a literal interpretation of the Bible untenable for thinking individuals. Questions people are asking are: What is evil? What is good? What is natural? Who decides what is good, evil, and natural? Who makes the rules and why? Who decides what is right and what is wrong? The idea that nature gives the answers to hard questions, let alone God's will for us, is no longer a valid modus operandi. What is natural is no longer as simple and clear-cut as it seemed to be as little as one hundred years ago. Natural law, which seemed to work and be accepted in the church of the '40s and '50s, now seems woefully inadequate.

Within Christianity, there are at least two approaches to natural law. One is traditional and based on authority, which attempts to justify traditional teachings through an appeal to God's will as if God's will is up for grabs! The second approach looks to contemporary experience and reason in light of science and newly gained knowledge. After all is said and done, openness, honesty, and dialogue among all concerned parties is the way to a more honest approach to natural law theory. (2019)

Natural Law and Related Topics

In religious terms, natural law is seen as a participation in eternal law, which, in turn, is seen as God's own mind. It is the law located between eternal law and human or positive law, which is the law that governs society. Some see it as a fundamental intuition regarding basic goods and right behavior. It is a deep common sensibility in relation to right and wrong. Given this definition, it is dependent on the existence of God. In any case, natural law presupposes eternal law for religious people. For many nonreligious people, God is not a necessary ingredient for the existence of natural law. Natural law is just that; it is natural; it is part of nature. Natural law is said to reside in man, placed there by God or based on inner sensibilities that we call human nature. These laws exist in both man and nature. For example, "Thou shall not kill" is a law residing in the hearts of men and women while the law of gravity or the rotation of the earth around the sun lies outside of man.

Human nature and natural law are two different entities, which are intrinsically connected. Human nature can be defined as general characteristics, feelings, and behavioral traits of humankind, regarded as shared by all humans. Just as with natural law, human nature is complex. Diverse opinions regarding human nature are held by many. Some feel human nature is basically good with an inclination toward evil while others believe it to be evil or maladjusted with a tendency toward good, etc. Many people treat human nature as a static reality because it makes reality easier to deal with when rules are hard and fast.

However, like natural law, human nature is dynamic and, therefore, difficult to define and not easily pinned down. Just as with natural law, there may be basic unchanging realities; however, so far, we don't seem to have the ability to ascertain in an absolute way, with unanimity, what they are in all circumstances and in all times. There is much disagreement, even in the somewhat simple definition of terms, let alone the reality behind these terms.

To make things more confusing, our forefathers spoke of human rights that they claimed were self-evident such as life, liberty, and the pursuit of happiness. These were considered to be self-evident rights of all men without exception. Life, liberty, and the pursuit of happiness are the most well-known of these rights, but there are many who hold that free speech, freedom of religion, and the right to bear arms are also among those inalienable rights.

I think we must give the founders credit over and above religious leaders in their modus operandi in coming to these beliefs. The founders used a posteriori thinking rather than a priori thinking in coming to their conclusions. That is, rather than observing reality and coming to conclusions, religions and theologians posited what they thought reality should be (oftentimes based on Scripture and inaccurate scientific data) and then looked for elements that would support their theory. The Founding Fathers looked at reality and reasoned from it what they believed were inalienable rights. In both cases, reason was an important part of the process but not always.

Pursuit of happiness can mean a multitude of things to different people. Although life and liberty are more evident than the pursuit of happiness or freedom of speech, all these rights are open to interpretation and in many cases have exceptions. Inalienable rights are those held to be rights that can never be forfeited. Are they seen by all people as fundamental rights of human beings? Are they seen by all people as the basis for moral interactions between people? Are they irrevocable? Did the founders know all the inalienable rights of individuals? Do we know all of man's inalienable rights? Do they ever change? Do they evolve? Are there exceptions? Are they semi-absolute? Does time and place matter in reference to these rights? Do we know all these human rights, and are they all self-evident? Does culture affect these rights? When universal health care is available to all, does it become an inalienable right? Did our forefathers purposely leave this question only partially answered? This is just a short list of questions regarding natural human rights.

If we throw conscience into the mix, these questions become even more complex. Conscience can be viewed as a feeling or voice seen as acting as a guide to rightness or wrongness of one's behavior. It is seen by some as the final and ultimate guide to correct action. But is a correct or true conscience really correct or true if it is not in possession of accurate information? An informed conscience often requires study and fact-finding. Judgment and insight into a particular issue are necessary in order to make a correct decision regarding appropriate behavior. The more we question, the more complex these discussions become.

When trying to figure right from wrong and good from evil it is incumbent on individuals and groups to approach the discussion with humility, reason, and judgment, recognizing the sensibilities within the nature of women and men. Even when this thoughtful process is used, interpretation of things that seem absolute can be cause for different people to come to different conclusions. Open, honest, and well-meaning people can and do come to different conclusions about what is right and wrong based on natural law and human nature. Even when the rules seem hard and fast, people interpret them differently. There is no absolute authority, be it an individual or an institution, who can honestly tell people what is the absolute truth and right action in all cases and at all times. Outstanding individuals and institutions can help guide people regarding this process but cannot be an infallible source of right and wrong and good and evil.

George Will, in his book *The Conservative Sensibility*, states that "*beneath myriad degrees of culture there is fixed nature which neither improves nor regresses.*" Whether George Will is correct or not, there seems to be little doubt that there are some general guidelines found in human nature that many societies accept as valid. We can certainly learn from nature at large that gives some clear and some not-so-clear guidelines. Human beings seem to have a propensity to simplify the complex. It is through constant observation, habitual interaction, critical analysis, and a sensitivity to history that we come to know what is right and wrong, what is good and what is evil.

The wisdom of those who have gone before us is no little contribution to the reservoir of human knowledge concerning these issues. This is an ongoing process, with time and circumstances being part of the procedure. It is through this process that we gather insight into natural law, human nature, and human rights. (2019)

Why Did God Become Man?

I believe that institutions, once formed, are subject to unintentional and sometimes intentional error and are plagued with corruption of one sort or another (lust for power, control, money, sex, etc.) This holds true for traditional religions as well as nontraditional and unorthodox religions. I am convinced that St. Anselm's answer to this most important question was an unintentional mistake given his background. The fact that he was born of royalty during the Middle Ages greatly influenced his theology and spirituality.

Because mistakes, distortions, and corruptions are inherent to religion and institutions, I do not embrace religions and institutions in an absolute fashion. The most fundamental concepts held about God seem to be distorted and insufficient. I, like Anselm, am a product of a Christian environment as it exists in a particular time and place and feels a new paradigm is needed. A new paradigm will in no way solve all the mysteries of God and religion, but if we are to grow in our understanding of God and religion, paradigm change is a must.

The Christian concept of God handed down to us over the centuries is in some critical ways deficient or confused. There seems to be a comingling of traditional theology with some deep-rooted misconceptions. We are working under a paradigm that is firmly rooted in Anselm's answer to this famous question. Misconceptions, mistakes, and distortions have strongly influenced Anselm's theology. These may not be seen as obvious problems by many because we have been raised with these flaws that have become part and parcel of our belief system. For me, the awareness of these misconceptions came slowly over many years. Some believers do see these flaws and still remain members of these religions and institutions. They have made adjustments that allow them to stay connected even though they are aware of these problems.

For many, these institutions are family; they are home. People tend to modify and adjust their beliefs, which may turn out in the end to contradict the beliefs of their church or religion. With this adjustment and accommodation, they are able to remain connected. The leaders (priests, ministers, imams, and rabbis) may demand strict adherence to theological and practical rules and regulations. Little do they know or understand the accommodations many of their flock have made. These accommodations allow people to be flexible and free enough to ignore certain aspects of religious belief, which, in some cases, if known by church officials, would invalidate their affiliation or end in excommunication.

I am a social and emotional Catholic. However, I no longer conceive of faith as a belief in dogmas and theologies that stress adherence to rules and regulations. For instance, by proclamation, the Catholic Church has declared herself infallible in areas of faith and morals. Rational, thinking people look at many of the Catholic Church's pronouncements as irrational and outdated in light of modern science, biblical interpretation, psychology, and spirituality.

Over the centuries, religions have added many layers of theological thought and speculation as if it were absolute truth. As time passed, rules and beliefs were multiplied. This process has obscured the real heart of religion and spirituality, as outlined in Marcus Borg's masterful book *The Heart of Christianity*. These are the things we must keep in the forefront: love, not hate; freedom, not domination; justice, not retribution; mercy, not retaliation; compassion, not inhumanity; sharing, not hoarding; tolerance, not intolerance; humility, not arrogance; peace, not chaos; patience, not short-temperedness; along with the understanding that God is a mystery beyond our comprehension. Many religious people see these above virtues as weaknesses, but these characteristics are most evident in Jesus and his gospel. These are the life-giving principles of religion and spirituality.

I am most familiar with the religions of Western civilization. When I speak of the concept of God, it is from this background, although I think this application is somewhat universal. The paradigm we live and operate under started to develop with Constantine when the church and state became basically one institution. Contradictions and misconceptions started to weave their way into the fabric of Christianity. We believed that God sent his Son out of love, and yet we act in many ways out of power and domination, which speaks volumes about what we really believe. We say God is a God of love, but in fact, many Christians see him as a God of retribution, one who seeks appeasement and reparation for offenses.

This was a deadly comixing of misconceptions and untested theology. The result was a distorted view of religion and spirituality. This faulty conceptualization of God leads us to demand retribution rather than forgiveness and mercy. We say God is merciful and forgiving, but we seem to value retribution over mercy and punishment over forgiveness. Is this in part because in our subconscious we have accepted Anselm's answer? Just below the surface, our faulty concept of God, which came to us by way of Anselm, is exposed many times by our true beliefs and actions. All of us act on occasion in contradiction to what we think we believe. Perhaps we see these virtues as aspirational, which allows us to do some terrible things to our fellow human beings. It is difficult to navigate the complexities of motivation, but we owe it to ourselves, our sisters and brothers, and God to examine deeply and in detail what we say we believe and how it relates to how we act.

Richard Rohr, in his daily meditations, speaks of the paradigm Anselm created to explain why God became man. Was it love, mercy, forgiveness, and justice? Yes and no. Certainly, Anselm would say God became man out of love, but in his paradigm, he, for all practical purposes, diminishes and almost ignores love as the prime motivating force for the Incarnation. He paints a picture of a God who requires equivalent atonement and satisfaction. He sees God as analogous to a king with infinitely more dignity than his subjects. He sees men as analogous to peasants of the day. He sees man's sin as analogous to a peasant's insult to a king. It was unthinkable for Anselm that a peasant could make reparation for an offense to a king or royal. The only solution to this dilemma, for Anselm, was for God to require someone of his stature to make amends—not what we would expect from a loving, merciful, and forgiving God.

Anselm believed the offense to God's dignity was so immense that only a divine being could repair the insult in an equivalent fashion. The paradigm was faulty and incorrect because it was slavishly connected to the narrow concepts of the day. This faulty paradigm has had a negative influence on Christianity to this day. Anselm saw God as a God of retribution and reparation rather than a God of mercy and forgiveness. It was only after reparation for this offense was satisfied by the death of his Son that man could enter again into a positive relationship with God. Instead of a theology of unconditional love, mercy, and willing vulnerability, a theology based on the feudal system of fear, retribution, and punishment became the most influential paradigm we have lived under to this day. The consequences of this theological choice have reverberated in a negative way through the halls of history. This paradigm has given us a false notion of justice in which we still see God as stern and demanding.

St. Francis of Assisi (1182–1226). The reason Jesus became man and died for us is love and all-embracing mercy, according to Francis. Jesus and his Father offered women and men a love and unity with themselves beyond our wildest dreams. Even though we have rejected God in the most violent way (crucifixion), we are still graced with love, mercy, and forgiveness, which is diametrically opposed to Anselm's vision of punishment, payment, and atonement. Here is the good news: God's response to this rejection was and still is one of forgiveness, mercy, and love, not punishment and abandonment.

Francis seems to indicate that mercy and love are the motivating factors for the incarnation with little concern for repayment and retribution. Hard to believe, but this is the unconditional love of God. The most fundamental answer to Anselm's question should have an intimate connection to the virtues of love, justice, mercy, compassion, tolerance, freedom, humility, peace, and patience. If this is so, then Anselm's paradigm is fundamentally flawed. His God of retribution, atonement, and punishment is a faulty creation of man's making.

Some might object by saying what about justice? For Francis, mercy trumps justice. Some may ask what about the Bible? Francis would seem to indicate that a reading of the Bible with the above virtues in mind leaves little room for condemnation and punishment. A prayerful and thoughtful reading of the Bible will radically change our concept of God and will bring us to a more loving, kinder God. All that has accrued to religion and spirituality is not necessarily true religion or true spirituality. True religion and spirituality are practicing these virtues with humility, selflessness, and believing in a God without malice or anger but rather a God who herself/himself divinizes these virtues and infuses Scripture with divine love.

This is, I believe, the new paradigm we are searching for today. Who knows what actually awaits us in the afterlife, but I have complete and absolute faith in the loving and merciful God of St. Francis, who will always extend to us unending, infinite love and mercy because we are his children, the daughters and sons of his creation. (2019)

Continuing Questions

One day ago, January 26, 2020, Kobe Bryant, forty-one years old, and his daughter Gianna, thirteen years old, were killed in a helicopter crash that also took the lives of seven other people. This was a significant event, especially since Kobe was an international sports figure. Even if he were not a famous sports personality, it was still a devastating event.

Although devastating, it was not a singular event in terms of disasters and suffering. On any given day in the United States of America, over seven thousand people die; throughout the world, some 150,000 people die from natural causes, accidents, and other mishaps. Millions of people suffer and die each year without the publicity of Kobe's death. Death and suffering are part and parcel of life, but they continue to raise questions about the existence of God and his potential involvement in the human drama.

Only two days before this terrible accident, I had completed an essay on belief and disbelief. Many philosophers and theologians and common, ordinary people grapple with the idea of a good, loving, merciful God who stands in juxtaposition to evil, suffering, and even death. Many religious people somehow seem to be able to live with this concept of the existence of a God that wills, or at least allows, suffering and evil. They even posit suffering as a necessary component of the nature of God. In Bishop Casper's book *The God of Jesus Christ*, suffering seems to be an important thesis. Whether his speculations are correct or not is really not the issue. The importance of the question is its universality; evil, suffering, and death touch all people.

After giving this question much thought, I continue to get stuck on the notion that even if this suffering is part and parcel of God's plan, it is still very difficult to accept. One aspect of this problem that disturbed me greatly is the thought that some might hold that the reward of everlasting life and happiness will be so incredible that it will wipe out all past trials and tribulations. However, the fact that this evil and suffering took place and caused real pain and real suffering for millions of people can never be taken back. Not even God can undo what has been done. Genocide, war, poverty, slavery, etc. cannot be undone! These things are real! Real people experience real pain and suffering. Anguish is experienced! All this has happened and is still happening and will continue to happen as long as mankind will survive. None of it can be undone! Where is the love? Where is the mercy? Where is the compassion?

All the answers we have formulated come up short. These questions persist; they continue to plague us. They truly remain unsolved, and all the philosophizing and all the theologizing has not, for many, produced an adequate explanation for God's existence or for the reality of suffering and evil and its effects, especially if God does exist. It is our fate and destiny to continue to struggle with these unanswerable questions. (2020)

Justice

While trying to examine the nature of God's love, the question of justice comes into the equation. If God exists and is actually all-loving and all-forgiving, what is the role of justice in the scheme of things? If an individual acts in a way that, in traditional Christianity, has been seen as worthy of eternal punishment, how do we justify an all-forgiving and all-loving God? Can God be just and all-forgiving and all-loving at the same time?

Justice can be defined as a morally fair and right state of everything in which all persons are treated equally without favoritism or prejudice. Justice demands a certain level of respect for the other. Within the concept of justice resides the doorway to the golden rule: "*Do unto others as you would have them do unto you*" (Matt. 7:12).

At a certain period in history, justice came to be associated with punishment that, in some fashion, would make up for the harm done to another. It was believed that punishment somehow and to some extent would restore balance to the moral order.

The Jewish and Christian scriptures are replete with the theme of justice. *"And what does the Lord require of you but to do justice, love kindness and walk humbly with God"* (Micah 6:8). The Bible calls for justice almost two thousand times. Jeremiah, Ezekiel, Isaiah, and Hosea all stress the absolute necessity for justice. Justice, of its nature, must be applied to religion, politics, social issues, and the like.

We will concern ourselves with two types of justice: retributive and restorative. Retributive justice, derived from the word *retribution*, emphasizes a system of punishments designed to exact payment for offenses with little emphasis on rehabilitation or reconciliation. It seems to be a negatively based solution to violations of justice. Restorative justice, from the word *restore*, on the other hand, seems to emphasize the endeavor to restore the relationship between offender and victim. It attempts to balance, through positive means, the harmony lost when the unjust occurrence took place. Restorative justice focuses on the rehabilitation and reconciliation of relationships. At the heart of restorative justice is forgiveness.

In Desmond Tutu's book *No Future without Forgiveness*, which deals with the horrendous injustices of apartheid, he states, "*Ultimately goodness and laughter and peace and compassion and gentleness and forgiveness and reconciliation will have the last word and prevail over their ghastly counterparts.*" He doesn't cling to anger or hatred. He has no need or desire for retribution but rather looks to restoration of relationships through a loving forgiveness. This does not deny that anger and hatred are not part of the process but a part that must be worked through until we get to forgiveness.

It appears, today, the emphasis in our society is on retributive justice. Society seems to be trying to make punishment equal to the harm done. In most cases, if not all, no amount of punishment will balance the scales of justice. Perhaps looking at punishment as a solution to the problem of injustice is the wrong approach. The role of justice is to set forth the minimum required of us with regard to judgment, fairness, and equality. Justice contains the seeds of love. True justice is the threshold of love. Justice at its apex is mercy, compassion, and forgiveness.

As human beings, we struggle with the question of justice and injustice. Between justice and injustice, there is, for us, a tension that always remains difficult. Ultimately, if we believe in God, we must look to the concept contained in James 2:13: "*For judgment will be without mercy to anyone who has shown no mercy; mercy triumphs over judgment.*"

No matter how difficult it is for us to acknowledge that God is a God of restorative justice, the facts point in that direction. He is a God who saves all, restores all. Christian Scripture seems to point overwhelmingly to a God who takes justice into account and ultimately comes down on the side of mercy, forgiveness, and love. Should we not rejoice? (2020)

Do We Really Want a Solution?

A couple of days before my birthday, I received a text message from a longtime friend and fellow essayist regarding a movement called NoNotoriety. A married couple, Tom and Caren Teves lost their son Alex in the mass murder in an Aurora, Colorado, movie theater on February 16, 2019. It is a sad fact that we, as a nation, have failed to address the gun safety issue in a broad and unified way. It is not just that we, over the last twenty years, have been unable to address the problem, but it is the fact that we, as a nation and as a government, have resisted mightily to even consider, in a meaningful and comprehensive way, how to deal with this blight on our nation and culture. Politically, we have not come together in a sincere, honest, and respectful way. I cannot believe that people of good faith could not come together in unity and openness to exchange opinions, ideas, and theories in an effort to present to the nation a plan that would be reasonable, rational, and respectful.

After all is said and done, we are talking about human life here. We are all sons and daughters, brothers and sisters, mothers and fathers. We are all related not only in blood but in humanity. We are presently twenty-some years since Columbine without a comprehensive solution. Even more terrifying is the fact that gun violence is worse than ever. How can this be?

As we approach the 2020 election, the issue of gun safety is still with us. This April 20, 2020, will mark twenty-one years since Columbine. Over these years, we have made little progress toward stemming the tide of gun violence in America. There is little doubt that this is a complex problem but a problem that could certainly be mitigated and possibly solved if not completely, at least substantially. As with health care, racism, immigration, and border security, we, as a nation, cannot come together to solve these problems. I believe there are some fundamental reasons for this situation. The main and most fundamental reasons are greed, power, and privilege sustained by the status quo.

Greed, power, and privilege among our politicians and others inhibit us from honestly seeking solutions to this and many other problems. Bills are rejected by either party, disallowing any discussion that might speak of a solution. Fearmongering, demagoguery, and the like are used to frighten people into seeing others as threats. Fear is generated on all sides of the issue in order to maintain the status quo. Why? What is the significance of the status quo?

The status quo, for both political parties, is in reality an important entity. The status quo protects wealth, power, and privilege. Both parties seek their agenda in spite of negative consequences for a large majority of people. Why wouldn't people in general and politicians, in particular, seek solutions to gun safety in this country? Why wouldn't Americans look to countries that have had gun control issues and have addressed, to a greater or lesser degree, how to solve or mitigate the consequences. We have not looked seriously at other countries that have dealt more successfully with health care, racism, and immigration. Are we so arrogant as to feel that we have nothing to learn from each other? We are not obliged to act like other countries, but perhaps we could learn from their experience.

It is my contention that the status quo that protects money, power, and privilege is the main cause for this lack of resolve regarding these issues. Individuals, corporations, and governments promote divisions among the common folks in order to foster their valued positions. Martin Luther King Jr. tells us,

> *The oppressor never voluntarily gives freedom to the oppressed... You have to work for it... Freedom is never given to anybody. For the oppressor has you in domination because he plans to keep you there, and he never voluntarily gives it up... Privileged classes never give up their privileges without resistance. It is not done voluntarily, but it is done through the pressure that comes about from people who are oppressed.*

You might think this quote of Martin Luther King Jr. does not apply to the issues of gun safety, racism, immigration, and the like. It, in fact, does apply to these conditions but is rarely recognized for what it is: oppression. It is through the status quo that institutions, businesses, and individuals maintain their wealth, power, and privilege. In many cases, fear of loss or a lessening of assets demands maintenance of the status quo.

We are all guilty—the left, the right, and all of us in between who do not seek equitable and fair solutions to our multiple problems. The word "oppressor," when applied to us, is offensive, and it should be. We cannot see ourselves or conceive of ourselves as oppressors. However, when we fail to seek equitable and fair solutions, even if unwittingly, we are not in fact insignificant oppressors. It seems to be incumbent upon all those who have privilege, power, and wealth to hang on to it with all their might. We can see that in this way, the status quo protects those in the privileged class and holds down the poor and disadvantaged. There is a moral imperative to bring those less privileged people into a more reasonable and equitable situation for our sake as well as theirs.

Regarding the gun safety issue, liberals have made only a limited effort over the last twenty years to sit down and seriously attempt to solve this problem. To stay in power, the left has allowed, consciously or subconsciously, a non-resolution of this issue to continue because it serves a purpose, which is the maintenance of the status quo that fosters and protects the position of wealth power and privilege.

MSNBC, Fox, and CNN are all guilty of fanning the flames of discontent because it is good for business. The common folks in this country have been the victims of this greed, power, and privilege—e.g., lies of the cigarette industry who had no regard for the common man's health, the banking industry who had no regard for the financial well-being of the poor and middle class.

Another example is Wells Fargo's account fraud scandal of 2016. Michael Milken—convicted of security fraud in 1989, released from jail and pardoned by President Trump in February 2020—is somehow worth $3.8 billion. Wow! College admissions scandal: perpetrators of this crime were all people of money, power, and privilege.

The list of abuse by people of wealth, power, and privilege goes on and on (e.g., Jerry Sandusky, Jeffrey Epstein, Anthony Weiner, Harvey Weinstein, and John Edwards). The list of institutions is also lengthy: Facebook, involved in the "fake news" scandal; Monsanto, the producer of harmful chemicals over years: DDT, PBC, and Agent Orange. Insurance company scandals like Cigna were investigated for artificially inflated medical costs, causing some consumers to pay as much as ten times the true cost of their medical services. Other companies that are more concerned about profits than consumer satisfaction are as follows: Sprint, Foxconn Tech, University of Phoenix, NFL, and Fox Entertainment, just to name a few. Their illegality impacts disproportionately the poor and disadvantaged.

This widespread lack of concern for financial health, economic, health, and emotional well-being is widespread but, in many ways, lies just beneath the consciousness of the average middle-class person. This is by design. Large numbers of people in the middle class are complicit in this oppression at least implicitly, if not explicitly. If a country with our resources cannot make real progress for gun safety in twenty years, I believe it is purposeful and not just because it is a complex problem. It somehow serves the right, the left, and the middle class to maintain the status quo. The poor are the only people who do not benefit from the status quo. We were able to put a man on the moon shortly after the Russians launched Sputnik. It seems to me that if we really wanted to solve these problems, we have the wherewithal to do so. A wall, a war, a difference of opinion, a diminution of rights, and denial of reality are not solutions to our problems. Rather communication, cooperation respect, hard work, tolerance, compromise, moral rectitude, and the recognition of injustice are the tools of correction. All these means of resolving problems are being cast aside by the lust for power money and privilege. If we do not seek the high road in these matters, we are dooming our nation and society to the long list of nations and societies that have been recorded as being on the wrong side of history, to say nothing of the grave injustices endured by our poorer citizens. (2020)

Paradox
What Is It?

Paradox is a seemingly absurd self-contradictory statement or proposition that when investigated or explained may prove to be well-founded or true. A statement or proposition that, despite sound (or apparently sound) reasoning from acceptable premises, leads to a conclusion that seems senseless, logically unacceptable, or self-contradictory. *"Truth is honey which is bitter"* (Oscar Wilde) or Matthew 16:25, *"For whoever would save his life, will lose it."* How can one hold two opposing ideas in one's mind and heart at the same time? It seems like a contradiction or an impossibility. Is it what we call ambivalence, or is it something more? I find myself in this state of being quite frequently. Can one believe in God and at the same time not believe in God? Can one believe and disbelieve simultaneously?

Whether God actually exists or not, and whether we believe in God or not can change everything and is truly relevant. The distinction between belief in God and the actual fact of whether God exists in many ways dictates our beliefs and behavior. I live with this tension on a daily basis. I don't see it as a negative but rather as a constant stimulus regarding truth-seeking concerning God, religion, and all reality. The deeper we get into this, the more complicated it gets. It can change our view of creation, our view of our final end, and everything in between and beyond, if there is a beyond. It feels like more than just ambivalence. There is a conflict between "evidence" that strongly supports both beliefs. We should realize that they are beliefs. This tension exists precisely because they are not provable facts.

I was raised in a moderately strict Catholic tradition. The question was not did God exist; that was a foregone conclusion. The fact is there was very little questioning going on in those days. There was virtually no questioning of God's existence or the validity of religion, at least not in a public way. The idea of asking a question like this was repressed; for most, it existed only in the unspoken recesses of the mind. It was a closet issue, similar to the question of gay rights.

I, like many, suffered from a sort of brainwashing. The pressure to believe without questioning was mostly unspoken yet enormous. I had accepted and embraced the notion of a personal God for most of my life and probably, in my heart of hearts, still do. My beliefs today are not as simple as they were as little as ten years ago. There are too many unanswered and perhaps unanswerable questions for me to accept religion and God as presented. A modicum of humility dictates a modest approach to these issues. The knowledge of mankind, although vastly greater than mine, is still limited and finite. Hubris is the gateway to ignorance. Excessive pride and unrealistic self-confidence can lead to self-deception and a distortion of reality. It took almost fifty years for me to seriously consider, in a critical way, my beliefs and their foundations and implications.

For the last twenty years (2000–2020) I have been considering the existence of God and how, if "he" exists, to make sense of the claims of religion, God's relationship to us, and our relationship to him. Considering my strong beliefs and background, there should be no surprise regarding the importance of this issue for me. I am no longer a traditional Catholic or Christian. I am, however, Christian in many ways. I do believe Scripture and much of Christian tradition have a great deal to teach us about living our lives in a loving, moral, and ethical way. It is the contradictions within Christianity and religion, in general, that cause and have caused philosophers and theologians to ask question after question about the truth of many religious beliefs and teachings. Is the need for something beyond ourselves so strong that we created God and religion, or is it that the existence of God and religion are so strong that it is impossible for us not to embrace them?

These questions are the basis of my dilemma; for some, belief without answers is what they are most comfortable with, and this, I believe, is a valid approach to religion.

Sometimes there are no answers, just faith. We should not live in fear and trepidation of a God who is beyond our capacity to know. It is good to live in optimism and hope rather than in despair and pessimism even though we live in an unsure reality. Some will reject this type of questioning out of hand, but for those who are willing, it can be a door to an honest evaluation of belief leading to a more thoughtful and reasoned approach to reality.

If we ascribe to the maxim "*life is a mystery to be lived, not a problem to be solved*," as Kierkegaard stated, then we human beings, more than likely in this lifetime, will never know all the answers to all the questions. (2020)

Free Will

As I started this essay, I read an article in *The Atlantic* magazine as part of my research. The article "There Is No Such Thing as Free Will" (June 26, 2016, issue) by Brian Cave is excellent, well written, well researched, thoughtful, and challenging. If you are interested in the notion of free will, it is a must read. My background as a Catholic and a priest firmly established my belief in the notion of free will. My objective here is not to discard free will or to denigrate scientific discovery but rather to raise awareness of the possible complementary nature of religion and science. This is not the first time that science and religion seemed to be at odds with each other. It is our obligation to investigate all possibilities while at the same time realizing that science and religion are not mutually exclusive in this matter. Scientific knowledge regarding free will is evolving and may help us understand this important concept. I am suggesting that we be open to seeing free will in a potentially different way.

We have, for centuries, held what we feel are hard and fast "rules" to live by only to find out, on more than one occasion, that through science, reason, thought, reflection, and dialogue, our positions have changed. We should not, out of fear, reject advances in scientific knowledge without at least giving them a fair hearing. What at first may seem like shocking new information, which seems to contradict what we have taken more or less as gospel, may give us new insight into the mystery of life and perhaps make our reality more truthful and honest. Because the concept of free will is so important, we should certainly hesitate to promote an all-out dismissal of free will.

Free will can be defined as the power of acting without constraint of necessity or fate, the ability to act at one's own discretion. Individuals to be held accountable for their actions must have the ability to act in true freedom or at least enough freedom to outweigh any impediments to that freedom. Exactly what free will is or means is an ongoing question. If we understood it and all its ramifications, much of the mystery of motivation, human behavior, the nature of man, and to some extent, the nature of God would be more clearly understood and somewhat less mysterious. It is critical to understand the importance of free will. It is the linchpin that keeps the wheels on the bus. Without it, would the elements of our modern moral structures and institutions be in peril?

Free will has been considered by philosophers and theologians for over two thousand years—Plato, Thomas Aquinas, Thomas Hobbes, Abelard, and Nietzsche, to mention only a few. Boethius (477–524) said without free will "*there (would be) no virtue or vice anymore.*" He also believed that free will was exercised only when we use reason and rational thought to come to our decisions. Thomas Aquinas also felt that reason, rational thought, and the action of the will were all necessary for free will to be properly exercised.

These qualifications of free will may prove to be of great importance as the scientific investigation continues. Certain impediments such as fear, ignorance, duress, intimidation, habit, and psychological and social situations are presently seen as mitigating factors to free will. Nature and nurture definitely factor into our consideration of freedom.

It is more widely believed today that we are not completely responsible for our success or failure (i.e., we actually stand on the shoulders of our ancestors). Are we sure that mankind has free will in the traditional sense? If so, how free? Is it possible that we could overcome genes and circumstances to be the directors of our own destiny? In Luke 23:34, these words give us pause to reflect: "*Father forgive them for they know not they do.*" Jesus seems to be saying there are, at least in this case, mitigating circumstances to a fully free act.

Sara Smilansky of Tel Aviv University advocates illusionism, which is the belief that free will is an illusion but must be ascribed to for the good of society. Some scientists believe our brains are a physical system, causing our thoughts and actions. As a physical system, it suggests that we no more will it to operate in a particular way than we will our hearts to beat. This can be a frightening thought, yet it is gaining in popularity because of scientific research. This is called determinism; that is, human actions are ultimately determined by causes external to the will with the conclusion being that man is not responsible for his actions.

If free will is a fantasy, what will happen to all those beliefs and institutions based on it. Could it be we are not as free as we think we are but hopefully not as restricted as some might suggest? We are speaking here regarding morality and moral decisions: the ability to make moral judgments and act upon them in a way that allows necessary freedom and responsibility. Scientific experimentation does show that those who believe in free will act in a more "moral way" than those who do not believe in free will. In fact, belief in free will led to positive behavior not exhibited in those who did not believe.

Free will has become a third rail issue since Darwin's *On the Origin of Species*, which challenged many traditional beliefs and led to the work of Francis Galton on nature versus nurture, which ultimately begged the questions now surrounding free will. If free will does not exist or is so diminished, is morality in jeopardy? If we are incapable of choosing freely right from wrong or good from bad, can responsibility be any longer assigned? If we are predetermined by nature or nurture, are we then more or less robots?

However, Sam Harris, a noted American neuroscientist, points out that determinism is not fatalism. For Harris, determinism is the belief that our decisions are part of an unbreakable chain of cause and effect. Fatalism, on the other hand, is the belief that our decisions do not matter because whatever is destined to happen will happen. Harris believes the consequences of losing faith in free will would be much less negative than many philosophers and theologians fear. Accountability and responsibility would be gone but so would blame, punishment, outrage, and revenge. He compares the response to Katrina and 9/11; if the response to 9/11 were the same as the response to Katrina, hatred and aggressive vengeance would have been less violent and destabilizing.

Perhaps new paradigms might be considered in our approach to free will. Bruce Waller, a professor of philosophy at Youngstown State University, believes we have, in any situation, the ability, even if we reject traditional free will, to come with varied options to make decisions without external constraints. He feels that determinism and free will are not opposites but simply describe our behavior at different levels. Although science is making great strides in this area, it seems to be leaning toward diminished belief in free will, yet by no means has it spoken the last word on the subject. We should not reject science out of hand. We should be open to new knowledge and new ways to think about things, but at the same time, common sense and the dictates of civilization require us to be cautious in evaluating the data. To prematurely dismiss such an important concept as free will could be catastrophic for society. (2020)

Would Religion Exist Even without God?

This is a big question! It is probably wildly presumptuous of me to consider this age-old and complicated question. It is even more presumptuous to attempt this in a short essay. Obviously, I am not trying to give an extensive explanation concerning why religion exists. I am rather trying to share some of my reflections on this matter. There are many theories, reasons, and opinions that philosophers, theologians, and religious leaders give in answer to this question. Here are just a few examples: Religion flows from the nature of the God-human relationship. Religion is the natural product of finite beings. Religion exists as a means to control the masses. Religion is an evolutionary process designed to cope with reality.

After much study and reflection on this multifaceted issue, I am probably no closer to a definitive answer than I was many, many years ago. There are, however, two threads that run through this discussion every time I contemplate this mystery. Religion, even if a figment of mankind's imagination, has strong reasons for existence. The two threads that I always encounter in this deliberation are hope and justice. They are universal, and without them, religion, in my opinion, would not exist. Without hope and justice, religion would be hollow and empty at its core.

Absent of hope, despair is always knocking at our door. Religion holds out the hope of existence and happiness beyond this life. It promises that death is not the end, that the possibility of happiness after death is real even if not guaranteed. It at least tells us that death and nonexistence are not necessarily one and the same thing. It can certainly help relieve us of the ultimate fear that death is the final end. The realization that this life is all we have and that we need to face many hardships and struggles along the way with no hope of our future existence can be, and is for most, a cause for depression and despair. Hope is an optimistic virtue that sees God as a loving compassionate being who, at a minimum, gives us a realistic chance to achieve that for which we hope.

Hope and justice are inextricably connected. Without justice, this world can be mean and cruel. Ultimate justice gives this life meaning. Without ultimate justice, the suffering and contradictions we encounter on a daily basis—as individuals, as a society, and as a world community—can bring suffering and despair. The death of an innocent child; war, collateral damage, exploitation, and abuse of the weak and underprivileged; economic inequality; and a host of other confounding inequities are examples. Justice without the realization of our hope is a fantasy, and hope without justice is a sham.

Mankind longs for life, for without life, he ceases to exist, at least in a conscious form. Women and men long for justice, if not for all people, at least for themselves. Inequity is conspicuously evil in all its forms; religion says you will have life and justice. In the end, these will triumph, and this is an enormous consolation and promise for those who believe; for those who do not believe, it is a real challenge. A God who cannot offer both hope and justice is a non-god. This is the minimum that religion can offer. Without these two attributes, religion and belief in God are inconsequential, but because they are so important to religion, they become a necessity for the majority of people.

It is hard to believe that most of us could deal with reality if the thought of hope and justice were a sham. Perhaps these two qualities have been placed in us by God so that we are inclined to search for him. If so, religion is real. If these are just natural inclinations of women and men, then religion, even though it exists, is not what it promises to be.

Of course, God, belief, and religion go hand in hand. So even if there were no God, there would still, in my estimation, be religion. In mankind, there seems to be a natural tendency to hope for something more and a need for ultimate justice. Without life after death, there is no possibility of true justice.

This is a real issue with which many of us must grapple. The reason or reasons we attribute to why religion exists will determine how we deal with life both on a conscious and subconscious level. It will affect the decisions we make as we navigate all the intricacies of life. If religion is true, all this makes sense; if not true, then we have no hope or justice beyond what this life deals us.

For most people, this is unacceptable. If some are capable of giving life meaning without religion, it is perhaps because for them, life has intrinsic value and dignity. If religion is false and yet one believes unwittingly, he or she is duped and shall never know the real truth, but if real, our deepest needs and desires will hopefully be fulfilled.

I believe these deep-rooted aspirations of hope and justice are two of the most basic reasons for the existence of religion and our belief in God. Our choice is between belief and religion as opposed to unbelief. Given the options, religion seems the better deal, and thus the large majority of people choose religion. In the end, we will have an answer. We are told when we enter through that final door, we will encounter either darkness and nonexistence or life, ultimate justice, and the fulfillment of our hopes (yet perhaps there is something in between that is beyond our power of discernment). For these reasons, religion will always exist. The alternative is almost too harsh for most to bear. Certainly, hoped-for life and ultimate justice are preferable to a fade to *black*. (2019)

Could God Have Done Better?

Could God have created a different and "better world"? If God is God, the answer is both yes and no. If the answer is yes, then the next question is, "Why didn't he?" If the answer is no, the next question is "Why not?" Before we get started, we have a bit of a conundrum. Let's not get into mental, philosophical, and theological gymnastics. Let us do as John Lennon of the Beatles did—just imagine.

Could God have done it differently? What if he created a race called the Cyber-H Race composed of cyber-humanic beings? These beings would be very much like the human race but lacking free will in certain areas. The truth of the matter is that we really don't know how free we are; it is a mystery for us. We are still working that one out. These beings would be able to do all the things that human beings do but only better. For example, they could learn faster, love more deeply, be more empathetic, be more merciful, be more understanding, and the like. You get the drift. They would have all positive traits as part of their nature. These traits would be natural to them, part and parcel of their makeup.

They would even have free will. They could choose among options. They would have likes and dislikes and make choices that would foster growth and development. The choices for growth and development would be almost infinite according to God's plan but would not include pain, suffering, and evil. They would be able to achieve all the possible benefits of pain, suffering, and evil through other more humane means. Free will would exist in a more real way than we experience it today. The only limitation on free will would be that it could not be an option to choose evil. It would only be exercised for mutual good or the good of others. *"Do unto others as you would have them do unto you"* would be the bedrock of the Cyber-H Race. It would be the foundation of his nature. Being happy, healthy, and holy would be fundamental to the nature of the Cyber-H.

How hard could this be for a God of unimaginable love and power? A God who has given different natures to different creatures could clearly come up with a nature to fit the bill.

For me, to even approach this issue in this way seems to takes colossal hubris. Job's suffering was seen by his friends as a sign of God's condemnation of Job as a sinner when in fact Job was a faithful servant of the Lord. My hope is that I am not seen as an enemy of God but rather a seeker of truth. There is much we do not know, but I can't believe God would want us to stop thinking and imagining; it is, I hope, an honest form of prayer, meditation, and reflection on the larger mysteries of life. If God is responsible for this creation then the Scriptures are certainly true, and my limited understanding has been betrayed. *"For my thoughts are not your thoughts, and your ways are not my ways, says the Lord. For just as the heavens are exalted above the earth, so also are my ways exalted above your ways, and my thoughts above your thoughts"* (Isaiah 55:8–9). (2020)

COVID-19 versus Racism?

Which in the long run will be more devastating? Besides poverty, COVID-19 and racism are at this time the most devastating and disruptive realities facing this country. This is probably the last essay of this book. It is only fitting that it concerns COVID-19 and racism, both of which have been front and center this year. It is interesting that we are in the year 2020, for it is with 2020 vision that we need to view these realities and draw from them some insight into ourselves, our sisters and brothers, and this nation of ours.

COVID-19 has dominated this year not only because of the havoc it has generated in terms of deaths (over 250,000), tens of thousands without work, thousands upon thousands going hungry, and the loss of educational opportunity but also because of the urgency and immediacy of the need for a resolution to the pandemic and its horrific consequences—all this happening in one of the most important presidential election years in our history.

The pandemic has pulled back the thin veil hiding the inequities that are preventing this nation from achieving its desire to be great. It seems that we may be missing another opportunity to transform a difficult situation into a self-redeeming event because of a lack of wisdom, judgment, leadership, and planning. There is no doubt that whether we handle COVID-19 in a wise and prudent way or not, the virus will dissipate, but at what total cost, we do not know. Whatever the cost, it is already too high. We will, I think, regain our fundamental stability in many of the areas that have been hardest hit but only with great effort.

Racism, on the other hand, will not dissipate as quickly or in the same way as some of the devastating effects of COVID-19 (e.g., the return of physical health for survivors, some semblance of economic stability, educational consistency, and the like). When COVID-19 is long gone and becomes, for many, only a memory, racism will still remain. It is and has been one of the most consistent characteristics and flaws regarding the stability of this Union. COVID-19 does not have the power to bring down this nation, but racism does unless we do something to lower the level of hatred, injustice, poverty, and inequity associated with race. Racism is an intransigent and long-standing fissure in the foundation of this nation, and if we turn a blind eye and a deaf ear to understanding and solving this self-destructing problem, we will be doomed to failure as a nation and society. I am personally optimistic that we will meet and solve this problem because I see in younger generations the desire and power, not only to recognize the inequities of racism but the will to bring about meaningful change. (2020)

What Does 70+ Million Mean?

There can't be more than seventy million selfish, angry, and stupid people in the USA. That just doesn't make sense. So the question is, why did so many people vote for Donald Trump? Why did so many of my friends vote for him? Why did my brother-in-law vote for him? Why did my neighbor, my mechanic, my college buddy, and so many other good and decent people vote for Mr. Trump? He clearly appeals to people's lowest instincts to satisfy his own personal needs and desires. Why would so many good and decent people vote for Donald Trump to be their leader when it is so obviously apparent that he is a seriously flawed human being. He is without a doubt, a divider of people using fear and hatred as a catalyst to further his ends. This does not mean that he did nothing right. He pushed to move a COVID-19 vaccine along with great haste, which was an important and positive step for which he gets little credit. He seemed to have a strong anti-war attitude, which was refreshing since all the Republicans and Democrats have gotten us into war after war after war—almost one hundred years of semi-continuous war.

Perhaps Mr. Trump is not only the cause of division and hatred but taps into what is already there. The answer to the question why did so many people vote for Donald Trump may only be fully answered in the future. We should all ask ourselves how we feel about the contentious issues of the day. Do we feel anger, fear, and a sense of impotence with regard to our future? Do we feel that our countrymen are our enemies? Have we lost or discarded our ability to question adequately and honestly our true beliefs and attitudes? We have seen hatred, anger, and selfishness as important contributors to the political unrest of the day. An examination of our country's history as a society will help explain how we got to where we are today. Racism and attitudes that flow from class distinctions are strong contributors to the more than seventy million who voted for Mr. Trump.

Yes, this country is divided, but there are good people on both sides. I am not talking about extremists especially ones who resort to violence and guns as a solution. I am not talking about selfish and hateful people on either side of these issues. These people may be forever lost, filled with ideas and feelings that are basically unchangeable and not acceptable to most of the people of the USA. You know that there are good people who hold positions different from yours on all sorts of political and religious issues. I think a partial explanation for why so many good people voted for Mr. Trump is that, to a greater or lesser degree, they are unable to distinguish accurately, negative from positive influences. Acceptance of our failure to question adequately the relationship between what one believes and how one acts and reacts is strongly avoided or denied. Some people can't imagine or just don't care to see the causes and extent of human suffering: "if it doesn't affect me directly, it has little to do with me." There is a moral disconnect that somehow relieves people of the obligations to care for our sisters and brothers. What is our obligation toward those suffering from starvation, small business and restaurant failures? What about mom-and-pop enterprises, the homeless, and all those in desperate situations? Become aware! We can't just let them suffer and die, or can we? It is consciously or subconsciously believed that laws, rules, regulations, traditions, judgments, and history are more important than people, and thus, these beliefs trump the exercise of virtues, such as mercy, justice, and equity. This is only one man's opinion, but I think it is a better answer to the question "What does 70+ million mean?" rather than people are only angry, selfish, and stupid, although a large number of Trump supporters seem to fit that description. (Nov. 16, 2020)

Conclusion: Where Am I Today?

The Christian ideal has not been tried and found wanting. It has been found difficult and left untried.

—G. K. Chesterton

The same could be said of Islam, Judaism, Hinduism, socialism, and most mainstream religions. After all, the study, reading, thought, prayer, and living over my lifetime, G. K.

Chesterton's statement seems to tell much about religion and about belief and practice. What we profess to believe does not always translate into practice in our daily lives. Jesus and his good news perhaps make a great deal of sense to us, but we find it difficult to implement.

Scripture, as a guide for my life, makes a great deal of sense to me. As I grew up, my understanding of Scripture matured from a literal interpretation to a meaning-oriented, nonliteral interpretation. The Jewish and Christian scriptures have become an important guide for my life. Conscience and Scripture have become my ultimate guide. I no longer depend on institutions to direct and guide me or to make hard decisions for me.

However, I would like to first say how important institutions were for me and can be for most people. They are formative and can help develop fundamental, foundational building blocks that will allow us to become integrated adults. Institutional support along with healthy home life and simply living life's experiences prepare us for true adulthood. My parents formed me in love and compassion; they encouraged openness and critical thinking. Fear and guilt played a minimal role in my life. Openness and honesty were always encouraged. With this type of support from family and from the Catholic Church, a strong independent foundation for adulthood was laid. As I learned from my parents and church, true adulthood is a combination of emotional, spiritual, and intellectual maturity with openness to diversity and the ability to challenge and question what appears to be gratuitous and questionable.

Institutions and systems can fail, just as individuals can fail. As adults, we have an obligation to recognize and challenge institutions when they fall short or become corrupt. All institutions and systems can fail badly, and all institutions and systems are compromised because power, money, and control drive them, to some extent, in one way or another. This is not to say institutions and systems don't have a place in society, but rather it says, as adults, we must judge institutions and systems with a critical eye. They are in many ways just as vulnerable to error and corruption as we are, or perhaps even more so. Thus, it behooves us to pick and choose from what they have to offer. In some cases, we have an obligation to challenge and correct these institutions.

What we say we believe is often betrayed by how we act and live, as was so keenly observed by G. K. Chesterton. When we make honest and fair-minded choices, we should be able to stand before God and ourselves without fear or guilt but rather with a sense of humble righteousness. No good and merciful God will punish us for an honest pursuit of the truth even if we miss the mark. For me, an important part of the spiritual life is the path and journey to right thinking and acting: value-based living. Being so committed to an institution or system that we lose the ability to evaluate and judge can be catastrophic. Jesus, Martin Luther King Jr., John XXIII, Gandhi, Confucius, Buddha, the Jewish prophets, and countless other leaders can help us on our journey to be better persons. Their philosophies, theologies, and ethics have withstood the test of time. We can also have a real impact on individuals and the larger community through our openness, truthfulness, and desire for integrity. With thought, reason, and critical judgment, we have the ability to choose the institutions we feel will help us move toward what is right and good. This also means we are not committed to believe or practice all an institution or individual proposes as truth. What it does mean is that with good judgment and discernment, we can and should separate what is valid and true from what is spurious and false.

As time has passed, I have become less concerned with orthodoxy and belief and more concerned with modern challenges and practices. I have become less concerned with outdated rules and regulations of religion and more concerned with the virtues espoused by religion such as mercy, kindness, compassion, justice, honesty, forgiveness, understanding, openness, tolerance, love, and nonjudgmental activities as expressed in almost all religions and spiritualities.

After approximately twenty years of work on these essays, I have come to a different place than I started from. It has been a long road from "then" to "now," but it has been a wonderful journey. *"And he went out not knowing where he was going"* (Heb. 11:8). Like Abraham, I set out on a journey, not knowing where I was going or where this journey would lead me; however, I was confident it would bring me to a better place. That confidence has been justified and fulfilled.

Since God, religion, and life are mysterious, these words of Richard Rohr are apropos even regarding mystery in general.

> *I see mystery not as something you cannot understand; rather it is something that you can endlessly understand! There is no point at which you can say "I've got it." Always and forever mystery gets you! In the same way, you don't hold God in your pocket; rather, God holds you and knows your deepest identity. When we describe God, we can only use similes, analogies and metaphors. All theological language is an approximation, offered tenta-*

> *tively in holy awe. We can say, "It is like…, or "It's similar to…; but we can never say with absolute certainty, "It is…" because we are in the realm of beyond, transcendence, of mystery. We absolutely must maintain humility before the Great Mystery; otherwise religion worships itself and its formulations instead of God."*

Humility must be exercised whether we believe or not. Arrogance and self-righteousness are the arch-enemies of humility and truth. We do not have the answers to these mysteries and perhaps never will; They are beyond our scope. *Only a mind that is closed is certain.* (Dean Spanley)

I hope this book has aided and will continue to aid you on your journey toward emotional, spiritual, and intellectual fulfillment. Hope and consolation are also the desired end of these essays. Perhaps some of these essays have answered some questions or allow you to view reality in a different and deeper way. Whether one believes in God or not is not the question. How we live our lives and treat our sisters and brothers is the question. The answer is "in everything do to others as you would have them do to you" (Matt. 7:12).

BIBLIOGRAPHY

Alexander, Michelle. 2010. *"Prisons: The new Jim Crow."* New Press.

Armstrong, Karen. 2007. *"The Great Transformation."* Anchor.

The Case for God. 2009. Anchor.

The Bible. 2009. Anchor.

Holy War. 2001. Anchor.

A History of God. Ballantine. 1993. The Letter to the Romans.

The Battle for God. 2000. Anchor.

A Short History of Myth. 2005. Canongate.

Albacete, Lorenz. 2002. *God at the Ritz.* Crossroad.

Angelou, Maya. 1957. *"I Know Why the Caged Bird Sings."* Atlantic Monthly Press.

Barclay William. 1957. *"The Letter to the Romans."* Saint Andrew Press.

Barron, Robert. 2017. "To Light a Fire on The Earth."

Bernan, Morris. 2006. *"Dark Ages America."*

Borg, Marcus. 1995. *"The Heart of Christianity."* Harper One.

Brown, Raymond. 1996. *"Reading the Gospels with the Church."*

"Catechism of The Catholic Church." PBS documentary (1988).

Campbell. Joseph. "The Power of Myth." Bill Moyers.

Carroll, James. 2001. *"Constantine's Sword."* Houghton Mifflin.

Cuomo, Mario. 1993. *"More Than Many Words."* St. Martin's Press.

Darwin, Charles. 1859. "On the Origin of the Species."

Dawkins, Richard. 2006. *"The God Delusion."* Houghton Mifflin.

Diamond, Jared. 2005. *"Collapse."* Viking.

Du Boise, W. E. B. 1935. *Reconstruction in America.*

Douglas, Fredrick, Booker T. Washington, and W. E. B. Du Boise. *"Black History Collection."*

Eger, Edith. 2013. *"The Choice."* Ebury Books.

Eldredge, Miles. 2005. *"Darwin in Discovering the Tree of Life."* WW Morton.

Ellison, H. L. 1957. "Exodus." Saint Andrew Press.

Gates, Henry Louis. 2019. *"Stony the Road."*

"Dark Sky Rising" (2019).

Gates, Melinda. 2019. "*The Moment of Lift.*" Flatiron Books.

Gibson, John C. L. 1957. "Job." Saint Andrew Press.

Goodwin Doris Kearns, 2019. "*Leadership.*"

Green, Brian. 2020. "*Until the End of Time.*" Knop Doubleday Publishing Group.

Haidt, Jonathan. 2012. "*The Righteous Mind.*" Pantheon.

Haught, Richard. 1996. "*2000 Years of Disbelief.*" Prometheus.

Heschel, Abraham. 1951. "*A Philosophy of Religion.*" Noonday Press.

"*God in Search of Man.*" Farrar 1955.

Hitchens, Christopher. 2007. "*God Is Not Great.*" Twelve.

Johnson, Elizabeth. 2011. "*Quest for The Living God.*" Continuum.

King, Martin Luther Jr. 2001. "*A Call to Conscience.*" Warner Books.

Malcom X. 2020. "*The End of White Supremacy.*"

Martin, James. 2016. "*Jesus a Pilgrimage.*" Harper Collins Publishers.

Merton, Thomas. "*No man is an Island.*"

Mecham, Jon. 2018. "*The Soul of America.*" Random House.

Neiman, Susan. 2002. "*Evil in Modern Thought.*" Princeton University Press.

"Learning from the Germans." Princeton University Press (2015).

Neuffer, Elizabeth. 1988. *"The Keys to My Neighbors House."* Picador.

Obama, Barack. 2006. *"Audacity of Hope."* Crown.

"Dreams from My Father." Crown (2004).

Sobel, Dava. 1999. *"Galileo's Daughter."*

Solomon, Andrew. 2012. *"Far from The Tree."* Scribner.

Stowe, Harriet Beecher. *"Uncle Tom's Cabin."* John P. Jewett and Company.

Twain, Mark. 1962. *"Letters from the Earth."* DeVoto Books.

Wilkerson, Isabel. 2020. "Caste." Penguin.

"Warmth of Other Suns." Penguin (2010).

Will, George. 2020. *"Conservative Sensibilities."* Liberty Hill Publishing.

ABOUT THE AUTHOR

Joseph Woerner was born February 20, 1941, into an Irish Catholic family in Jersey City, New Jersey. He was ordained a priest of the Archdiocese of Newark, New Jersey, in May of 1957, was educated at Seton Hall University, and received a degree in sacred theology from Catholic University in Washington, DC. He was a parish priest for six years, stationed as St. Peter's Parish and Orphanage in Newark, New Jersey, for three years. During his time in Newark, he taught religion at St. James High School, also located in Newark, and was responsible for the continuing education of the sisters assigned at the orphanage at St. Peter's Parish for almost three years. He moderated adult education programs and taught religion at Holy Trinity High School in Westfield, New Jersey. After leaving the priesthood, he worked as the assistant director of admissions at Newark College of Engineering, now known as the New Jersey Institute of Technology.

In 1973, he resigned from the priesthood, married Marilyn Williams, and together raised three boys. As a salesman for Black Millwork Inc., an Andersen Window distributor, he retired in 2007 as a valued employee after thirty-two years. While a parishioner at St. Mark's parish in Sea Girt, New Jersey, he organized and moderated a Bible study group for ten years, during which he started writing essays on religion and related topics. At present, he continues to write essays on religion, politics, and current events.

CPSIA information can be obtained
at www.ICGtesting.com
Printed in the USA
BVHW080032010223
657531BV00006B/58

9 781685 702748